SENSE OF OCCASION

SENSE OF OCCASION
HAROLD PRINCE

APPLAUSE
THEATRE & CINEMA BOOKS
An Imprint of Hal Leonard LLC

Published in 2017 by Applause Theatre & Cinema Books
An Imprint of Hal Leonard LLC
7777 West Bluemound Road
Milwaukee, WI 53213

Trade Book Division Editorial Offices
33 Plymouth St., Montclair, NJ 07042

Printed in the United States of America

Book design by Lynn Bergesen, UB Communications

Library of Congress Cataloging-in-Publication Data is available upon request.

ISBN 978-1-4950-1302-7

www.applausebooks.com

For Judy, Charley, and Daisy,
whose inspiration and generosity
immeasurably made all of this possible.
My love always.

AUTHOR'S NOTE

From the age of eight, when my parents took me to see the Mercury Theatre's production of *Julius Caesar* starring Orson Welles, I knew there was something special about the theatre that could not be duplicated anywhere. Of course, there was no television then, but there were swell movies (not "films" in those days) and we lived for the radio. Never underestimate how potent radio was, for the simple reason that it invited your imagination: there were just those voices and you filled in everything else. I always felt that applied to the theatre as well; less is generally more because the audience is complicit with live actors—we fill in the blanks. You can't do that in a movie theatre or sitting before a television screen. And all of that I define as a heightened *sense of occasion*.

In addition (and this is less important), I remember when we dressed in the best we had for live theatre because we regarded it as an event of special importance. I sat in the second balcony of the magnificent Empire Theatre on Forty-First Street and Broadway to see *Life with Father* in "the suit"— one with matching jacket and trousers and a white shirt and tie. I remember my heart beat faster as curtain time approached—anticipating a rare and precious occasion.

INTRODUCTION

2017

In 1970 John Fisher, editor of *Harper's Magazine*, invited me to write a book about my short career in the theatre, from office boy to assistant stage manager to producer to director/producer. I declined because my career *had* been so short, which is precisely why he made the offer. He saw that the theatre might be in for a seismic change because of the advent of television, and he asked me to chart the beginnings and effect of that change and, perhaps, to predict where it was going. I procrastinated. And then, I reconsidered. But still I didn't deliver. I expect *Harper's* lost interest by the time I wrote *Contradictions* four years later. It was insane arrogance to write *Contradictions* in 1974, but in a way it wasn't, of course. It was just much too soon, but in hindsight I'm glad I wrote it.

Now, more than forty years later, I'm ready to revisit the book and to complete it—to see where I was right in my assessments and where I was wrong. The reflections on the first twenty-six chapters are all new material, and the remaining nineteen chapters cover the period from 1974 to the present.

I don't want this to seem like the grumblings of a grumpy old man who is nostalgic for the Broadway of the *good old days*. I am an optimist, and I hope my comments will be taken as an invitation to the new generation of wannabes to invest in a viable and productive artistic future. "The theatre is dying" was a punch line in Oscar Hammerstein's lyric in the musical *Me and Juliet*—and indeed the theatre has been dying for as long as it's been living, so its problems are not irrevocable.

I don't expect to make friends with many of my observations about the dangerous direction the theatre has taken, but it is not my intention to offend anyone.

My comments about shows and collaborators are rarely in chronological order. That job was taken care of excellently by Foster Hirsch in his book

Harold Prince and the American Musical Theatre. Rather, I offer here occasional anecdotes and additional insights into what I have experienced over the course of a long (seventy years and counting) career . . . ouch!

INTRODUCTION
1974

I get a lot of mail from theatre enthusiasts—many of them in universities, some, unbelievable as it may seem, still in the lower schools—with questions about the creative and business areas of the theatre today. I've worked almost exclusively on Broadway or on touring companies of plays which originated on Broadway, so the questions usually apply to Broadway theatre.

Though my work in New York has been predominantly on musicals, most of my opinions apply equally to plays without music—just as, surprisingly, most of the questions I receive extend to nonmusical theatre.

The most popular and least possible question to answer by mail is: "What is producing?" It is generally followed by: "What is the difference between the producer and the director?" I have a form letter for those questions, and the more specific and stimulating ones I answer individually.

In the last couple of years my mail has tripled, and this year my letters often come from people who are doing doctorates on theatre and contain dozens of questions.

This book, then, grows out of my desire to cut down on my mail.

Also, I've been working in New York since 1948, and this is as good a time as any to take some stock and come to some conclusions with respect to the way the theatre is going and just how invalided the theatre is. And, perhaps more personally, what my future in the theatre might hold. So in collating all these questions and asking more, I've come to some conclusions, and ordered out of chaos the tangle of information, of experience, of surprises and disappointments, frustrations.

I've had a unique life in the theatre, uniquely lucky. I went to work for George Abbott in 1948, and I was fired one Friday that year from a television job in his office. I was rehired the following Monday, and I've never been out of work since. Perhaps Neil Simon's play *The Prisoner of Second Avenue* got to me as profoundly as it did because the leading character came home one day and announced that he'd lost his job. I suppose I'll always live in unreasonable, lunatic fear of losing my job.

So this book grew out of hundreds of letters written and a dialogue between me and Annette Meyers, who has been my secretary and my assistant and something of a devil's advocate for fourteen years. She came to my office an English teacher from New Jersey. She has learned just about everything there is to know about how we do our shows, and she has seen the theatre enter this confusing and harrowing period of change (which I hope is documented in the text to follow). She is married to an actor-writer, which means that she is probably privy to information and attitudes to which it would be difficult for me to be exposed. This familiarity with the other side—a term I deplore because the lines which separate and departmentalize the theatre are taking a terrible toll on it, particularly today—has qualified her to frame some of these questions in a way that has caused me to look at aspects of the theatre that I generally ignore.

There are very few anecdotes in this book, and a modicum of names get dropped. It isn't glamorous, because I don't think the theatre is—not in terms of diamonds and sable. People lament that fact, but I think it is neither to lament nor to celebrate. Times have changed and the theatre with them.

To simplify things, I have presented the material in chronological order, starting with something about myself and then launching into the twenty shows. I have taken them one by one, and in the course of each one I have tried to analyze what I learned, first at George Abbott's elbow and then at Jerome Robbins's, and then at all those other collective elbows: the authors', composers', lyricists', designers', choreographers', the actors', and the company managers'. The first of the shows is *The Pajama Game*, the most recent, *Candide*.

The first version of this book covered 650 pages. I have eliminated everything about each show which was routine—operational redundancies. What remains is what remains interesting to me in the continuing learning process which is "doing" plays. And, hopefully, in what remains are answers to most of the questions I am asked.

The book dictated its own title. We started it three and a half years ago, and about halfway through Annette began to collect instances in which I changed my mind totally, reversed myself 180 degrees. I have a predilection for oversimplifying. It makes my life more pleasant. I am an optimist—which also makes my life more pleasant. Annette Meyers enjoys threshing up the contradictions and she endures pessimism. Somewhere, probably, between the two of us exists a measure of reality.

Contradictions as such don't bother me too much (what is it Emerson said?). The only one from which there seems no respite—*the ultimate contradiction*—is born of my desire to work ALL THE TIME and my fear of working just to keep busy.

I don't know.

SENSE OF OCCASION

CHAPTER
1

We were privileged, upper-middle lower-rich class, Jewish, both parents from German families which settled here soon after the Civil War. There was never any question that I would go to college, that I would travel, that I would go to the theatre early and often. Mine was a family addicted to theatre, and still there was no effort to encourage me to work in it or to discourage me, and at no time was there any to push me into finance. So I didn't have to resist something I *would* have resisted.

I was always preparing myself for this. I fantasized a lot as a kid; most kids do. Some kids don't, but I did. And my fantasies took the shape of the life I'm living now. How many people can say that?

I've had theatre ambitions all of my life. I cannot go back so far that I don't remember where I wanted to work. The only difference is that what I wanted to be was a playwright, and that still stands me in good stead. But I am not a playwright.

Saturday matinees were part of a New York Jewish child's intellectual upbringing. I spent mine in the orchestra with my parents or up in the top balcony of the Empire Theatre with a school friend or by myself. My allowance went for theatre tickets rather than ball games, and I saw Orson Welles (when he was twenty-one) do *Julius Caesar*, Burgess Meredith in *Winterset*, Bankhead in *The Little Foxes*, Schildkraut and Le Gallienne together in *Uncle Harry*, not great, just marvelous. I saw the usual kid stuff: *White Horse Inn*; I saw *The American Way*; I saw something called *In Old Virginia* at the Center Theatre, and there was a sequence in which a whale swallowed Jonah. I thought that was something.

I wasn't as interested in musicals, and by the time I got to the University of Pennsylvania, I wasn't interested in them at all.

I ran a radio station which I had helped form at the university, writing weekly adaptations of plays, pirating everything—O'Neill, Maxwell Anderson, Odets, and so on—and I would direct those and act in them sometimes.

Also, I wanted to be a novelist. I wrote novels beginning early in my teens and continuing through college. I remember working at a Smith-Corona portable till four or five every morning. In that period I wrote four novels and as many full-length plays. I wish I knew what became of all that material. Just to see.

I was not a drama major. There was no such thing. And I don't believe in it. I don't approve. Everything theatrical at Penn was extracurricular. I took a liberal arts course: English, psychology, heavy on history (still my favorite subject), philosophy, and I read plays—many plays. I think it's fine to study drama if you want to be a scholar, a critic, to teach. I do not think you get much valuable, practical experience in college dramatic programs. Maybe they are getting more practical and less self-congratulatory, less social, but I think probably on a postgraduate level.

I was a fair student. I went to college when I was barely sixteen and finished when I was still nineteen. Too fast, I think, but to compensate I came to appreciate that I had gotten the beat on my peers. I was working for George Abbott when I was twenty.

I never believed in the apprenticeship system, so I never tried summer stock. I don't think that kids going to Westport, Connecticut, putting on blue jeans and oxford shirts, and splattering paint all over themselves are learning a damn thing about the theatre. They're learning what a lot of fun Arlene Francis is and what a lot of fun you can have in Westport, Connecticut, during the summer. There's nothing tidy, comfortable, social about the experience of learning your craft in the theatre.

I was very bad about looking for work. I was shy and as silent as I am presently loquacious, so I fooled myself into thinking I was "making the rounds" by writing plays and having *them* make the rounds instead. One of these reached the desk of the head of the script department at ABC-TV. He had heard that George Abbott was organizing a small experimental TV unit and arranged an interview for me with someone in the Abbott office. I went straight over there, and I never left. We still share an office, and it is only across the street from the one I entered twenty-six years ago.

At the time of the Abbott office interview, I remember I said I could not imagine what I could do to earn even twenty-five dollars a week, so I offered to work "on spec" for nothing. I offered to leave at any point if they discerned in the quality of my work that I was not being paid. That amused somebody, and I went to work for nothing. Two weeks later I was raised to twenty-five dollars a week, and I stayed at that figure for six months.

I did a little of everything. We soon had three shows on television, the most prestigious of them *The Hugh Martin Show*, an original musical which George Abbott wrote, featuring Joan McCracken and Hugh Martin, the Hugh Martin Singers, Butterfly McQueen, and Kaye Ballard. It supposedly took place in Hugh Martin's living room. It was modest. It appeared on NBC Sunday nights at seven. Abbott wrote the first one and directed it, and then he let me write the second and direct it. He simply approved what I was doing and went away and let me do it. Soon I got into a battle with Kaye Ballard, the comedienne on the show. I was a nervous kid in those days, nervous, ambitious, apprehensive. It was irritating to observe how quickly I moved, how intensely I worked. After all, you never know when someone's watching. We clashed, and Hugh Martin (who had brought Kaye into the show and was a great friend of hers) went to Abbott and insisted I be taken off the show, and Abbott refused. Martin put it to Abbott: Prince or the show. Abbott chose Prince; the show went off the air.

Actually, the television operation annoyed Abbott for many good reasons. There was SO much activity: many shows on the air, much hysteria in the office (Abbott prefers CALM), and no money coming in—a poor combination. So one Friday Abbott disbanded the television department.

It was three in the afternoon, and I went straight to what is now the DeMille Theatre on Broadway, where I sat in a cold sweat till well past midnight. I'd lost the best job in New York.

On Monday morning, when I went back to empty my desk, Bobby Griffith, who was George Abbott's production stage manager, told Abbott that he'd been unhappy for some time with his assistant and requested he replace him with me. So I had a new job, and it paid seventy-five dollars a week. The show, a revue called *Touch and Go*, had originated at Catholic University in Washington, D.C., and was written by Jean and Walter Kerr.

Everything began to move quickly. I worked nights as second assistant stage manager at the Broadhurst and days in the Abbott office, running the switchboard, casting, messengering—the works. And there was a show in Boston called *Tickets, Please!* with Paul and Grace Hartman, which was in some trouble. Its director had been fired and Abbott called in. Abbott wanted a stage manager to take with him to Boston, and as Bobby Griffith was in London, staging an edition of *Touch and Go*, I went to Boston, where I became first assistant stage manager and where I met the Hartmans.

Nights I worked on their show, and days I wrote a play with Ted Luce, who had written much of the *Tickets, Please!* material.

The show ran a season, and by the end of its run, Ted and I had written a comedy-murder mystery called *A Perfect Scream* that the Hartmans optioned, and I had joined the Dramatists Guild. (The Hartmans separated after *Tickets, Please!* and our script is filed away somewhere—but where?)

Next I went on loan to the Leland Hayward office to cast the new Irving Berlin musical *Call Me Madam*, so I was at Hayward's every morning at nine thirty, went to the Coronet, where the Hartmans were playing in the evenings, and went home after the performance to finish writing the play.

It was understood that I would be Bobby's first assistant on *Call Me Madam*, but the Korean War started and I was among the first drafted (my photo appeared in the New York *Daily News* over the caption "Korean Threat").

I got drafted (and it was exactly like being fired), but not before I had met Ruth Mitchell, Hayward's stage manager on *Mister Roberts*. One day Ruth dropped by the office, a sensational-looking woman with a silly black poodle on a long leash. She was and remains very glamorous.

At that time I also met Howard Lindsay and Russel Crouse, two gentlemen of the theatre, who from then on became our friends, rooting for us— eventually investing with us—genuinely enjoying the way our lives were going. They were something.

I never got to work on *Madam*. I went to its opening night and I reported at 10 Church Street for induction, the reviews under my arm, the following morning at five thirty.

I slept practically the whole two years, not just in bed but on my feet. I was stationed in Germany, assigned to an antiaircraft artillery battalion. Actually it was not such a bad time. Being thwarted in "progress" tranquilized me. I still think of those two years as real years. My life before and since hasn't been too heavy in the reality factor. When I left for the army, George Abbott said there would be a job waiting for me when I got back, but I refused to count on that—despite a stream of friendly and informative letters from Celia Linder, his secretary.

I was billeted near Stuttgart, and my evenings I spent in a place called Maxim's, a sleazy nightclub in the bombed-out ruins of a church. It was 1951; in 1966 that club reappeared in *Cabaret*. Ultimately, the years in Germany were to qualify as a business deduction.

I arrived after two years by troop ship to Hoboken on October 8, 1952, which happened to coincide with Abbott's opening a play called *In Any Language* with Uta Hagen and Walter Matthau. We were given passes for that evening, and I went straight to the Cort Theatre in uniform, arriving fifteen minutes before curtain. I walked on the stage. George Abbott was sitting on a chaise in Raoul Pène du Bois's elegant Roman set, Bobby Griffith beside him. Abbott looked up and said, "Are you back already?" and I said, "It's been two years." And then, "When do you get out?" I said, "Next week." And he said, "Well, come in next week. We're doing a new musical with Rosalind Russell based on *My Sister Eileen*."

My Sister Eileen became *Wonderful Town*, and during that first year of its success, Bobby and I hatched plans for one of our own.

REFLECTIONS ON CHAPTER I
OF *CONTRADICTIONS*

I made no mention of a nervous breakdown in *Contradictions*, but I did have one when I was fourteen and wrote about it in the foreword to Foster Hirsch's book. It lasted a blisteringly hot summer in New York (there was no air-conditioning then). My family had been hit by the Depression, and in quick order we lost a place in Westchester, a beautiful apartment on Seventy-Seventh Street opposite the Museum of Natural History, our cook, our driver, and my mother went to work designing hats for the then-famous Hattie Carnegie. I remember asking my parents whether I shouldn't get some help from a psychiatrist, but they dismissed it, attributing it to puberty! I remember asking Benny, my best friend at school, whether he had similar problems, and he dismissed it with, "Are you crazy?!" Which I was. By the end of the summer, the black clouds dispersed, and when I returned to school I had changed. The desire to work in the theatre had become an obsession to the degree that I wondered—worried, really: If I didn't find a life in the theatre, how the hell would I live?

When I first returned to New York having graduated from the University of Pennsylvania, I didn't know how to find a job, and it terrified me. An actress friend of my grandmother's (who had been a star at the turn of the century and now lived in a nursing home) recommended that I pay a visit to Chamberlain and Lyman Brown's offices—they had been hugely successful actors' agents. Their office was in an old Broadway building that housed Actors' Equity as well.

I had no experience directing except for one play I had written myself at the University of Pennsylvania (parenthetically, it was given the annual award for best direction). I made a list of all my favorite plays, some famous and some quite obscure, and at the head of the list I typed, "Plays directed by Mr. Prince." Beside every play's name I put the name of a theatre and its production dates. I picked theatres all over the country, far from Broadway—remember, there was no Internet then and little opportunity to check up on me.

Having done that, I took myself to the Brown office sans appointment. The office resembled the Collyer brothers' living room—very dusty, brown, flaking walls, with photos of stars of another era: Fritzi Scheff, Walter Hampden, the Barrymores (you get the point). There was a small gate separating the waiting room from the receptionist, who was also turn-of-the-century. I introduced myself to her as a young director, handing her the list of plays I had directed—well, rather, the plays I wished I had directed—and then asked to meet Mr. Chamberlain Brown. She said he was a very busy man, but she would show him the list and perhaps he would get back to me for an appointment but not to count on it.

At that moment, from the door behind her desk, a voice shouted, "Who's out there, Effie?" "A young man," Effie replied. "He says he's a director." Mr. Brown: "Has he done much?" "His résumé says so." From behind the door: "A director! Effie, send him right in."

She buzzed the little gate that separated me from the Promised Land, and I went into Mr. Brown's office, résumé in hand. He was on the phone. He gestured to me to hand him my résumé, and immediately this followed:

"You won't believe what just happened! It's this young man who I've been hearing so much about. He's a brilliant young director and everyone's talking about him. He has a list of plays he's directed that will knock your eyes out. And he just walked into my office." (Pause.) "Yes, I'm serious. He's standing right in front of me." (Pause.) "I'll ask him. Mr. Prince, can you go over to this producer's office? He called me five minutes ago to say he's lost his director and he needs a replacement to direct the summer season in Franklin, New Jersey. Are you interested?"

He handed me a piece of paper with an address of an apartment in Queens. I left the office and, an hour later, was hired on to direct eight plays that summer in a school gymnasium.

The first two plays were *Angel Street* and *John Loves Mary*—both recent Broadway hits. I put together a cast of available actors, a number of rather good actors, one of whom would be featured in the film *From Here to Eternity* playing a burly villain. But who was I to be choosy? I cast him as a handsome young leading man in *John Loves Mary*. Those first two plays sold out, so I'd rescued the company from disaster—well, not quite, because I made a bargain with the producer to pick the next two plays.

The first was Lula Vollmer's *Sun-Up*, which had been produced by the Theatre Guild in the twenties. I directed it on multiple stages with the audience surrounded by the action, which was an audacious decision in those times. Predictably, the audience was confused. The following week I directed A. A. Milne's *Mr. Pim Passes By*. No one was amused. I bankrupted the company and hitched my way back to New York. The next interview I had was with someone in George Abbott's office.

When I started at the office, I believe I did a good imitation of J. Pierrepont Finch (Robert Morse's character in *How to Succeed in Business Without Really Trying*). Though Abbott's office opened at nine and closed at five thirty, I arrived at eight thirty and could be seen working (well, doing something!) until six.

I realize that my presence in the office was abrasive. I was smiley and enthusiastic and overenergized. So, recognizing that, one morning I wrote at the top of my desk calendar (for an entire year!): "WATCH IT!!!"

Abbott was dabbling in television, having hired about three people (including his then wife) to explore the possibility of producing television shows.

We produced a game show called *Charades* at NBC on West 104th Street with Tom Ewell, the stage and screen star, as its master of ceremonies, and I was the jack-of-all-trades. My job was to corral young Broadway actors, rehearse in the afternoon, followed by a camera rehearsal, and before the show itself, take them to dinner in the commissary. Among them were Julie Harris and Carol Channing. Both ladies had enormous appetites. Channing had just been discovered in a revue called *Lend an Ear* and soon thereafter became a huge star in *Gentlemen Prefer Blondes*. Her eating habits changed remarkably, as did her physical profile, and to this day she brings her own food to all meals.

Charades was welcomed, and so Abbott agreed to write and direct *The Hugh Martin Show*. Hugh Martin was the composer of not only *Best Foot Forward*, an Abbott success, but also the movie *Meet Me in St. Louis*. I was Abbott's assistant.

Once the first show had premiered, receiving fine reviews, Abbott confessed that he didn't enjoy the assignment and had asked a team of famous playwrights who were working in California to write the second script. It arrived on a Friday after Abbott had left the office, scheduled for a first reading with the company on Monday. Seeing the script on his desk, I read it and I knew he wouldn't like it. Come early Monday morning, I heard a moan from his office, whereupon he summoned me to tell me the script was terrible and that now, dammit to hell, he had to write one himself. Whereupon I replied, "Mr. Abbott, I read it on Friday, and over the weekend I wrote a new script. Would you like to read it?" He did, and he liked it; furthermore, he told me I'd be directing it as well. He would come in at the end of the week to see how it went and make suggestions.

So the second show was all mine, but there was *only* a second show, because that cast couldn't handle all my unbridled energy and there was no "WATCH IT!" to warn me. Despite the fact that the second show went rather well, they wanted their Abbott and, for damned good reasons, couldn't accept me. It was an either-or confrontation, Abbott chose me, and NBC pulled the show.

I owe Kaye Ballard an apology, because at an earlier time I told this story and blamed my firing on her. I don't know where that information came from, but it was inaccurate. In retrospect, I'm sure I got on everyone's nerves, not least of all Hugh Martin's—brilliantly talented and always a sweet and gentle soul. I was a pain in the ass.

During *Touch and Go*, I made my first Broadway appearance. A member of the chorus was sick and his understudy was sicker. The curtains had risen on a first-act finale: *Hamlet* as adapted by Rodgers and Hammerstein. It was called *Great Dane A-Comin'*. Hamlet had been slain, and an angel from heaven with furry wings descended to the stage . . . that was me.

Bobby Griffith let me call the cues during some performances of *Touch and Go*. It should have been a great training experience. However, I've come to realize I never would've been a first-rate stage manager. The show was structured in the old-fashioned way—sketches, solos, and chorus numbers, each separated by a traveler (a curtain) which closed while the orchestra played enough utility music to give the stagehands time to change the scenery. Invariably, I would lose patience and open the traveler before the stagehands had finished their job, which meant they had to duck behind couches and chairs for the length of a scene. On occasion I even caught a stagehand exiting. I believe this indicated my early desire to direct. In other words, despite George Abbott's famous reputation for moving shows at a brisk clip, I had my own ideas. In hindsight, I'm wondering how the hell I kept that job.

I made my second appearance in *Tickets, Please!*, a revue starring Paul and Grace Hartman. I sat in the bleachers at a roller derby. The show featured Jack Albertson as a radio commentator. Grace Hartman sat next to me as a fan as her husband, Paul, hawked soft drinks to the crowd. Each performance they conspired to break me up, which I did, and after every performance they called the cast together to scold us for being so unprofessional for laughing onstage.

I came to cast *Call Me Madam* with no prior experience. George Abbott's casting director, Bobby Griffith, was in Europe reproducing one of his musicals, and Bill Hammerstein, who cast for Leland Hayward, was in London similarly occupied. So Abbott suggested I interview at Hayward's office for the job. I got it, and I started from scratch—well, behind scratch. I called agents and introduced myself, and there were auditions regularly. The show starred Ethel Merman and Paul Lukas, and I was to concentrate on finding the male juvenile lead. It was the time of *Oklahoma!* and *Carousel*, so everyone was a Curly. Gloria Saphire, who was one of the best of the agents, in frustration yelled at me over the phone, "Young man, we've sent you everyone. What the hell are you looking for?" And I replied, "Me. I'm looking for me. Someone who's graduated from college, wears horn-rimmed glasses, has a brush cut, and doesn't look like he belongs on the stage." And that's how we found Russell Nype.

Some years later, Ruth Mitchell was reintroduced to me by Jerome Robbins and became the production stage manager of *West Side Story*. She stayed on for the next forty-plus years, earning an "in association with" billing on most of my shows.

I took George Abbott's name off the door of my office only ten years ago, when we moved to a new suite. By then, he had been dead for over a decade. My wife, Judy, said it had ceased to be an homage and had become simply macabre.

I waited forty-three years to write another play, but more about that later!

CHAPTER
2

Bobby Griffith was producing a television show for the Ford Motor Company when he read in the *New York Times* the review of a book called *7½ Cents* about a strike in a pajama factory. He phoned me from rehearsals, suggested I read it, that he was too busy, and we might have to move quickly. I did and we did. By two o'clock we had made an offer to Harold Matson, the author's agent, for the musical rights. Subsequently, Leland Hayward tried to obtain them, and there were other similarly prestigious offers, but Harold Matson, displaying intuition for which he is highly respected, chose the fellows with the enthusiasm, if little else.

Abbott was not interested. He was not attracted to it: it seemed drab, and it was about a strike, and this country was in the throes of the witch hunt. The notion of strikes, strike leaders, capital, and labor, and so on—all of that tossed around the stage for laughs when everybody was being pilloried by the McCarthy committee—seemed crazy. Still, Abbott agreed to direct it if we got it properly adapted. This, I'm convinced, purely out of affection for Bobby Griffith.

Every major writer of musical comedies in those days was asked, every major composer and lyricist—there's no point in naming them, *everyone*, and they all turned it down. Meantime, Abbott had been thinking and one day suggested that we send for the novelist, Richard Bissell, to see if he might be interested in collaborating with him.

Bissell was living in Dubuque, Iowa, a man with a business to care for and a wife and lots of kids. It took him four days to pack his belongings, pile his family into a station wagon, and move to Connecticut. Permanently.

Abbott's contract on that show and subsequent shows was more than fair. Naturally, he wrote his own contract, which was for a smaller percentage of the profits, a lower royalty, than the younger successful directors were getting. And there was no nonsense about billing size, position, no mandatory "boxes" surrounding his name.

We had no money, not for options, not for *stationery*. George Abbott provided everything. He gave us an office, the telephones, and we did our own secretarial work, and that's it. Although he must have kept a record of all of it, he never billed us. After *The Pajama Game* opened, we began contributing to the rent.

Frank Loesser introduced us to Dick Adler and Jerry Ross, who'd already had songs on *Hit Parade*, one of them Tony Bennett's "Rags to Riches." Adler and Ross wrote three audition pieces on spec—"Steam Heat" was one; the opening, "Racing with the Clock," another. The show was theirs.

The dancer Joan McCracken recommended Bob Fosse (then her husband), an aspiring choreographer, for that assignment. Fosse had choreographed his portion of "From This Moment On," a Cole Porter number in the *Kiss Me, Kate* film, but as I regarded this debut as my once-in-a-lifetime chance, I was afraid to count on him. So we asked Jerry Robbins to back him up, and he agreed in return for a co-directing credit, which I knew was unacceptable. Abbott asked me what had happened, and I told him of Jerry's demands, to which he replied, "Oh, Hal, give it to him—everyone will know who directed the show." So we did, and this became Jerome Robbins's first directing credit.

Rosalind Russell, the star of *Wonderful Town*, introduced us to her husband, Frederick Brisson, who joined us as a producer. The partnership lasted two more shows.

We capitalized *Pajama Game* at $250,000 and raised our money the conventional way. We auditioned for backers in borrowed living rooms.

Freddie Brisson gave an audition early on, and George Abbott told the story exactly as it was—in other words, strikes and more strikes. In that one night we eliminated every major theatrical investor in the country and were forced to canvass people who didn't normally invest in shows. All told, there were eleven auditions, which is not really that many. I would tell of Romeo and Juliet in Iowa, eliminating the strike, eliminating the pajama factory; Adler and Ross would play the score and sing, augmented by four singers from *Wonderful Town*; and Bobby and Freddie would "sell."

Edie Adams offered us her living room. We took two bottles of Scotch there and some potato chips, and did so well that we went back again. Twice.

In those days (and, incidentally, again today), there was little money coming in from record companies. Though Columbia eventually recorded the album, it did so reluctantly.

When the show went into rehearsal, at the Winter Garden Theatre, we were still $28,000 short. The money we had raised was in escrow and could not be touched, so Abbott advanced us the $28,000, which Freddie raised to pay him back.

Bobby Griffith and I hired ourselves as stage managers. We needed the salaries. Until recently, producers weren't paid a nickel until a show had recouped. They existed solely on an office expense of a couple of hundred dollars a week. Once a show paid off, they split the profits equally with the investors. But it took only fourteen weeks in 1954 to return the $169,000 which *The Pajama Game* cost. Today the figures are simply too high; it takes so much longer to recoup that producers receive a percentage—usually 1.5 percent, occasionally more—of the gross weekly receipts.

It took a year from purchasing the novel to opening the musical, which is not long.

In New Haven, Boston, and New York, *The Pajama Game* was an instant success. Still we had no money. So on opening night in New York at the St. James Theatre, we saw our show from the wings while we worked it. We heard the applause. We shared the showstoppers over the intercom system: "That went well, God, didn't that go well!" and so on. When the curtain came down, we crossed the stage and embraced each other.

I was getting $125 a week, and he was getting $250, and we'd go into Sardi's and someone would call, "Lend me a few hundred thousand, will you!" A month later, Bobby Griffith saw *The Pajama Game* for the first time. It was six and a half months before I did. He quit stage-managing it and I stayed on.

Going back a bit, we opened in New Haven and then moved on to Boston. I think Boston is the best place to try a show out because the audiences are more sophisticated and enthusiastic about the stage. Business is good, if the show is. And the critics then were singularly helpful, discerning, intelligent. And fun to read.

It may come as a surprise that of two newspaper reviews for *Company* in Boston, one was a rave (Kevin Kelly) and another was a terrible pan (Elliot

Norton). Still, with a very small advance, we picked up each week we were there and sold out the last. That's a theatre town.

I like to go to New Haven for similar reasons. And to Washington, D.C. What changes the Arena Theatre complex and the Kennedy Center have wrought in that town!

I haven't tried out in Philadelphia since the 1950s, when the level of criticism was dangerous, encouraging audiences to support the wrong shows, not to be discerning. When *Fiorello!* played there, *Saratoga* did the business, and when *She Loves Me* was there, *Tovarich* sold out.

But it has changed; the *Zorba* national company was interestingly reviewed and did business. Reviews of *Company*'s touring production were highly critical and unhappily accurate. More recently, we opened *A Little Night Music* to a discerning response from audiences and critics.

The Pajama Game opened in New York on May 13, 1954, with an advance of only $40,000, which meant it could survive one week. On May 14, there was a line of four hundred people at 9:00 a.m. waiting for the box office to open. And the following day we distributed a 20 percent check with the reviews. We did this for some years with subsequent hits. But it was simply a trick. We deliberately overcapitalized our shows so that if we had a success we could mail a check the following morning. It seemed to our investors a profit distribution, and though they knew the difference, they went along happily with the feel of it. Our first shows were capitalized at $250,000 and cost under $170,000. Today, think what we would have to raise to ensure an overage. In fact, costs have so spiraled that I occasionally undercapitalize (the figures appall me), running a personal risk every time I do a new show.

And I have never believed in the overcall provision.

It's just that I wouldn't want anybody coming back to *me* for more money, particularly when a show's in trouble, and, really, money rarely affects the outcome.

In William Goldman's book *The Season*, which is a survey of the Broadway season of 1967–68, he pointed out that I was the youngest producer in the theatre in 1954. With the exception of Kenneth Waissman and Maxine Fox (*Grease* and *Over Here*) and Stuart Ostrow (*1776* and *Pippin*), at forty-six I am still one of the youngest—a dangerous state of affairs. He also suggested that though I was one of the most successful producers in the theatre, my

16

only nonmusical success was Phoebe and Henry Ephron's light comedy *Take Her, She's Mine*. Too true.

Some time after *The Pajama Game*, Bissell wrote a book which became a musical called *Say, Darling*, in which the boy producer, Sam Snow, was played by Bobby Morse, who looked exactly like me in those days. He still looks like me; it is I who don't. I was disturbed when Bissell wrote his book. I thought it was a cheap joke to characterize the boy producer as an amusing yes-man, a dilettante, who hung around 21 with a lot of beautiful babes. I couldn't get into 21 those days. I've never been a dilettante. Yes, I shaved at my desk. Yes, I paced the floor when I talked on the telephone. Yes, I was nervous, am nervous. Yes, it was even an amusing and sympathetic performance, but I couldn't see it at the time. I was too concerned with making a serious reputation, learning from Griffith and Abbott how to be good in this business because we had to be to do what we wanted in the theatre without interference, artistic interference. We had to put behind us forever the backers' audition, the patient and false consultations with the people with money about scripts and scores and casting. So any character imputations threatened me, perhaps irrationally.

I became a producer because fate took me there, and I was delighted. I used producing to become what I wanted to be, a director. (Ultimately, I hired myself, which is more than anyone else would do.) In those days, to ameliorate my frustrations as an observer, I would make a list pointing out everything that bothered me. Perhaps there would be 150 items. Out of deference to the director, I would offer one or two or even five of them at a time when he wasn't preoccupied. Obviously, half of the 150 were taken care of before I got to mention them.

I learned how remiss directors are about going back to see their shows. Abbott does some, but not enough, and Jerry Robbins almost never goes back.

I always had it in the back of my mind to put in the director's contract that his royalties stopped if he didn't see his show at least once a month. But I imagine he wouldn't have signed that contract.

Years later, as an incipient director, I used to look in on *Fiddler on the Roof*, and though I knew I could help keep it fresh, I ran up against Jerry Robbins, who, unwilling to return to it himself, tied my hands, preferring that the stage manager keep it *exactly as it was*. Well, exactly as it was is not always fresh. Today, in my dual capacity, I can return and restage. I totally changed the last scene in *Cabaret* twice during its Broadway run. Perhaps because I had better ideas, perhaps because the actors needed new moves, new readings. Obviously, the stage manager is at a disadvantage; he cannot alter direction which has gone stale.

I have never dropped in unannounced to take notes on a show I directed. Such deceit implies mistrust of the actors. Instead, I give notice, so that if someone is feeling ill, at least he'll call up the necessary reserves of adrenalin to give his best performance. That way I can see where the company has unintentionally gone wrong, embellished unwisely. Lost pace. I can see what really has become of the play, what values have been lost (or found!), and set it right.

Most important, I learned early when to say yes and when to say no and to base those "business" judgments on "artistic" criteria.

REFLECTIONS ON CHAPTER 2
OF *CONTRADICTIONS*

The advance of *The Pajama Game* was $15,000, not $40,000. That means that the show could have run for a performance and a half.

The Pajama Game cost $169,000, and *Damn Yankees* cost $162,000. This is somewhere in the neighborhood of the budget for shoes and wigs on a current Broadway production. Today, you can produce an independent feature film for what it costs to do a one-set straight play on Broadway.

Initially, Gwen Verdon turned us down, expressing her preference for remaining Jack Cole's dance assistant. She came to our office, strikingly beautiful with a shock of red hair in an Afro, charming and subtly sexy. She was irresistible. I don't recall how we finally persuaded her to do the show, but it was a tough sell.

Over the years, Gwen's experience as an assistant choreographer persisted. So, despite a string of huge Broadway successes, and after having been married to and then separated from Bob Fosse, Gwen continued as a glorified dance captain, protecting Fosse's choreography in New York and on the road. I've always observed sort of a sadomasochistic relationship between dancers and choreographers. Dancers punish their bodies, and choreographers legendarily wreak havoc on their favorite dancers. Chiropractors, osteopathy, and crutches contribute to their commitment to dance.

When the curtain rose on *Say, Darling*, Bobby Morse, pacing, was on the phone with either a star or an agent and shaving with an electric razor at the same time. Playing the rather feckless womanizer, he had a hell of a lot more charm than I. He was, to quote my wife (who had seen the show as a young girl), "adorable." The audience greeted his performance uproariously, so much so that I was ticked off when I realized they were laughing at me. During intermission I made my way to the lobby, expecting people to recognize me. But no one did. And then I knew: You can't have it both ways, can you? So I came to like *Say, Darling*.

For many years, I worried about being taken seriously. So whenever I was aware I was being photographed, I always scowled. If you look at my picture on the cover of the few books that have been written about me or in interviews, you'll see a fellow with no sense of humor.

It may be useful here to point out the obvious: popular music used to be theatre music. In 1954, when *The Pajama Game* opened, there were three number-one *Hit Parade* songs in its score. "Hey There" went number one even before anyone had seen the show. It was followed by "Hernando's Hideaway" and "Steam Heat." *Damn Yankees* provided two number ones— "Whatever Lola Wants" and "Heart." When theatre music ceased to be popular music, it encouraged me and my collaborators to seek more unconventional subjects. We could get much more serious, eventually moving into opera territory.

CHAPTER
3

A couple of weeks after *The Pajama Game* opened, Albert Taylor, an agent at William Morris, brought Douglass Wallop's novel *The Year the Yankees Lost the Pennant* to Abbott. It was, again, an implausible subject for a musical—baseball. Except for Ring Lardner's *You Know Me Al*, baseball had been anathema on the stage.

Abbott read it and agreed to direct it, providing Brisson, Griffith, and Prince produced it. Taylor became associate producer. The score for *Damn Yankees* was written by Adler and Ross. Fosse was choreographer. This time Abbott shared authorship with Wallop.

We had no difficulty raising money then or for many years. One hundred fifty-five people invested in *The Pajama Game* and in *Damn Yankees*, and many of them are still there twenty shows later. We never held another backers' audition (well, not as of 1974, anyway).

Even today, a letter announcing a play, its author, and the name of the composer and choreographer (often they are all new names) accomplishes the job. But it isn't as easy as it was the first seventeen years.

When we cast *Damn Yankees*, Mitzi Gaynor was offered the leading role first and turned it down. Zizi Jeanmaire was in New York at the time and also turned us down. Gwen Verdon was in Paris. She was our third choice.

On *Yankees* a great deal of material was rewritten on the road. More than one-third of the score was jettisoned. All the ingredients for panic were there, but Abbott worked calmly, and day by day everything improved except the ending.

When the show opened in New York, on opening night in fact, the plot called for Gwen, who'd been playing a beautiful witch, to be turned into an ugly hag at the curtain. The reviews for the show were good, but it came as something of a shock to us that the audience resented our turning the girl they'd fallen in love with into an old crone.

We went home with the reviews that night. We had a success, though how big a one we couldn't tell. At about six the next morning, I called Bobby Griffith to say the show was long and there were a number of things obviously wrong with it in New York that hadn't bothered us in Boston, specifically the ending. And how in hell, if he agreed with me, were we going to get George Abbott back into rehearsal? Bobby, too, had been tossing and turning all night and suggested we call Abbott at nine and ask for a meeting in the office. But by eight o'clock, my phone rang and it was Abbott, and he'd been up all night, troubled by the length of the show and the final curtain.

So we met at Dinty Moore's for breakfast. We couldn't locate our stage manager, so Bobby, George, Adler, Ross, and I divided up the cast phone numbers and called a rehearsal for that afternoon, at which time a number was taken out of the show (we'd gotten away with that one in Boston, but *not* in New York), another number previously in the second act was placed in the first, and the end of the story was altered. On its second night, the show was twenty minutes shorter and stayed that way for a thousand performances.

We asked Walter Kerr back to rereview it, and he liked it more than he had originally.

The only other lesson to be learned from that show was that despite the pretty good reviews, there was resistance to the baseball theme. Our advertising had been keyed to a picture of Gwen in a baseball uniform. "Saucy" was the word. Still, we never sold more than $250 worth of tickets a day during the first four weeks of the run. So our success suddenly looked to be a disaster until we changed the ads to a picture of Gwen singing "Whatever Lola Wants" and excised all references to baseball, even changing the color of the ad from ballpark green to red. One Monday morning three and a half weeks later, there was a long line waiting for the box office to open.

Bobby Clark played the devil in the national company, and he was miscast. We needed a male star to tour (or thought we did). I had worshipped Bobby Clark from early childhood, and the possibility of doing a show with him was irresistible. Abbott expressed serious misgivings that we were casting a comic personality rather than an actor. He urged us to disregard the box office aspects and find a *believable* devil.

Well, except for the absence of his painted-on eyeglasses, Bobby Clark was Bobby Clark, and though the tour was immensely successful, it was because of him rather than *Damn Yankees*. Often the reviews said that there would be no show without him, that it wasn't much, but at least it served as a vehicle for him. Meanwhile, the show had been playing in New York over a year and won all the awards.

Years later, I was talking to Zero Mostel about *A Funny Thing Happened on the Way to the Forum*, and the authors objected on grounds that Zero was an actor and not a vaudevillian. Since we couldn't get the vaudevillian of their choice—Phil Silvers—they agreed, reluctantly, to go along with Zero. In *Forum* he played the slave. He was the actor. The story prevailed, and I think the show was a greater success because of it. The same applied to Ray Walston in *Damn Yankees*.

It is not unusual for material to get short shrift, for otherwise good material to seem inferior, in the hands of a dazzling personality. Stars have a way of saving themselves at the cost of the material.

Not simply to put them down: I mean stars get to be stars generally because they're good, and if the best person for a role happens to be a star, then he should be cast.

But I think one of the best things about the theatre is that the star system doesn't really work. It's beginning to happen in movies, I think, to the artistic advantage of those movies. We have always been able to do shows like *West Side Story*, like *Yankees* with Gwen, that create stars. There's no question that we sacrifice an element of security, the guarantee of a run, if the reviews are poor.

On the other hand, it's an advantage I'd happily forgo in return for the star's creative demands. The presence of a star often perverts the material of a show so that you're giving somebody more to do than the part really requires. And the star system and the whole business of giant advance sales boomerang almost invariably. What the public anticipates with excitement is generally disappointing. Now, why? Because to have a point of view about something makes it that much more difficult to be surprised by it, and the likelihood of its point of view being the same as the creators' is slim and not even a good idea.

Ballyhoo leads to disappointment. Most of the shows I've done have not had advance sales, because they've not been based on particularly familiar material and they have not been star vehicles. So—no advance, but plenty of opportunity to surprise.

I've come to believe the astronomical advance is a precursor of disaster. Take a look at the shows that have gotten the biggest advances over the years: *Breakfast at Tiffany's*, *Mr. President*, *Jennie*. And *Dear World*. You can go on and on and on.

Very few shows open on the road in really good shape. But the ones that arrive in New York successfully are the ones that were polished, properly edited, rewritten, and handled well, and that depends very specifically on *professional* behavior in collaboration. So, if you find it, it's precious. Hang on to it.

Hang on to it, that is, until you sense that familiarity has dulled the stimulus of the collaboration.

Damn Yankees wasn't as good as *Pajama Game*; probably the next wouldn't have been any good. Then Jerry Ross shockingly died, and the decision was out of our hands.

REFLECTIONS ON CHAPTER 3
OF *CONTRADICTIONS*

Apropos the road, it was conventional in the 1950s and 1960s to send out national companies that were inferior copies of the Broadway originals. In theatre parlance, sets are often referred to as "flats." Well, these sets really were *flat* and whenever they opened or closed a door, the set shook.

As for casting, you cast either with a once-famous performer or someone who looked as much like the original star as possible. For example, we selected someone with bright red hair to play Gwen's role in the *Damn Yankees* tour instead of Chita Rivera, who had auditioned brilliantly. The devil was played by Bobby Clark, once a huge Broadway star who worked with eyeglasses painted on his face. In *Damn Yankees*, without the eyeglasses, he played with all the idiosyncrasies that made him a star. The show suffered.

Claudia Cassidy, the critic for the *Chicago Tribune*, understandably took offense at the quality of touring companies and became fixated with blasting anything that came through Chicago. Of course, we despised her, but we also knew how right she was. And she prevailed. The quality of touring productions improved, and today a road company is every bit as good as its Broadway counterpart and sometimes even better. Further, these productions contribute substantially to a show's profits.

CHAPTER
4

After the first two shows, we let a season pass. I don't think we were gun-shy. Nothing interested us. In 1956 we heard a score written by Bob Merrill for MGM, an updated version of Eugene O'Neill's *Anna Christie*, to star Doris Day. Doris Day indeed.

Someone had had the lunatic notion to take the story of a prostitute, written in the late 1920s, in a period of economic calamity, and move it up to 1955, leaving the rest intact. We offered to take it over for the stage, to backdate it, to help romanticize the story. It became *New Girl in Town*.

I've done two musicals involving prostitution—*Tenderloin* and *New Girl in Town*—and the subject is not romantic and rarely comical, and our materials were too conventional, our vision superficial.

Ultimately *New Girl in Town* succeeded at the box office, but not on the stage, because the principal reason for doing it was that we hadn't done anything for over a year and were dying to work. We sneaked through with a hit, and there is little pleasure in that.

A lot of musicals are created for no better reason, and often they work. But they have never worked for me. I'm stuck with "why am I doing it." And in fact, all plays that I see suffer the same criterion. I did not enjoy *Mame*. Why did they bother? I see that it's amusing, and I appreciate the polish, the talent involved. But the why anyone bothered, the *why* consistently gets in the way.

That doesn't imply that all musicals need be trenchant. God knows, *A Funny Thing* wasn't, but it had classical antecedents and it was conceptualized.

MGM was eager to unburden their *Anna Christie* onto us, to let us try to solve their problems. But first we had to see O'Neill's widow, Carlotta Monterey. Abbott paid the visit. She was charmed by him. We negotiated the rights easily and for reasonable terms. We then acquired the score, of which we were able to use only half because the contemporary material was useless in the new scheme of things.

I thought Gwen would be good for the lead. I remember George Abbott was somewhat resistant. She was a dancing star and it bothered him. But Gwen wanted to play it desperately, and she was right to want it. It would show off aspects of her acting which she'd never shown before. It would stretch her.

We had heard Thelma Ritter was scheduled to play the Marie Dressler role in the MGM version. A wonderful idea, so we took it.

The best thing about that musical was the meeting of those two ladies in a bar. It was the best scene and it contained no music, which was symptomatic of what was to be wrong throughout the musical.

Very sensibly we set up guidelines to avoid traps. George had been reluctant to cast Gwen, not because she couldn't play the role without dancing, but how would audiences feel if they went to a musical *Anna Christie* starring Gwen Verdon and she didn't dance? And Anna mustn't dance. We all agreed with that—Bobby Fosse and Gwen, all of us, agreed with that. No matter what, this woebegone, negative, misanthropic wharf rat must not be choreographed.

All well and good *until* you get into a bit of trouble and reach for the crutch. We're a little boring in there, *Gwen, put on your dancing shoes.* Which is exactly what happened. And the more dancing we added for Gwen, the more we hurt the show. *New Girl* was far better in rehearsal, when we stuck with a concept, conscious of risking the wrath of our audience.

George Abbott has never been a man to set someone dancing without motivation. In this respect, "the Abbott touch" has been consistently misunderstood. Dancing characters dance, doors are slammed *only* when characters out of emotion would slam them, and there is no such thing as a funny reading of a line.

There is a kind of deliciously unmotivated musical, a cherished memory of yesteryear which some of our critics lament the loss of. Not I. I think that shows in which songs are utterly unmotivated, in which characters react inconsistently for laughs, mindless and pleasantly entertaining though they may be, through overpraise dangerously inhibit the future of the musical. I think *Hello, Dolly!* is one of those shows.

I think that *The Matchmaker* is brilliant source material for a musical. I think also that show was blissfully conceived, that it moved brilliantly. I don't think anybody in the world could have done it as well as Gower Champion, and I don't think it's *The Matchmaker*. I believe I would have preferred *The*

Matchmaker, because there are tensions in that play and because there are people. Carol Channing is an artist. She has powerful style and you can relax and let her take care of you. She also makes you smile, inside and out, but she isn't Dolly Gallagher Levi, not Thornton Wilder's Dolly Gallagher Levi. She can play this musical called *Hello, Dolly!*

Now, there are serious pitfalls in my preferences, and they tend to take the fun out of an evening.

A beautiful example of a show which was mindless, and as far as I'm concerned worked marvelously, was *Bye Bye Birdie*. What a good time. What a really good show. But try to apply to its characters consistent human motivations; try to direct them in those terms. I know if that show had found its way into our office, and I'd loved the score as much as I ended up loving it on the stage, I would have destroyed it. If I'd been the director, I would have destroyed it, and if I'd been the producer, Abbott might have seriously damaged it, because all of us fed on the kind of logic harmful to the spirit of *Bye Bye Birdie*(s).

Birdie is one of the few mindless musicals I love. *Guys and Dolls*, another, is one of the best musicals I have ever seen.

But give me *The King and I*.

For *Anna Christie* MGM initially wanted 2 percent for the basic rights, but we fought that: 2 percent is too high. Though as much as 3 percent has been paid for basic rights, and the Shaw Estate exacted enormous terms for *Pygmalion*, that doesn't alter my position. I would have turned down the Shaw Estate and looked elsewhere. I still would.

A play should be budgeted so that it can exist at 60 percent capacity.

We held out in our negotiations with MGM and ultimately settled the rights for a total of 2 percent to both the motion-picture studio and the O'Neill Estate. And though that show ran not quite thirteen months and generally well below capacity, it returned its investment and realized a substantial profit.

But what is *Anna Christie*? And what should it have been? *Anna Christie* is an opera, and that is all you can truthfully, faithfully make of it. An American opera. Probably it would not have run a year *had* it been an opera, but that, aesthetically, is what it should have been. The book tried valiantly to lighten relentlessly serious material.

29

As soon as we opened out of town, we knew we were in deep trouble. Something we couldn't turn to each other and say in New Haven. Instead we set out to make a *better* evening of it, to make a hit out of it, but (and this despite Abbott) the panic had set in, and panic decreed that Gwen change costumes and reappear every few minutes in a new musical number—singing, dancing, turning increasingly into the workhorse, bailing all of us out of a shared embarrassment. Mind you, she wanted the new material. She wanted new dances. She, too, had panicked. (In fact, no one girl in the company could handle Gwen's chores. Three understudies were assigned to cover the role simultaneously!)

The most important days in the birth of a musical are the day you decide to do it (and that's when we got into trouble with *New Girl in Town*) and the day *after* you open out of town. Few shows open in good shape. The amount of work you can accomplish is extraordinary. But not if you panic. The fellow who goes to bed right after the opening performance out of town wakes up fresh in the morning, moves slowly for a couple of days, and then says, "Now here's what we're going to do"—that fellow collects his stability (because he's got to be exhausted, having been through the extended rehearsal period) and gathers objectivity. I learned that from Abbott.

And, too, Abbott listens to people. I learned from him that you should, in fact, listen to everybody. Of course, you're going to listen to a lot of fools, but listening doesn't mean acting. Turn off the fools. But when the same observation comes up over and over again, doesn't that suggest *perhaps* you're receiving good advice? Don't be stubborn: listen. You really aren't threatened. You won't act if it contradicts your better judgment.

Abbott's work, even when it fails, *never* gives you a feeling of uneasiness. It has foundation. You never sit in a theatre and think, Oh, God, what's going to happen? You know people are going to make entrances and exits like professionals. You are in good hands.

Gwen, meanwhile, got sick. She was sick from exhaustion, and sick from conflict. There was a dance which had been designed for a scene in a brothel; Abbott and the producers objected to it as pornographic, an artistic miss. The movement possibly was lovely (Gwen and Bobby Fosse thought so). Erotic, yes. But it had been imposed on the play. We had entered a musical brothel, our prostitutes became dancers, our Anna Christie, Gwen Verdon.

30

Now every line from the original play which survived the adaptation gave us trouble. Gwen got sick and all work stopped.

For the first time, we were confronting each other rather than collaborating, Verdon and Fosse on the one side, Abbott, Griffith, and Prince on the other. I believe it's impossible for an actress who is learning new lines and lyrics, rehearsing dances, and appearing constantly onstage scene after scene to remain objective in such a crisis.

We reached a poor compromise: the ballet was out in favor of another version. Gwen got out of bed, and Bobby rechoreographed. The outcome was a pale imitation of the original. Still as out of place, but inoffensive. So much for compromise.

I have no regrets about *New Girl*. I think the lessons learned were worth the trouble and we were paid for them. *New Girl* remains for us unique in that respect: a hit which I must consider a failure.

I never worked with Bobby and Gwen again; at that time the troubles we shared became imagined betrayals. Panic divided us, and we took sides. What was wrong was that we had collaborated on the wrong project. It takes time to accept that.

Even though *New Girl* ran 439 performances, nobody came to see a "Brisson, Griffith, and Prince show" for as long as that partnership existed. Mostly the reviews assumed that George Abbott had produced them. And later when Bobby Griffith and I were sole partners, there wasn't a sense of a Griffith and Prince stamp either. We got our share of publicity, but neither of us was a television personality. We never gravitated toward that. Perhaps with *Cabaret*, because I had directed it, people were aware of my involvement as they had not been before. Add the phenomenal run of *Fiddler* to subsequent shows, and I think some people do come to see a musical this office does. But, and this is as good a time as any to say it, Broadway is not the place to look for loyalty from the public, and sad as that is to the ego, it is one of the best things you can say about Broadway.

Every time Richard Rodgers goes to bat, with all the affection and gratitude that people feel for what he has achieved in the past, in a sense he is still going for the first time. There is nothing to parallel films, where you can make a good picture in 1953 and work the balance of your life *because* you made a good picture in 1953! Sounds ruthless, but it's good for the theatre. And for artists.

REFLECTIONS ON CHAPTER 4
OF *CONTRADICTIONS*

Years later, as a result of my producing *New Girl in Town* (adapted from *Anna Christie*) and directing *The Great God Brown*, I was given the prestigious Monte Cristo Award from the Eugene O'Neill Theater Center. I'm particularly grateful for that because I've since visited this amazing facility, taught a class there, and was taken on a tour of O'Neill's home in Waterford, Connecticut, the setting of his masterpiece *A Long Day's Journey into Night*.

Apropos the break-even figure, in the 1950s, we budgeted our shows so that at 60 percent capacity they could repay their investment and show a profit. How times have changed.

CHAPTER
5

New Girl was the last Brisson, Griffith, and Prince show.
Propinquity began us, and when *Wonderful Town* closed, Freddie Brisson
moved back to California, and the distance finished us. The effort of sharing
decisions with a partner on the West Coast was time-consuming and seemed
fraudulent on our part.

The partnership officially ended when we took over *West Side Story*.

West Side Story had been owned by Cheryl Crawford, in association with
Roger Stevens. Stevens had financed the formative years of that project.
When Miss Crawford bowed out, Stephen Sondheim brought us in. He and
I had first met in the audience on the opening night of *South Pacific* in April
of 1949. He was there with his mentor, Oscar Hammerstein II, and Mary
Rodgers introduced us.

It's curious, that. Steve was a composer whose reputation had reached
me all the way from Williams College, where he had written book, music,
and lyrics for a show called *Climb High* (which was the story of a young man
with aspirations to act on Broadway).

Steve reminds me that soon after we met, I reasoned with him over a
bacon, lettuce, and tomato sandwich in Walgreen's that we were the natural
inheritors of the theatre we were entering. I've always been an optimist,
Steve a pessimist. (I guess both of us are wrong.)

Back to *West Side*. The most interesting part preceded our involvement.
West Side was originally dreamed up in 1945 by Robbins and Arthur Laurents
as a story about a Jewish girl and a Gentile boy on the streets of New York.
Soon after, Leonard Bernstein joined them, and for a time Betty Comden
and Adolph Green were to write the lyrics and Leland Hayward to produce.
Sondheim didn't join them until years later. During the twelve years before
Bobby and I became involved social, conditions had changed in New York,

and Laurents altered his libretto to a conflict of Puerto Ricans and Caucasians on the West Side of Manhattan.

That musical was brought to George Abbott to produce, and he turned it down. It was then offered to us and, based on the script, we turned it down without hearing the score.

I never appreciated how artful Arthur Laurents's book was until the play went into rehearsal—how concise, how important, in particular, the language he was able to invent to remove it *just enough* from real street language so that it would be at one with Robbins's dances. We turned it down, and Roger Stevens picked it up in conjunction with Cheryl Crawford, which brings us back to Boston and *New Girl in Town*.

We were going into our last tryout week there, Gwen Verdon was out of the show ill, rehearsals were stymied, and I was on the phone with Steve. It was 3:00 a.m., and I had documented our woes to the last detail. Eventually it occurred to me only politely to ask Steve how things were going with *West Side*. With six weeks left before scheduled rehearsals, Cheryl Crawford had called the whole thing off. I sympathized. What else could I do? I had my own problems.

I said good night, lay awake a few hours, then phoned him back and suggested Bobby and I fly to New York the following Sunday, meet with the creators, and hear the score. (Bernstein was very proprietary about that score: no one was supposed to have heard it, though I knew every note of it via Steve.) If we were happy with each other that day, they would have to agree to leave us alone during the remaining week in Boston, during the New York previews: they would have to wait until after *New Girl* opened. They agreed.

We flew into New York, had a marvelous meeting with them. Sondheim and Bernstein played the score, and soon I was singing along with them. Bernstein would look up and say, "My God, he's so musical! A *musical* producer!" I simply grinned, stopped singing temporarily, forgot again, and got complimented again.

Putting *West Side* out of our minds, we flew back to Boston.

Parenthetically, in those days I stayed on the road the entire time. The New York office was run by Carl Fisher, our general manager, and I would sit in on most rehearsals. They do get boring, so you go for intermittent walks.

But you never know when you'll be needed, and you must be there every morning for conferences. Abbott likes daily conferences. It's important for a director not to isolate himself from his collaborators, and strangely, most of them tend to, to protect themselves. The musical is the most highly collaborative form there is.

It was difficult to come out from under Abbott's protective arm. On the other hand, he gave us his blessing easily. George Abbott is a secure man. *New Girl* opened on May 14, 1957, and we met with Robbins, Bernstein, Laurents, and Sondheim at 10:00 a.m. on May 15. And *West Side* was cast, financed, booked into a theatre, and in rehearsal two weeks later than originally scheduled. This was only the first time that Steve Sondheim would come to my rescue and I to his, as we shall see later.

West Side was unique in that it was so incredibly prepared. Robbins is one of the most prepared people I've ever known. The contrast between Robbins and Abbott is interesting. Robbins apprenticed to Abbott in his earlier days. The very first shows he choreographed Abbott directed, and so a lot of the respect, sound-headedness of Abbott's organization, lack of emotionalism, lack of patience with theatricality offstage—this sanity influenced Robbins, has influenced me, has influenced others. But Abbott is less apprehensive than Robbins about material, and Abbott's shows are more often than not created on the road. He leaves a lot undecided until he sees a show in front of an audience. Consequently, it is not uncommon for Abbott to throw out a third of the score and substantially rewrite the script. It's his mentality.

Robbins, on the other hand, would like the opening-night reviews in his hands before he goes into rehearsal. He is gun-shy. He hates to go into rehearsal. He's the fellow standing on the edge of a precipice; you, the producer, have to push him over (which naturally makes you responsible if the show fails!). But when he finally goes, of course, it's galvanic.

West Side opened in Washington, D.C., in better shape than any show I've ever seen, much less worked on. Seven weeks later it opened in New York, and it was substantially the same. Robbins kept busy on the road because he's predilected to fixing.

Laurents kept writing, but little of it got into the show. The dance for the number "Somewhere" simply didn't work, and Jerry eventually improved on it.

Robbins has been called a "method" director. Actually, he likes to dabble in it. He did in *West Side* and later in *Fiddler*. During the rehearsal period of *West Side*, he related the cast thoroughly to their gangs. Half were Jets and half were Sharks. They traveled in packs away from the theatre. They were young and inexperienced, and identification improved their acting. *West Side* had no chorus. Each gang member had a name and history. Each cut out newspaper accounts of gang rivalries; they covered the rear walls of the Winter Garden stage with them.

There was a character in the script called Anybodys, played by Lee Becker, who was rejected by both gangs, so the cast rejected her. She took her lunch hour alone.

There was only one major crisis on *West Side*. It followed a disastrous first run-through, perhaps three weeks into rehearsal. The show was slow, lugubrious, somewhat self-conscious, IMPORTANT. Too much introspection, no impulse, no energy. Fear struck.

Laurents and Robbins, who worked well together—not always calmly, but productively—discussed it, and Jerry was persuaded to remove the method, discard the improvisational atmosphere, and resort to old-fashioned line readings. And the company snapped to so quickly that at the next run-through, less than a week later, the show was in good shape.

I am certain, however, that the earlier process gave the play its legs.

I feel some impulse to clarify the comment on Laurents and Robbins working together well, if not calmly. Laurents is a nag, astute, perceptive, persistently pressuring, assaulting, sometimes brilliantly, and Robbins understands this. He is capable of causing similar abrasions in his relationship with actors. This is not uncommon among choreographer-directors. The whole relationship between dancer and choreographer contains powerful elements of sadomasochism.

That process doesn't work for me. I need to have fun in rehearsal. I need the laughter, no matter how emotional things get. I shy away from contention. Contrary to my peers, no show for me is the most important thing in the world.

We gave a performance for the "gypsies" (an affectionate term given to dancers and singers in an earlier time, when living out of trunks was the mainstay of the commercial theatre), sans costumes, scenery, or orchestra. I have never heard such a reaction. To this day I tend to prefer these performances to the finished ones, probably because the audiences are sophisticated, predisposed in favor of friends in the cast, and unprepared. Certainly, production values should and can enhance. The trouble is that so often they don't. I've never seen a show that was made a hit by its scenery or costumes (Oliver Messel's work for *House of Flowers* and Christian Bérard's for *The Madwoman of Chaillot* were equally ravishing). However, I have seen shows that were seriously injured by the wrong production.

In the case of the gypsy run-through, what people are responding to is an evolutionary process, which, if you've handled your rehearsals properly, comes at the perfect time. Your first audience is ready and your actors are primed for a first audience. The good in a production takes stage center, and the flaws are excused; after all, there are how-so-many weeks to go, not to mention *the scenery, the costumes, and the orchestra.* I'm surprised so few productions use the gypsy run-through. Perhaps they are afraid they are not ready, but rehearsal schedules should be gauged so that you are ready the day before you leave for Boston or New Haven or Philadelphia. There's really no postponing it, and occasionally a New York audience can affirm something about your material that you won't feel confident about again until you return to New York.

A Funny Thing Happened on the Way to the Forum had a triumphant gypsy run-through. It opened a week later in New Haven and died. It died again (and worse) in Washington. A play designed for laughter played to silence for four weeks, and all we had to keep the actors and creators going was the memory of the bare-stage run-through in New York. It sustained them.

Also, the gypsy run-through gives you extra days while you're setting up the show out of town to fix things that clearly don't work in front of an audience.

Apropos the value of designing: I remember I didn't have much patience for the blue jeans Irene Sharaff "designed" for *West Side* at the cost of seventy-five dollars a pair (today they would cost $200). I thought, How foolish to be wasting money when we can make a promotional arrangement with Levi Strauss to supply blue jeans free for program credit. So I instructed the wardrobe mistress in New York to replace them as they wore out with Levi's, not with costumes. A year later I looked at *West Side* and wondered,

Why doesn't it look as beautiful as it used to? What's happened? What "happened" was that Sharaff's blue jeans were made of a special fabric, which was then dipped and dyed and beaten and dyed again and aged again, and so on, so our blue jeans were in forty subtly different shades of blue, vibrating, energetic, creating the *effect* of realism.

Digressing, there is a famous drop which Lem Ayers designed for the finale of *Kiss Me, Kate* and which to my eye was a construction of black and white diamonds. I found it visually thrilling. Subsequently, working with Lem on *Pajama Game*, I asked to see the sketches for *Kiss Me, Kate*, in particular the black-and-white one, which wasn't black and white at all. It was black and white and green and red and maroon, and there were other colors, controlled and interpolated to create the *effect* of black and white. Black and white would have died on that stage. The additional colors energized it.

Jean Rosenthal was lighting designer for *West Side Story*. It was the first time we had worked with *any* lighting designer.

Credit Jerry Robbins. Credit dance theatre, which depends more on lighting than scenery.

When I started with Abbott and until *West Side*, Bobby and the company electrician, George Gebhardt, lighted our shows. It was a matter of lights up for the scene, and lights down for the song. Lights up again after the song, with George Abbott shouting from the orchestra, "More light on those faces—this is a funny scene." And when the laughs didn't come, still more light. (There weren't lights powerful enough to get *those* laughs!)

To give you some idea of how unappreciated lighting design remains, our most prestigious designers receive a weekly royalty of seventy-five dollars.

Though *West Side* received unanimously favorable reviews in New York, many were lukewarm. It was another musical, lurid, perhaps, lacking in heart, and of course, the dances were stunning. We sold out for only a few weeks. I went to the box office the morning after it opened, and instead of the hundreds of people I expected, there were only three people waiting to buy tickets.

As a rule, critics do not predict art; they follow it.

More specifically, our drama critics did not understand the score. It is axiomatic that when a composer writes the score for his first show, though the show may be a success, the score is rarely recognized. Invariably he must wait for his second success for his first good reviews. In the case of *West Side*, Bernstein was applauded, Sondheim wasn't even mentioned, and Laurents's book was largely ignored.

Walter Kerr called *Cabaret*, the first success I directed, "a stunning musical, brilliantly conceived," but neglected to mention the director. I was paid back when I did *Zorba*—disproportionately, perhaps—for all the years that I didn't get reviewed.

As for the reviews that costumes and scenery inspire, I think they are discouragingly undiscerning. Critics are impressed by certain reputations (and not others), usually reputations that come from outside: Leonard Bernstein's reputation, Burt Bacharach's reputation. Visiting royalty. They're not *not* of the theatre, but they're not working in the theatre regularly.

Barring total approval in a review, I covet controversy. I wish there were more critics. I wish they weren't "trendy."

Too often, critics disregard the ambitions of a project, settling for limited horizons. I don't want them to admire something with pretentious aspirations. That would be absurd. But when they measure that which is attempting to achieve something and succeeds 70 percent in achieving it, equally with something which is attempting nothing but to amuse in old-fashioned terms and achieves it 100 percent, then they have performed irresponsibly. It is easier to document laughter, hilarity, than the stimulus of ideas. If a serious play is lucky enough to be controversial, to cause a storm, then it may succeed. But why should that be mandatory? If a critic is intrigued by a serious play, he is obliged to write intriguingly. That takes writing talent.

The question of a critic's credentials is another thing. One theatre critic is also a dance critic; why is he there? One critic was a newscaster; why is he there? I really don't know, and I don't even care. If he's there to review theatre, and he's intelligent and loves theatre, those constitute credentials as far as I'm concerned. On the other hand, he still must write well or speak well or, in the case of television, project well. I'm one of those people who think it is possible to review a show in fifty seconds. You can read quite a lot of words in fifty seconds, and you can transmit quite a lot of emotion in that time. TV critics need not be pundits; I'll save weekends for scholarly tomes. This morning, tonight, I simply want to know whether to go down to the box office and buy tickets. Immediately—yes, or no.

The subject of critics and criticism, which commands so much space, doesn't deserve it. Nothing new has been said for thousands of years. Without critics, people wouldn't know what to see. Good reviews sell tickets.

Enough said.

West Side played about a year and a half on Broadway; then we made an error. We calculated we had run out of our audience, so in a last-ditch effort to keep going until the road tour started, we lowered prices and initiated a two-for-the-price-of-one policy. Immediately we sold out; we had run out of one audience and *into* another. Ticket prices were too high even then for a substantial segment of our audience which indeed is interested in going to the theatre. Our pricing then and now doesn't cover a wide enough range: I know there are cheap seats, but too few and rarely ever in the orchestra. Theatregoers don't want to climb stairs. I don't necessarily agree with them (I mean, the balcony *can* be fun), but what in hell is gained by our obstinately ignoring the realities! Put more popular-priced seats downstairs and you'll sell out. And a full-price empty seat is emptier than a half-price full one. The economics are simple enough: you must gross a certain amount to ensure operating expenses and a fair profit to recoup your investment. It can be done by keeping a wider spectrum of prices. This way I believe we would do away with the two-for-one policy, which is seriously damaging the theatre.

Anyway, we pulled *West Side* out of New York perhaps six months too soon.

It was too late to change our plans and stay. We had to book theatres, advertise, sell subscriptions well in advance. It takes a peculiar talent to know when to close a show, and this office is short on that talent. I'll save that until later.

Our road tour lasted less than a year. Business was very good on the West Coast, disappointing in Chicago. Chicago is generally disappointing with Broadway touring shows. It supports its local theatre. "Second City blues," I think, accounts for some of it. That and the fact that the quality of touring productions had been inferior for so many years.

We came back to New York, and I persuaded Bernstein to conduct the overture reopening night, and the critics to rereview us, with the result that we received the reviews we should have gotten in the first place. This time around the book was special, Sondheim was credited, and the show had a place in history. Further, they implied they had felt that way about it the first time around. But they hadn't.

We played another six months. Ironically, we would have played even longer had I not gotten into a dispute with the musicians' union. We were playing the Alvin then, and it had booked a new musical. The Broadway, a bigger house, was available, and we could have moved, dropping prices and enlarging our audience. Probably the show would have run an extra six months. However, it was no longer a moneymaker. It was alive, providing employment. From a producer's and investor's point of view, there were no more profits in store, perhaps even some small risk in the move.

We went to the musicians' union and explained that if we closed at the Alvin Theatre on Saturday, we would be able to open again on Wednesday or Thursday of the following week at the Broadway. We could not afford to pay the actors, musicians, or anybody else for the intervening days, and I asked for a concession. They turned me down. We produced statements substantiating our position. I suppose they figured that our ego was so great that we would keep that show running even at a loss. They were mistaken, and *West Side Story* closed. The musicians were out of work, and so for that matter were the stagehands and the actors and everybody else.

Unions, not just theatrical unions, seem to operate on the theory that to allow the exception is to weaken the whole structure of the contract with management. "Give them an inch and they'll take a mile." I know management provoked it, and I am a unionist myself, but conditions *do* change.

Unhappily, negotiations with the musicians have not changed (see *Candide*, page 187). I have my problems with the actors' union, as well. Long ago I ceased going to Actors' Equity for concessions. Occasionally, I would present their council with problems which I was naive enough to believe we *shared*. I was invariably turned down.

In the old days, we always gave everybody a raise the day a show returned its investment. We can't afford to do that anymore, because the union is too busy ruling that a chorus person carrying a tray is in fact playing a waiter and must be paid accordingly. Or that somebody leaping inches off the stage in a dance is risking life and limb and so is entitled to hazard pay. We sit down and argue strenuously these absurdities, and ultimately it degenerates into my winning some points and losing others, and finally someone says to me, "Don't you understand, these rules are not made for YOU, they're made for the crooks we have to deal with?" And I can't help but think, Why, then, don't you make special rules for me?

Everyone considers *West Side* a classic, yet in that year 1957–58, it did not win any major awards.

West Side Story was never appreciated in those terms until it was made into a movie. For the stage version, Jerry Robbins won a Tony as best choreographer. I think they would have had difficulty avoiding that! But the show lost out to *Music Man*, which ran years longer than *West Side Story*.

But awards are like that. They give them out and it is nice to collect them. Much nicer than watching the other fellow collect them. Nevertheless, it is wrong to think they are an accurate measure of achievement. They can be; they often are not. It seems to me equally wrong to make a big deal of refusing to accept them: that gives them the importance they're not supposed to have.

What awards are is publicity. They are good for the theatre industry, fleeting fun for the individual, and only occasionally good for the play. This has changed some since Alex Cohen took over the Tony Awards, which are watched by forty-four million people.

As for the film, United Artists was the only interested buyer. They bought it for $315,000, which was very little in those days, plus a piece of the profits. But profit participation in films has always been a chancy business: don't count on any. *West Side Story* was the exception. Though the Broadway production recouped its costs, and increments from the tour, stock and amateur rights, and the cast album provided some profit, the film as of today has been worth over $3 million to the production. And there will be more.

REFLECTIONS ON CHAPTER 5
OF *CONTRADICTIONS*

"America," Chita Rivera's showstopper, was staged by Peter Gennaro. In the intervening years, Rivera has been quoted saying that much if not all of her dance material was choreographed by Peter Gennaro.

As of the end of 2015, *West Side Story* has returned 1,521 percent to its investors.

Since I quit producing in the 1970s, I think it's fair to say that it irritates me when I'm referred to primarily as a producer. My pal Sondheim must have felt similarly annoyed when he was identified for many years as a lyricist. It doesn't happen to him anymore, but to me, well, occasionally.

In 1958 I was invited by the Eisenhower administration to do what became the first light entertainment show that ever played in the East Room of the White House. (Since then there have been similar shows for many administrations. In the case of President Obama, even more frequently.) At the time, I put together material from *The Pajama Game* ("Steam Heat"), *New Girl in Town*, *The Music Man* (with the child star Eddie Hodges), and *West Side Story*.

Peter Gennaro and Pat Stanley wore sneakers while rehearsing "Steam Heat," which left great black lines on the polished floor. Predictably we also made rather a lot of noise, and at one point there was a call from upstairs that Mrs. Eisenhower was resting. Despite all this, it came off well, and there's a wonderful picture of all of us ranged on the staircase below the Truman Balcony.

CHAPTER
6

Only one theatrical poster is missing from the walls in my outer office. I haven't had the guts to hang it.

After *West Side Story*, Bobby and I read and liked a straight play by Jess Gregg called *The Sea Shell*, later changing the title to *A Swim in the Sea*.

It was about incest in a fatherless Southern family. The principal role called for a strong lady star in her sixties, a Laurette Taylor type, perhaps Shirley Booth or Helen Hayes. So we sent it to the Misses Booth and Hayes, and they returned it. Simultaneously we sent it to the appropriate directors—Elia Kazan, Joshua Logan, Harold Clurman—and they too rejected it.

The rejections continued coming in until we had exhausted lists of third and fourth choices. Eager to see it through (we had started it, hadn't we?), we arranged to try it out in winter stock in Palm Beach at the Royal Poinciana Playhouse. We reasoned that the play, littered with compromise casting and direction, would shine through a faulty production, that we would be able to fix it, based on seeing it, and to interest the right people to reconsider and do it on Broadway.

We had entered a companionship with self-deception, not unique in the theatre but unprofessional and lazy.

In order to try out in Florida, there are certain requirements. The play must have few sets, preferably one, to be designed by the theatre's resident designer and executed by apprentices, a small cast (room for apprentice walk-ons, perhaps?), and laughs, but the essential requirement is a star. So we persuaded Peggy Wood, television's *I Remember Mama* and (for the sophisticated Palm Beach audience) Noël Coward's star in several musicals and more recently *Blithe Spirit*—a brilliant actress if cast in the right role.

Nevertheless, Miss Wood was miscast. She knew it. She agreed to play it only for the two Florida weeks. Then, perhaps, if it were rewritten, but that was a long shot. Anyway, it was a chilly New York midwinter, and Florida was warm and we couldn't get hurt.

Truly we couldn't get hurt—not financially. In return for a small stake in a future Broadway production, Palm Beach would pay rehearsal costs, cast salaries, and furnish the set (suitable for transport to Broadway), costumes, and elegant social and sociable full houses. How could we lose?

In addition to Miss Wood, we cast two relative newcomers, George Peppard and Inga Swenson, as the incestuous progeny.

Audrey Wood, Tennessee Williams's agent, recommended a young director named Elliot Silverstein. How do you choose a director whose work you've never seen? On a third person's recommendation? Subsequently, Silverstein directed the film *Cat Ballou*. We were not so fortunate.

A Swim in the Sea wasn't all that bad in Florida. Considering the compromises, and the ten-day rehearsal period, the reviews were pretty good, but then, local newspapers are predisposed to encourage their local theatre. *No one gets hurt.*

The trouble is that when no one gets hurt, when you limit the chances you take, indemnify the production, you go lazy, the "sure thing" evaporates in the same atmosphere of self-deception.

But the reviews in Florida were nice, and it had been costless and painless— so we came to New York.

Peggy Wood wisely refused to come. So did George Peppard. Inga Swenson reasoned hers was the best role in the play and a fit debut, regardless of what became of the play. Probably she was right.

And Elliot Silverstein wanted to come. So he did.

We signed Fay Bainter, who expressed grave misgivings, to replace Miss Wood (we showed her the Florida reviews), shipped the economy set to New York, and raised $100,000.

Griffith and Prince up until now had had four sizable successes, so it was difficult, impossible perhaps, to conceive of failure.

At the start Bainter and Silverstein loathed each other.

To replace Peppard, who had been excellent, we compromised on a charming Tony Perkinsish fellow with modest talent and little experience.

At the least, our venture into eclecticism demanded a perfect cast, sensitive direction, a production, if it was to have a chance. We gave it nothing but $100,000 and an opening in Philadelphia.

The play didn't work. Reviews were awful. The first of two weeks I kept to my room in the Warwick Hotel, to my bed actually—Oblomov. At the end of that week, Bobby and I decided to leave the play in Philadelphia—more accurately, to leave Philadelphia and to leave the actors there to play out the final week.

For Inga Swenson it was particularly painful because it was to be her debut on Broadway and she was good. As it happens, it merely delayed her inevitable success in *110 in the Shade*. For Fay Bainter it was a reprieve. For Silverstein it was probably a disappointment. It would neither have hurt nor helped him if we had let it come into New York. For Jess Gregg, the playwright, it was a great disappointment because he was deceived into thinking that something badly produced was better than nothing. He was wrong, but what alternatives had he? Griffith and Prince had optioned it.

As for us, the minute we knew we were closing the show, it was easy to leave the hotel—indeed, a relief to have had a flop. Moreover, we deserved it. And it was painless. Pain is a play you love that closes, but pain is not a failure. Curiously, we felt baptized. A failure lent credence to the events of the past three years and gave us a feeling of continuity.

Inadvertently, the disaster provided us with the means to further impress our investors. We returned 52 percent of their money with a letter saying we had closed in Philadelphia, had chosen to return the remaining capital and deprive them of an opening night on Broadway.

Actually, investors should take failures in stride. What they shouldn't take in stride are insufficient profits from successes.

Incidentally, we gave the scenery to the University of Pennsylvania in exchange for carting it away. Another economy.

REFLECTIONS ON CHAPTER 6
OF *CONTRADICTIONS*

I regard the material for *A Swim in the Sea* as excellent and Jess Gregg as a first-rate playwright who never experienced the success he deserved.

A Swim in the Sea was produced in London more successfully.

I've directed a number of plays over the years, but it's clear I'm not regarded as being as successful a director of plays as I am of musicals. I regret that, because as I've said earlier it's plays that lured me into the theatre, and I think in a number of instances I have done a good job. I've come to believe I should've directed *A Swim in the Sea*. Some years later when I brought over *Poor Bitos*, an Anouilh play which had been a success in London starring Donald Pleasence, he urged me to take over the direction of it. I couldn't or wouldn't, and though I admired the original production, I realized only after it closed swiftly on Broadway that I would've done a better job. It would not have been so realistic; it would have been abstracted, and that would've been better for the play, which Pleasence seemed to know, but at the time I didn't.

CHAPTER

7

Arthur Penn called, asking me whether I'd be interested in an idea for an original musical. Over lunch at the Coffee House Club he handed me a piece of paper on which he had written the name Fiorello La Guardia. He had researched La Guardia's private life as well as professional career. There were surprises. Half Italian, half Jewish, Fiorello was at once warmhearted, ruthless, sentimental, intransigent, musical, a distracted father to his family, an omnipresent father to millions, endlessly petty, and immensely generous, a human being of heroic size.

I had always been fascinated by the personal lives of Churchill and Roosevelt. And it was some surprise to find that Fiorello shared their paradoxical inability to cope with their private responsibilities while solving the problems of the masses by using precisely the same human criteria they should have been bringing home.

Bobby loved the idea and suggested Jerome Weidman, who had written *I Can Get It for You Wholesale*, as a possible librettist.

Weidman was interested. We met in Rowayton, Connecticut, at Bobby's house—Weidman, Penn, and I, Penn agreeing to guide the writing and ultimately direct the musical.

At this point, we sought permission from Marie La Guardia, Fiorello's widow. La Guardia had died in 1947. Though interested, she was anxious to protect her husband's reputation and arranged a meeting with friends of hers and the late mayor's at the La Guardia home in Riverdale.

We offered to outline roughly the course of the musical as soon as we knew it, but withheld editorial approval. Our intentions were honorable, but in order to make a good evening of it, we had to illuminate the martinet in Fiorello, his ruthlessness on behalf of his principles, and so on.

It was also in our plans to tell Fiorello's personal story in terms of his two marriages. It was Penn's idea that in the first act our leading lady would play his first wife, the beautiful Thea, who died in childbirth in the 1920s.

In the second act, taking place years later, the same actress would play Marie, his secretary and assistant during the clubhouse era in New York politics. He would marry Marie at the final curtain. Questionable larger point: you always marry the same woman.

We proposed the outline to Mrs. La Guardia and her friends, who agreed to think about it and let us know. The next morning she phoned and said go ahead. The immediacy of the reply was characteristic of Marie La Guardia.

The first scene Weidman wrote was of a poker game among wardheelers in a clubhouse and ran thirty minutes, every minute of it rich in ethnic Italian American political history. Weidman then went on to write a second scene for the second act, using the same characters. They'd aged and the city was in the grips of Jimmy Walker's fraud and corruption. Encompassed in these two out-of-context scenes, Weidman had captured the tone, the peculiar vitality of the era, the style of our show.

It was time to interest a composer-lyricist. Bobby and I had recently seen a musical, *The Body Beautiful*, with an interesting score by a new songwriting team, Jerry Bock and Sheldon Harnick. Bock had written *Mr. Wonderful*, the previous year, for Sammy Davis.

I had known Sheldon Harnick as a composer and lyricist, particularly of special material. Tommy Valando, the music publisher, teamed them up. Subsequently, he did the same thing for Kander and Ebb.

On legal advisement, since we had yet to sign an agreement with the La Guardia people, and fearing pressure from them that we come up with Richard Rodgers or Irving Berlin, we suggested Bock and Harnick write three songs on spec, omitting to tell them the idea of the show they were asked to work on. We gave them the clubhouse scenes, which were not clearly defined La Guardia material. They agreed.

Meanwhile, I trimmed the first clubhouse scene from thirty minutes to seven and Bock and Harnick musicalized most of Weidman's dialogue into "Politics and Poker."

Bobby and I liked it so much we decided not to wait for the additional songs but to make it official, to tell them what the show they'd been working on for two weeks was about. Whereupon they wrote "On the Side of the Angels," the opening number.

The key songs in a score are so often the first to be written. This was true of "Wilkommen" in *Cabaret*, of "Company," of "Racing with the Clock" in *The Pajama Game*. Probably it's a very good idea, as they establish (or should) the ground rules for what is to follow. The tone, style, concept, and often the point of the evening. Oscar Hammerstein said most musicals are made in the first five minutes.

Weidman wrote quickly. The material poured out of him with no evident difficulty. And from the first, Arthur Penn seemed disappointed. He wanted it deeper, psychologically deeper.

But Weidman wasn't writing Penn's *Fiorello!* His, and Bobby's and mine, was a more nostalgic subject, a lament for a bygone manageable New York, for the loss of heroes, of the innocence of speakeasies and payoffs and gang wars. Penn wanted more; more internal conflict; deeper, more disturbed interpersonal relationships. He had had them in *The Miracle Worker* and *Two for the Seesaw*, and he wanted them in this, his first go at the musical form. I believed then and still do that he wasn't leaving room for music and dance, and, further, that Fiorello was the wrong subject for such treatment.

It's not that there exist rules about such things, just a *feel* of what identifies a project, of when the surprise is a surprise and not a violation. Since that time I believe I have proven a predilection for what Walter Kerr calls the "dark musical." So it was in *particular* that we disagreed, not in principle.

We parted amicably, Penn retaining an author's interest, and we turned to George Abbott to direct.

Abbott rejected the idea of Fiorello as subject for a musical. In fact, over the years Abbott disliked most of the ideas we had for musicals and said so. Fortunately, he has no difficulty changing his mind.

We arranged an audition for him of both numbers, and he loved them and the Weidman scenes. Nevertheless, our plotting, particularly over the thirty years we planned to cover, seemed unmanageable. One morning he announced, "You know what's wrong with your plot, don't you?" What? "That business about one woman playing both wives—that won't work. I'll tell you what it should be. It should be—" He was hooked.

What he suggested was that we take the Marie La Guardia character, introduce her as his secretary in 1914, though she hadn't met him until much later, and tell the story of both women concurrently. This would have meant that Marie, probably in her middle fifties in 1958, would have had to be in her middle eighties.

We presented the solution to her apprehensively. She laughed and agreed to it because she's that kind of a lady. She knew how old she was, and she knew the larger aims of the play. And if that was the way to make the story work, then that was all she cared about.

Weaving the two stories simultaneously made it possible to cover the history of our city from the sweatshops through World War I, Prohibition, the Seabury investigations, to World War II.

The Abbott collaboration, extending to co-authorship with Weidman, worked easily: Abbott would outline a scene, Weidman would go home and write fifty pages overnight, and then Abbott would edit, rewrite, and structure the total.

The only actor who came to mind for Fiorello was Eli Wallach, and he wanted to do it. He wanted to sing. We worked with him. He has energy, he looks both Italian and Jewish, and while he doesn't look like Fiorello, he would have seemed to. Curiously enough, Wallach is thin and Fiorello for most of the period of our play was skinny. (Once we asked Marie La Guardia whether there was anyone she wanted to play her husband, and she replied wistfully, acknowledging the impracticality of it, "The only entertainer who ever really reminded me of Fiorello was Frank Sinatra.")

Unfortunately, Eli Wallach lacked the vocal range required by the score. He offered to study, but he never would have made our rehearsals in time. There were no other candidates. We decided to find someone unknown, someone who looked as we remembered Fiorello, someone whose anonymity might prove an advantage in recreating a familiar historical figure.

In the years since *Fiorello!* either Alan Arkin or Dustin Hoffman, both established actors, could play Fiorello brilliantly, but in the 1950s there was nobody we knew who looked remotely like him.

Judy Abbott, who was casting for us then, had seen Tom Bosley in an Off-Broadway play, at the Phoenix, I think. He did not look like the young Fiorello, but he was familiar to us. He was a young man, a little heavy, round and jowly—not really Fiorello—better than that: a caricature of Fiorello. He read for us countless times, so often in fact that each successive reading was a disappointment. This happens when an actor is obliged to reaudition for a role. Having little or no coaching from the director, the actor naturally surmises with each recall that he has been deficient in some particular, that the powers are looking for something additional, *different*, from him, and so he searches in desperation for a new approach, and for every good reason he gets further and further from the true intuitive choices he made originally. Such was the case with Bosley. Nevertheless, we stopped auditioning him (in time!) and gave him the role.

Let's stay with the subject of audition procedures. They are assailable on every level—except, can you think of another way of casting?

Obviously, if you have seen an actor in a variety of performances or in a role similar to the one you're casting, if you sense his potential, then you can forgo a reading. But it takes a staggering self-confidence on the part of the director to cast someone for something he hasn't seen him play, on talent alone. I have known George Abbott to do that, and sometimes I put it down to impatience rather than self-confidence.

The unavoidable danger of auditions is that some actors, quick and brave and shallow (we once called them "radio actors"), give you at a first reading all you're ever going to get.

Other actors, some of the best, can't.

Abbott, having seen Marlon Brando in *A Streetcar Named Desire*, wondered why his casting office hadn't brought Brando around for auditions. Griffith hauled out the files showing that Brando had auditioned for Abbott half a dozen times and had been rejected.

Then, too, in the sense that the director has something in his mind as yet uncommunicated to the actor, it's sometimes impossible for an actor to give a pertinent audition. I'm thinking of Joel Grey in *Cabaret*. Grey, "born in a trunk," singing in clubs and hotels since childhood, shared experience with the MC, recognized the gaucheries, the hollow laughter, the courage and vulnerability of a performer in a sputtering limelight. But our MC was middle-aged and German and androgynous, and all of this Grey (or whoever) had to convey with a few lines from an opening monologue and nothing more.

No one could have auditioned specifically for that role. Instead, Grey sang and danced American style, and I told the authors I wanted him and to trust me. And they did. They don't always, but I've never been more certain of what I was asking, more willing to take full blame if it failed.

Unique in my casting experiences involved the lead in *Take Her, She's Mine*. We auditioned dozens of ingenues without success. Rehearsals were scheduled in a few weeks, and desperately Phoebe and Henry Ephron, the authors, and I examined the same worn audition lists in search of a surprise. One girl's name kept appearing and next to it the words "No Show." Apparently because of illness, she'd had to cancel repeatedly. She became our *idée fixe*. We persuaded her agent to coax her out of her sickbed and up to our office. Reluctantly, Elizabeth Ashley appeared, beautiful and pale, too ill to audition, and she left. Abbott turned to us and said, "What do you think of that girl? Don't we want her?"

So much for auditioning. The point is, why not? Given the fallibility of the whole system, why in hell not? It seems to depend on how desperate you are.

Fiorello! was a picaresque musical, creating special problems (see *Candide*, page TK). We needed news footage to bridge periods of time in which the personal story wasn't dramatized.

For example, Fiorello proposed to his first wife on the eve of his departure with the Expeditionary Forces in World War I. She withheld her decision, choosing to wait until he returned from the war. So nothing *moved* for them during the war. You can't exactly ignore a war, and we chose to span that time via news footage.

There was little film on Fiorello during that period, only ten seconds of him shutting his desk in Congress and leaving for Europe, but I found stock footage from a silent feature about pilots in World War I, of a squadron standing proudly in front of its plane, one of whom I chose to identify as Fiorello. And then in the film *Wings* I found a shot of a pilot complete with goggles, machine-gunning to earth a German plane. No one questioned that he wasn't Fiorello.

Oh, the blind faith of audiences! Have you ever noticed that when you see a play or a musical, nothing ever appears to go wrong? Actually, there are very few performances in the living theatre where something doesn't go wrong. A piece of scenery flies up or down mysteriously in the middle of a scene, or an actor misses his entrance (unforgivable) and the audience takes it all on faith, motivating everything SO it comes out all right.

We made a lot of changes in *Fiorello!* during its out-of-town tryout. New numbers were written, some of the best jettisoned. The relationship between Fiorello and his women became lugubrious and sentimental. Righting it cost us a beautiful number, "Where Do I Go from Here?," which Marie sang in the first act. It is not unusual for the potentially popular song in a score to end up in a trunk somewhere.

Perhaps the most effective song written on the road was "Little Tin Box." It came at eleven or thereabouts (when the curtain went up at eight thirty). We were somewhat mired in the sad period of Fiorello's life. He'd lost his first wife and child in childbirth, and politics was going against him, and to make it even jollier, we were in the Depression. Faced with all of that, Bock and Harnick wrote a second song for the wardheelers, a companion piece to "Politics and Poker." And it stopped the show cold. Hastily, Abbott and Weidman tied up the love story and Fiorello was on his way to City Hall.

I remember hearing about eleven o'clock numbers all my life. Though I don't care much for formulas, I would settle for an eleven o'clock showstopper every time. Those don't even hurt operas.

The major flaw in *Fiorello!* was the inclusion of the subordinate story of the policeman and the flapper. Primarily they supplied comic relief, in the 1950s a necessary part of the design of a musical. Ado Annie and Will Parker in *Oklahoma!*, the Carol Haney–Eddie Foy parts in *The Pajama Game*, and in *Fiorello!*, Pat Stanley and Mark Dawson.

There must have been a way to construct *Fiorello!* without relying on the formula. Nevertheless, consider its accomplishments. First, by creating subordinate characters, Abbott was freed from the constraints of the historical characters. And the subplot accommodated dance where dance was difficult to find.

The character of the policeman represented Tammany Hall, synthesized corruption in the city, spanning along with Fiorello the entire period of the play. Life rarely provides similarly convenient relationships, and he was an amusing villain, leavening a heavy second act.

How to achieve all this without him? I have yet to figure that out, but if we were doing *Fiorello!* again today, we would have to.

The reviews were ecstatic. All of them. And the show won every award you can win, including the Pulitzer Prize. But it ran only a couple of seasons, and that well may have been my fault.

There'd been so much talk about the price of theatre tickets; in those days tickets were only seven dollars, and people were beefing about that. The Broadway Theatre with a seating capacity of 1,800 was available, and after one year at the smaller Broadhurst, we decided to move the show to the Broadway, lowering our prices to five, four, and three dollars.

We retained our original company, had won the Pulitzer Prize, and we spent substantially to advertise the new scale.

Astonishingly, we did not increase the number of tickets sold at the Broadhurst by one. We filled the same number of seats but at the lower price. You figure it out. I simply assume the price of tickets wasn't the problem in 1961 after all.

There is another reason for *Fiorello!*'s abortive run. In the spring of 1960, Actors' Equity and the League of New York Theatres—representing producers and theatre owners—entered into negotiations which dragged on for weeks. There had not been an actors' strike since the famous one in 1919 which spearheaded the formation of Actors' Equity. Though I wasn't around in those days, I remember seeing photos of Marie Dressler fighting to wrest some measure of dignity from the oppressive clutches of the likes of George M. Cohan.

This wasn't the first threat of a strike early in the life of a show of ours. In 1954, weeks after *The Pajama Game* opened, a strike meeting was called at 1:00 a.m. in the basement of City Center. Though its co-producer, I attended because I was also its stage manager. The session was a responsive reading starring Ralph Bellamy. He would scream, "Strike!" and the membership would scream back, "Strike!" In other words, he received a referendum to take back to the negotiating table. When the meeting was over at 5:00 a.m., we emerged and the members of Equity formed a gantlet for me to walk through as they sang, "Seven and a half cents doesn't mean a hell of a lot," and so on.

Well, there was something extra in the wind in the spring of 1960 and I don't think it was the existence of a particularly inequitable contract. (More likely, it was the absence of a serious play that season.)

In the old days, Equity was composed of two unions: one representing actors, and the other, chorus members. In many instances they have entirely different interests. In 1955 the two disparate branches of the union were joined, giving chorus members a heavy edge in negotiations.

Negotiations, which had begun in a small room either at Equity or the League, as we approached the May 31 deadline were moved to more spacious quarters in the Manhattan and Astor Hotels. Fledgling lawyers representing both sides were replaced by the senior members of their law firms and the rhetoric flowered, and we were increasingly subjected to bigger and better scenes. It is anticipated that the actors might rage and fulminate, particularly the ones who had been out of work for a stretch, but the producers matched them. The lawyers, however, were the stars, and when news teams from the television networks appeared in the hallways outside the negotiating room, we were doomed. Given the spotlight on the six and eleven o'clock news, they were reluctant to leave it. What followed was, in Equity terminology, a "lockout." It was in response to a plan of the actors to strike one show on Broadway at each performance. This way they would retain their employment and be paid out of the union strike fund for the performance missed. The producers, realizing that the public would stay away from such Russian roulette, replied: you close one, you close all. We were blacked out.

Broadway, which finds itself hard put to get space in national magazines, was suddenly on the covers of *Time* and *Life*. We were the object of television cameras for eight playing days, but also of pressure from the Restaurant Association, the Hotel Association, the Fifth Avenue Association, the Sixth Avenue Association, the Broadway Association, and so on, to get this strike settled because, after all, it was killing *them*.

Coming as the strike did in the beginning of the summer, it made people reassess their plans to vacation in New York. And while the strike lasted only eight days, thanks to the press, in the public's mind it started before it actually had and lasted well after it was settled. Also, the beginning of a strike gets the publicity, not the end of it. The cover of *Life* was a blacked-out Broadway; when the lights went on again, *Life* was elsewhere.

The strike killed the momentum on Broadway. The impetus which makes for "tough tickets" was wiped out, and when we reopened there was considerable confusion from people who had held tickets for those canceled performances. Many soured on Broadway for that season and chose to take refunds instead of exchanges. I believe the 1960 strike cost *Fiorello!* six months on Broadway.

I am reminded of another episode during the blackout. Bobby and I were having a drink at Sardi's while across the street members of the *Fiorello!* cast were picketing the Broadhurst. Bobby had had one too many and was feeling grim about the state of the theatre and lecturing me on how times had changed and what it used to be like when he toured the country with his wife, and how spoiled we all were, not just the kids on the picket lines, but all of us. And he dredged up his favorite maxim, that the only theatre is a hungry theatre. Impulsively, he left the bar, crossed the street to reason with them. I followed. He was standing on a chair provided by the box office, and the kids, carrying their inflammatory signs, had stopped pacing and were ringed around, hearing him out on the subject of forty years in theatre—drink and frustration rendering him incoherent, all except the emotions, which were clear enough. The kids paid him more than respectful attention. They adored him. And when he decided he had finished, having repeated himself over and over, he climbed down and I guided him back to Sardi's. Crossing the street, I said, "Bobby, if you keep it up this way, you'll be dead in a year."

Commitment to the theatre is a wonderful thing, but it costs. We love working, and we are frustrated by those business elements which we must respect in order to keep working creatively. Union regulations frustrate us because we ask, and I think with some justification, How can you regulate creative activity? The trouble is that some amount of regulation is necessary, that artists are taken advantage of because they are artists, that entrepreneurs can be sons of bitches.

At the heart of it, I think, is an indictment, not of a particular union, but of contemporary unionism. In the old days, a committee from management met with the designated union leadership and over a period of time and anguish, it was hoped, would emerge with a fair and viable contract, which would go to membership for ratification. The fight, painful and debilitating, would be fought behind closed doors by experts, and when the doors were opened and recommendations made, there was some assurance that they would be accepted.

Today the situation has changed, and you can spend weeks in negotiations, come to terms at five thirty one morning, and the union team returns to its membership, holding a fistful of hard-won concessions, only to be rejected. The next thing that happens, because the negotiators have bargained realistically, is that additional days are required, wasted, juggling the contract so that it looks to the hotheaded membership that rejected it originally as though improvements had been made. Meantime, there is either a continuing strike or the aura of one hanging over the industry.

Because of all this, I felt in 1960 that we had established a strike pattern and that it would be unavoidable in subsequent negotiations, and sure enough, the next time we sat down, it happened again. But the strike of 1964 lasted a Sunday and cost only a Sunday matinee performance.

I remained convinced that every three or four years, depending on the contract, there would be a strike, and I was wrong. Ten years later, in 1970, Gerald Schoenfeld and Bernard Jacobs, representing the producers and theatre owners, were able to keep an untheatrical lid on the Equity negotiations, arriving at a contract well in advance of the deadline, limiting publicity in the papers to a notice of the ratification of that new contract. Unhappily, it took a gasping Broadway to accomplish this. (Again, in 1974, a contract was negotiated without a strike. Perhaps a strike would have been preferable.)

Nothing I have said about the 1960 strike is news to anyone in the industry. Nevertheless, in 1970, negotiations between the Off-Broadway management and Equity precipitated a strike similar to ours ten years earlier. It and the contract which emerged, in my opinion, crippled Off-Broadway for all time.

There is more I would like to say about negotiations in general with Equity, and it involves issues that are not economic ones. For example, I have heard a dancer suggest, in negotiations, our putting a clause in the contract that will "protect us from sitting around while the directors and choreographers do their thinking. Why don't they do their homework at night?" Very depressing indeed.

Another characteristic of labor negotiations is the acceptance of certain excessively sophisticated rules of the game, such as: there is no relationship between the negotiators' private behavior (in session) and public posture (before the membership). Another: all that transpires during the course of a negotiation is respected as secret. I am reminded that at the height of the blackout, with obduracy on both sides of the table and not much reason for convening, as the deadline for the strike approached, someone got the good idea to bring in Moss Hart, who was president of the Dramatists Guild, as an impartial negotiator. Many of the other theatrical unions were suddenly involved—stagehands, musicians—and one of them induced him to call a secret meeting at One Fifth Avenue, at which time the producers were persuaded to make their best offer, and it was summarily rejected by the union.

Hart left the meeting in despair, and the strike began. Ten days later when the strike was settled, the accepted terms were those which had been offered before the strike behind the closed doors at One Fifth Avenue.

Years have passed—for all I know, fifteen years is not enough time to violate the confidence of that session, but I choose to, not because I point the finger at one or another negotiating committee, but because I don't think the incident is unique.

In the course of a recent labor negotiation which resulted in a crippling strike—not in the theatrical industry—one of the two principal bargainers was drunk throughout negotiations. When I asked impatiently of friends in the press why they didn't report what they'd seen—that, for example, one critical session had to be canceled because a negotiator couldn't be awakened from a drunken stupor—I was informed that there were certain unwritten laws which must be respected. Why the hell should they? I'd like to know.

REFLECTIONS ON CHAPTER 7
OF *CONTRADICTIONS*

Actually, I met Sheldon Harnick's brother before I met Sheldon. Jay Harnick was a singer and an actor who subsequently became a producer. He was one of four singers in our backers' auditions for *The Pajama Game*. To one of the auditions he brought his mother, whom I complimented on Jay's talent. She said that if I thought Jay was talented, I should meet her other son. Her "other son" turned out to be Sheldon Harnick, and it was the beginning of a happy and lasting collaboration and friendship.

Some years later, I tried and failed to get a musical libretto from William Saroyan, the Pulitzer Prize–winning playwright of *The Time of Your Life*. We'd meet in the afternoon, settle on an assignment, perhaps a love scene of three pages that would introduce a musical number. Saroyan would work all night and the next day would present me with a hundred pages. Saroyan was a brilliant and uniquely quirky master of words. I regard his literary accomplishments with more than respect—I'm dazzled by him. But he was no collaborator.

Tom Bosley went on to TV stardom in *Happy Days*.

Apropos strikes: I'm a union man myself, though I've been "management" in the past. I'm an active member of the Stage Directors and Choreographers Society. I know unions are vital to the employer/employee formula. Today, less than 10 percent of the country is unionized, and it has seriously damaged the fabric of our society. Hopefully, the pendulum will swing back and we'll have more unions, with a greater number of members, and—here goes—strikes!

In the intervening years the League of New York Theatres became the Broadway League.

I was president of the League of New York Theatres in 1962. It was always a peculiar hybrid—a marriage of producers and theatre owners, in other words tenants and landlords. Where else in the world is there such an organization? But for a time it worked because there was some equality of power. David Merrick could have six or more plays simultaneously running on Broadway, Hal Prince, three, and Feuer and Martin, two. And there were many other producers.

There were so many successful producers that the landlords were balanced with their tenants, which meant that at that time the tenant could negotiate his contract for a theatre. It depended entirely on their project, and therefore every contract was different. Frequently, theatre owners competed to invest in shows.

Slowly but surely, in direct relation to the escalating cost of producing, the theatre owners now dominate the league. Contracts are pretty standard for any theatre, and the theatre owners proudly keep lists of shows in waiting for an available theatre. The attraction of a movie star goes to the head of the line, but most of the plays looking for theatres line up in a queue.

Do I think this condition will continue? Well, it may be wishful thinking, but I don't think so. I think as theatre gets more and more expensive to produce and to see, and as fewer and fewer productions return their investments, we may see a rejiggering of proportions again. But more importantly, the marriage of landlord and tenant is *wrong*—the tenants should have their own organization.

Finally, one of the best songs written for the *Fiorello!* score, "Where Do I Go from Here?," never made it to the show. It was to be sung by Marie La Guardia in the first act and has been recorded frequently; among its best interpreters was Peggy Lee. In creating a musical, you often have to jettison beautiful musical material simply because the composers come up with a more pertinent number or there's no time for it in the show or . . . I can't for the life of me remember why this one didn't make the final production; it's that wonderful.

CHAPTER
8

We had such a good time doing *Fiorello!* that we could not bear splitting up after it opened—so we did *Tenderloin.*

A friend at Random House sent me the galleys of a novel about the Tenderloin, that section of New York City in the 1880s named by the vice barons for its juicy pickings. It dealt with the relationship between a hellfire-and-brimstone aging minister and a young, charming, and unscrupulous gutter rat. The period was pretty to look at, the source material all too predictably musical.

Unlike the previous projects, *Tenderloin* was a natural. Everyone saw a musical in it. Producers bid for it, investors fought to finance it.

Today I suppose I can imagine *Tenderloin* as a stepping-off place for a parable of contemporary morality, the young leading man utterly amoral, triumphing, a forerunner of J. Pierrepont Finch in *How to Succeed in Business without Really Trying.*

It would be a good idea to cushion a realistic statement about contemporary corruption in pretty times gone by, but we did not do that. We fictionalized the period, romanticized the events.

Years later, *Cabaret* to its creators was a parable of the 1950s told in Berlin, 1924. To us, at least, it was a play about civil rights, the problem of blacks in America, about how it can happen here. Walter Kerr, who admired *Cabaret* and said so, accused us of deluding ourselves. Perhaps. But the point is, it was there for us while we were creating the show.

Tenderloin's score was a good one. The book never settled on a tone. We had as good an opening number as I have ever seen—as good as *Forum*, or the train scene in *The Music Man* or, for that matter, "Wilkommen"—called "Little Old New York Is Plenty Good Enough for Me." It was sung by the panhandlers, the pimps, the fixers who inhabited the Tenderloin.

The minister bent on closing down the brothels, saloons, and gambling casinos (in other words, cutting out the fun) turned out to be not an ideal character for a musical. Bobby and I did not help things by casting Maurice Evans in that role. Abbott preferred Hugh Griffith, the eccentric character actor probably most remembered for his appearance in the film *Tom Jones*. He would have given us the lunatic characterization the show begged for, but Bobby and I insisted on the Shakespearean star because it was offbeat casting. Evidently we hadn't learned from the Bobby Clark experience.

On this rare occasion we made the benefit ladies happy, and *Tenderloin* opened with an enormous advance sale. It was what the public wanted to see. Or *thought* it wanted to see.

The public rarely knows in advance what it wants to see. Eventually, it rejects what it anticipates and embraces what comes as a surprise.

Clearly, we were the wrong producers for *Tenderloin*. The whole notion of wrong and right producers is in discard today; the personality of a producer's work, his identity, is missing, and it seems to me therein lies one of the sicknesses of Broadway.

We made the first mistake in choosing to adapt *Tenderloin* as a musical. And then we just went on making mistakes. We had reconvened the creative team so we could be together.

Then we picked Cecil Beaton to do the sets and costumes, and Beaton did a beautiful job, but for the wrong show. It was tasteful and chic. It should have been vulgar. Beaton had the idea that we should make up the girls in the brothel stylistically, with masses of black grotesque makeup. So we took some of the prettiest girls you ever saw in your life and made them ugly.

Seven months later, we closed the books on *Tenderloin* only 25 percent in the red. The enormous advance meliorated the loss.

We never again did a show because it would be popular. We did, however, go back to work too soon. I may never learn that lesson.

REFLECTIONS ON CHAPTER 8 OF *CONTRADICTIONS*

We did not so much make a mistake in choosing to produce *Tenderloin* as we did in choosing *ourselves* to produce it. Merrick and Gower Champion would have knocked the ball out of the park, because of course it wouldn't have been about real hookers, but would've been a joyous *musical comedy*.

It should be noted that *Tenderloin* broke our string of successes from *The Pajama Game* to *Yankees* to *New Girl* to *West Side Story* to *Fiorello!* Reality hit us like a ball-peen hammer. In addition, I did not know at the time how much of a toll its failure had taken on Bobby Griffith. He died of a heart attack soon after.

Because of *Anna Christie* and *Tenderloin*, I've come to believe that hookers are not musical comedy material. They're tempting because they're flamboyant and sex is supposed to "sell," but when they're central characters in a musical, audiences are conflicted—they're not as amused for moral reasons, and I get it.

There's something I might as well take up now: from rather early on in my producing days, I began to respect metaphor as the spine of a musical book to such an extent that over the length of my career I've sometimes imposed a metaphor where none belonged. A number of my shows, especially the ones I directed, were inspired by issues—many political—and the basic material didn't invite or support a metaphor. *The Pajama Game* was always a show about a labor union strike as far as I was concerned, but believe me, its audiences didn't take it that way. It would never have been such a success had I directed it. *Damn Yankees* is one of the few shows that doesn't illustrate my obsession with metaphor. For that matter, neither did *She Loves Me* or *On the Twentieth Century*. But most of the rest of the musicals have.

CHAPTER
9

We hurried into the next, an adaptation of *A Call on Kuprin*, a science-fiction adventure written by Maurice Edelman, a member of the House of Commons.

The plot dealt with Russia's efforts to put a man in space. Jerome Lawrence and Robert E. Lee, who had written *Inherit the Wind*, set to work adapting it. Donald Oenslager designed a series of extraordinarily realistic sets: the chess pavilion in Gorky Park, the roof of the American Embassy, a dacha in the Crimea, and so on.

We budgeted a prohibitive $150,000 for a cast of twenty-six and a backstage crew equal to that of a full-fledged musical.

We were in Israel opening *West Side Story* when the script arrived with a note from Abbott saying he liked it and that when we returned we could cast for a spring opening.

Spring openings for serious plays are notoriously dangerous. You can't gain momentum enough, opening in April or May, to get you through the summer. It's a good idea to open a straight play in the fall so that it can run the full season, in which time it ought to have paid off. Serious plays traditionally don't play as many continuous performances as comedies and musicals.

However, we were in a hurry. *Tenderloin* had closed and the best thing to do was go back to work immediately.

Henry Fonda was the natural choice for the leading role. Henry Fonda was not available. We signed Jeffrey Lynn.

The night of the first preview in Philadelphia, the Russians, upstaging us, sent their Sputnik into space.

We had lost a race with the headlines. All the mystery, the glamor of the story evaporated. By the end of two weeks in Philadelphia, even I had grown weary of reading about the Sputnik. Newspapers were a nickel then, and *Kuprin* was old news.

As for racing with the headlines, there is a good reason why topical theatre is rare today. The speed of communications is primarily responsible, and you are safer dealing in abstractions, in metaphors. Once again, the theatre needs language, imagery, imagination, to separate itself from the realism of the six o'clock news.

This brings to mind apparently contradictory advice I collected soon after *The Pajama Game* opened.

Joe Fields, an author of *Wonderful Town*, warned, "Don't get so successful you begin to equate yourself with success."

On the other hand, Lem Ayers said, "Don't let early success make you gun-shy. Keep going." He and Saint Subber, when very young, had co-produced *Kiss Me, Kate*, and the phenomenal success had paralyzed them for a number of seasons.

The *Times* review for *Kuprin* was excellent, yet we sold one ticket (not even a pair) between ten o'clock, when the box office opened, and noon. The public wasn't interested. Instead of closing at the end of that week, we played another week, losing $20,000. I have heard it argued that authors have a right to an audience and that the investor, if he is going to lose most of his money, won't mind losing all of it.

But Broadway cannot survive that way. (I keep reminding myself; I doubt I'll ever learn.)

REFLECTIONS ON CHAPTER 9
OF *CONTRADICTIONS*

It is no longer true that you can come in too late in the season with a serious play. Today, all the plays and musicals vie for an opening date as late in the spring and as close to the Tony Award nominations as possible. It implies that critics and the public forget anything that opens in the fall. So explain, please, the success of the longest-running shows on Broadway: *Chicago* (opened in November), *The Lion King* (opened in November), *Mamma Mia!* (opened in October), *Jersey Boys* (opened in November), and *Wicked* (opened in October). And *The Phantom of the Opera* opened in January. In other words, none of the longest-running shows on Broadway opened in the spring.

Tenderloin and *Kuprin*—the one-two punch and it wasn't yet over.

CHAPTER
10

Bobby Griffith and I met James and William Goldman when we were doing *Tenderloin*. They tried to help some in the writing of it, but it was too late. Still, I acquired from Jim the script of a play he had written, *They Might Be Giants*. It was about a wealthy American with a Sherlock Holmes fixation, and about his family, who sent him to a psychoanalyst to have him declared insane so they could get their hands on his money. A fascinating play, beautifully written, imaginatively constructed—THEATRE.

Early that season, I had been exposed for the first time to the work of Joan Littlewood via her production of Brendan Behan's *The Hostage*. I was crazy about it. The sure yet impulsive way she maneuvered currents of reality and fantasy compatibly in one play was something. And I admired how she cued in fragments of songs—the show had many—and how they erupted from rather than grew out of moments. They had the abrasive effect of attacking when you least expected, creating such life.

Sondheim and I talked about that play then and for years, and a decade later the songs in *Company* were cued out of a conscious debt to *The Hostage*. We were in Boston with *Tenderloin* when I read Jim Goldman's play. I promptly scrawled a note to Joan Littlewood on some Touraine Hotel stationery, saying something like, "You don't know me, but I do know you and this is a play I'm enclosing which I think is extraordinary." I mailed it to her in London, and by the time we got back to New York, there was a reply. "You're right. I agree with you. Let's do it." And that was that. We scheduled rehearsals in June at the Theatre Royal Stratford, in the East End of London.

What made me take an American play about American people to an English director? I wanted to work with her. At the time I didn't know how much she relied on improvisation and how little on fixed material. She'd done the play I've just mentioned and *Fings Ain't Wot They Used t'Be* and *A Taste of Honey*, and they were wonderful. But the Behan play was reported to have been less than one act long when she went into rehearsal and *A Taste of Honey* similarly a string of scenes, with no cohesive theatrical shape.

Fings was the first Lionel Bart musical, and together they improvised it in a kind of freewheeling style, a precursor, perhaps, of Tom O'Horgan's *Hair*. What was so marvelous about all that was a curious irreverence and sloppy excitement—nothing constipated there.

The trouble was Jim Goldman had written a play. A tight, carefully polished play. I've never seen what Joan Littlewood did with Shakespeare. I would be inclined to guess, not very much. She doesn't take to discipline. The Goldman play was the wrong one to send her.

Meantime, *Tenderloin* opened in New York and hobbled through the winter months, and *Kuprin* opened and closed. We had yet to meet Littlewood. Then, early in June, Bobby Griffith, who was playing golf with George Abbott, collapsed on the ninth hole at the Westchester Country Club and died the next morning.

Giants went into rehearsal in June as scheduled. There were too many things for me to do in New York, so instead of being in London for that period, I managed to get away three days before the scheduled London opening.

Jim Goldman greeted me apprehensively at the stage door and ushered me to a seat in the rear of the second balcony. Joan didn't like producers much.

Littlewood's image of producers was Billy Rose. She referred to me: "When that Billy Rose gets here from New York . . ." but Jim assured me it would change when she met me.

The rehearsal I watched was confusing. As I became oriented, I realized that the leading man's lines were being spoken by a woman. Odd. It is part of Littlewood's technique to switch the roles around to give the actors a sense not only of their roles but also of the total experience of the play. A valuable exercise, no doubt, but we were three days from an opening.

Jim didn't seem perturbed when I expressed surprise. At the end of that rehearsal, he took me down to meet Joan Littlewood. It was immediately clear that they'd fallen in love—artistically. He was a playwright and her theatre, in the still bombed-out slums of East London, was run on a sound Bolshevik line. (Littlewood was the chairman.) Together they constituted a phalanx I could not shake. I didn't even try. I was too late, so I backed away and let it all happen.

Not surprisingly, two days before the scheduled opening she asked for one more week's rehearsal. They had had almost two months.

I spoke with Avis Bunnage and Harry Corbett, the leads in the production and longtime Littlewood actors, and on their advice I forced the opening date. After all, it was the East End, and Littlewood had always done her best work after an opening. Our reviews down there wouldn't affect a subsequent move to the West End after she'd fixed the production. This was Littlewood's pattern, and unless I forced her to open on time, the exercises would continue. All of this had been borne out by previous productions of *The Hostage* and *Sparrers Can't Sing*.

That decision was my sole contribution as producer.

She didn't like it, but once it had been made, she pushed herself to be ready, which simply wasn't possible in the two remaining days. But I had discounted this opening as the equivalent of New Haven, so in that context I wasn't too apprehensive.

We opened with the predicted disaster, and Littlewood accepted full responsibility for it.

For her, however, this had not been the same as the previous Stratford openings. She had fashioned those plays, in a sense co-authored them. This one had come to her total. Goldman chooses his words carefully, directs his scenes with precision, even providing detailed stage directions. All of this she admired, but it was contrary to the best of her experience.

Instead of improvising chaos, she should have mounted his play.

One of her masterpieces, *Oh, What a Lovely War!*, a musical revue about World War I, was rough-hewn, abrasive, and improvised. *Giants* was a well-made play and not her forte. She knew it only too late, and out of her upset at letting Jim Goldman down, she closed her theatre and fled to Nigeria. *Giants* was the last of the Theatre Royal productions for many years, the last of that acting company.

Returning late on the afternoon of the day we closed, I found her waiting for me in the lobby of the Savoy Hotel, wearing, as always, the tam-o'-shanter and tartan skirt which were her uniform, clutching a string bag containing a head of cabbage, some apples, turnip greens, and a Georgian silver flask inscribed in memory of *Giants*. Littlewood and *Giants* had closed the most audacious English-speaking theatre company of the 1950s, and I had introduced them to each other. (Predictably, Littlewood came home and is working again in that theatre.)

Jim and I returned to New York, and he suggested I direct it. I agreed eagerly, but I knew there was something wrong with the play. The Little-wood production had so obscured what was *right* that I arranged a reading of it.

I sent it to George C. Scott and Colleen Dewhurst, who seemed perfect casting to me, offering them the leads. They accepted at once. There had never been any equivocation when it came to Jim's script.

About this time Mike Nichols asked me what my plans were for *Giants*. Mike had yet to direct a play. It figured in his plans and he would love to start with *They Might Be Giants*.

Arrangements for the reading went forward. We rented a room at the Astor Hotel, assembled a cast including Scott and Dewhurst, and though they read well, I got no closer to what was wrong with the play.

The reason was I couldn't hear them. Instead, I kept hearing the performance I had seen in England. Those actors, their voices—I kept seeing *their* moves. I hadn't liked that production, still I couldn't shake it off. It was indelibly in my head.

A few years later I did *She Loves Me,* and eight years after that I was asked to make a film of it. I was excited, and we cast it well with Jerry Orbach and Joan Hackett. The Hungarian government offered unheard-of cooperation, to the extent that they would restore sections of Budapest, restaurants, and hotels to what they'd been before the war. And once again I couldn't start fresh. I couldn't seem to move away from the original stage production. It became a game of trying to recall what we'd done before, remembering too much on the one hand and not enough on the other.

I've always been amazed at directors, the classical ones usually, who can reinterpret plays over and over again in a lifetime. I can't do that now. I would like to someday.

I certainly couldn't do it with *Giants*. Unhappily, I told Jim as much at the end of the reading in the Astor. True, I could hold forth for hours about Littlewood's mistakes, but given the chance, I couldn't take advantage of them. And because I couldn't, reluctantly I relinquished the play.

Scott and Dewhurst picked it up, but subsequently dropped it. Kermit Bloomgarden optioned it for a time. It went that way from hand to hand, but it never got to Broadway.

I don't know what happened with Mike Nichols. Probably then it was too late. As for the others, I suspect in each instance they discovered something was wrong with it, and, as with a brilliant puzzle, the solution for it was always out of reach.

Because of the London production, Bobby and I retained the motion-picture rights. In 1968 they were purchased by Universal for a film starring George C. Scott and Joanne Woodward, and directed by Anthony Harvey. There was no cash in front from our point of view, but we would participate once the film was made. It was, and we did, and since then we have recouped all the money we lost in 1961. Which is probably the only time in my life that will happen.

REFLECTIONS ON CHAPTER 10
OF *CONTRADICTIONS*

The Touraine Hotel was my choice of digs because, as a stage manager, I received a free room in return for recommending the apartments to our cast. I hadn't absorbed the fact that I could stay wherever I chose.

Joan Littlewood was as unconventional as she was brilliant. I regard *The Hostage*, *A Taste of Honey*, *Fings Ain't Wot They Used t'Be*, and *Oh, What a Lovely War!* among the most successful and potentially influential theatre pieces I've ever seen. The problem is they *couldn't* be influential because no one worked as she did. She was a co-author of all of those plays. There are rumors that she started one of them with little more than a dozen pages and improvised the rest with the actors.

Actually, few know this: George Abbott went into rehearsal with Nanette Fabray and Phil Silvers in *High Button Shoes* with a fragment of a script, and he too improvised the rest of it from the first day of rehearsal. It became a box office hit.

I had forgotten that my first choice for the film of *She Loves Me* was a young Barbra Streisand. But she was rejected out of hand. The American money hadn't heard of her and had doubts as to whether the camera would love her. To this day I regret that film was never made.

While I'm on the subject of directing films: when I finally got around to it, I realized how ill suited I was to the task. I was too old to start from scratch and clearly not interested enough to learn the craft or to shadow a first-rate film director. I had beginner's luck with *Something for Everyone*. But in that case I had a great script from Hugh Wheeler, solid gold in cinematographer Walter Lassally, and platinum with Angela Lansbury and Michael York.

Some years later, I went back to the well with *A Little Night Music* and I think I made a mess of it, and not only because I had a hard time working with Elizabeth Taylor. My excuse for all of this is boredom—the amount of time between setting up a shot and actually shooting it can amount to hours. I'm not that fellow.

However, working with two stars, Angela Lansbury and Elizabeth Taylor, I did learn something about film acting. Angela, who is stage-trained, projected: I understood what she was doing as she was doing it. It was epic theatre, as Meyerhold and Piscator defined it. It's where I shine, and it was thrilling to watch Angie in front of the camera. With Elizabeth it was entirely different. I would often have to turn to the cameraman to ask, "Did she do it?" It was so little I couldn't see it. Usually I had to go to the rushes to see if I had gotten what I wanted. Nonetheless, she knew how to act for the camera, and when she was good, she was very good.

I did make an attempt at one other film. I had an idea for a film version of *Follies* that I tried to sell. It would be about the last days of Metro-Goldwyn-Mayer. We would give a gala party on the sound stage at MGM and invite every movie star in the world (and design it as a benefit for the actors' home in Woodland Hills). I wanted to use the documentary filmmaker D. A. Pennebaker to shoot the stars attending the reunion. And then I wanted to place the story of *Follies* in the middle of all this! Thanks to John Springer, the famous Hollywood publicist, I heard from Bette Davis and Joan Crawford, who said they would like to be in the film: Davis wanted to sing "I'm Still Here," while Crawford would sing "Broadway Baby." Springer said, "Can you imagine those two women singing those songs? Perfection."

I went to see Dan Melnick at MGM and tried hard to sell him my idea. But he turned me down. A year later, MGM produced *That's Entertainment!* My concept for a film of *Follies* is the one movie I know I could have made because it invited so much improvisation and I wouldn't have gotten bored.

CHAPTER
11

For the first time in seven years, the New York office was quiet. We had nothing on Broadway.

After *Kuprin* closed, I realized that, at least temporarily, the prospect of a next project did not excite Bobby. In truth, he took the closings worse than I. He seemed to have lost his resilience. He announced he wanted to slow down his activities, proposing I do some shows without him. The firm would continue, but he would function in an advisory capacity, retaining a minimal interest in shows that were "mine."

Today it is clear to me that it scared him how massively he had over-reacted to the failure of those plays, and before it was too late he meant to put time in the areas of his life it had been so easy to neglect. That's a problem shared by everyone who has a string of luck in the theatre. Success generally comes early (though Bobby was in his late forties), continues in stretches, and has a way of disappearing just when you need it most—when, paradoxically, you'd most appreciate it and you have nothing to fall back on.

His announcement of intention to slow down came in conjunction with the script for a musical I had read by Burt Shevelove and Larry Gelbart, based on the farce plays of Plautus, and called *A Funny Thing Happened on the Way to the Forum*. Sondheim had written the score and Jerry Robbins was set to direct. David Merrick was to be the producer.

The authors were having trouble moving it. Perhaps Merrick was reluctant—I never knew. Anyway, if it was available, would Bobby and I be interested in doing it?

Bobby wasn't enthused. I was. They went about arranging a release from Merrick, and I sent the script to Phil Silvers, for whom it had been written.

Judy Abbott, our casting director, had meanwhile read a play of Phoebe and Henry Ephron's called *Age of Consent*, later retitled *Take Her, She's Mine*. It was a light comedy loosely based on the Ephrons' life with their four daughters. Particularly it dealt with their eldest, Nora, and the inevitable pain a father feels handing his daughter over to another man. We optioned it.

At this point, Phil Silvers turned down *Forum*. All those togas didn't seem funny to him.

But then, a lot of people had trouble reading that script. Six months later, when we offered it to the American Theatre Society (a board made up of producers and theatre owners) for Theatre Guild subscription in Washington, they would not even accept it for consideration.

There was no urgency with *Forum*. Though still very much involved with it, Robbins wanted considerable rewrites, and characteristically was reluctant to set a specific rehearsal date. So we sent the script to Milton Berle, agreeing to settle for an easy summer.

Less than a week later, Bobby collapsed. Tommy Valando drove me to Parkchester Hospital, where Bobby was resting easier. I returned to New York, to be awakened at six thirty the following morning. I raced back, arriving an hour before he died.

It is still difficult to analyze my relationship with Bobby. A brother, maybe, and certainly (in the area of stage-managing) a teacher, a patient one, for I was emotionally ill-suited to that job. But he covered for me during those years, and I got out and into producing before anybody caught on. A friend. We loved each other. Ironically, he helped me in very real ways to calm down, to enjoy my life, more, in fact, than he was able to enjoy his own. He was generous, the delight of the panhandlers in front of the Lambs Club.

Michael Stewart, the playwright, once referred to Bobby and me as "the nice one" and "the loud one." I was the loud one.

The only area in which Bobby treated me unfairly involved my growing desire to be a director. It was the one thing in the world he didn't want me to be, and he didn't face it.

He was going to semiretire, but he wasn't going to open the door for me to direct. He had always said that he was going to direct, even before I knew him. But he hadn't. I do not believe that he would have been a particularly good director. It had become his curious, quiet failure, something which really didn't bother him—not until I became interested.

In 1960, after *Fiorello!* and before *Kuprin*, Roger Stevens asked me whether I would be interested in directing a musical version of *Juno and the Paycock*, providing the authors, Joe Stein and Marc Blitzstein, agreed.

I talked to Bobby, and he suggested that we should co-direct our own productions. He had a true and unerring sense of what was honest acting; I had a stronger sense of what was good material. He had a better facility for working, dealing with people. I had the edge on him with respect to taste and the physical aspects of a production—the scenery, costumes. We collaborated well, but when it came to direction, we could hardly have been co-directors. I postponed directing.

After Bobby died, Abbott told me that for the past year he had felt Bobby's and my partnership coming to an end. I tend to disagree, but I am sure that insofar as the issue of direction was involved, we were on some sort of collision course from which he would have had to back away. Given Bobby's age, and his desire to take things easier, I believe I could have pushed through what I wanted. After all, I was twenty years younger. On the other hand, it would have taken time, and his death in June settled it.

We buried Bobby, and I took his desk out of the eight-by-ten office, knowing that I could never take another partner. Instead, I restructured the office, making Ruth Mitchell an associate. Carl Fisher, who had been our general manager, took on that area of the business which had fascinated Bobby and bored the hell out of me. Bobby had been more proprietary than I, constantly looking over their shoulders, often unnecessarily. I was to lay the responsibility on them and turn to directing.

I read somewhere that one of the reasons for my success has been an ability to accept the failures. Not true. The truth is that Ruth and Carl, Annette and the rest have always been able to close ranks around me, cushion me, buffering the world outside.

Sycophancy?

It's not the same thing, because while they may be shielding me from the outside, they don't shield me from me.

I like give-and-take. I don't like being in a room by myself. I can't even think sitting down! Probably that is why I take to direction, and that's why my direction is invariably on my feet and on the spot. I don't prepare beforehand where the actors are going to move, and we don't sit around a table for days and talk. It wouldn't be fun, and I wouldn't know how.

And we have fun.

Bobby's death cast me out into a world I had easily avoided. I had seen Bobby from nine in the morning to eleven at night, six days a week (on Sundays he was his family's), since 1953, inadvertently to the exclusion of friends and business associates. All that changed.

I went to Europe and in Paris met the girl I was to marry a year later. I entered into an intensive period of psychoanalysis which lasted a couple of years. It wasn't so much that I had ceased to enjoy life beyond the theatre and the office, but a free-floating anxiety born of the events leading up to Bobby's death, the fear I saw created by two shows failing and bankruptcy in his personal life. I wanted to do something about it before it was too late.

I came back from Europe in August and went to work on the Ephron play, which Abbott had agreed to direct. We set Art Carney and Phyllis Thaxter as the parents and a cast of young people, including Elizabeth Ashley.

There was nothing especially interesting during the course of producing that play. It opened in Boston to marvelous reviews and plenty of laughter. When we arrived in New York, we seemed to have left the laughs in Boston, not to mention the good reviews.

More specifically, *Take Her, She's Mine* played the Shubert in Boston, with a seating capacity of 1,700. The size of the theatre made for a bigger, broader performance. That, plus the greater decibels of laughter, created a perfect relationship between the stage and the audience for the easy, good-natured superficiality of the material. In New York we played the Biltmore, seating 948. The actors were forced to modulate their performances. Laughter was cut by half, and the play begged for more serious scrutiny.

We worry too much about intimacy. A year later, I refused to move *Forum* (the intimate musical) into a large theatre, only to see it thrive on the road in a theatre twice the size of the Alvin.

Reluctantly, I moved *Cabaret* from the Broadhurst (1,153) to the Imperial (1,452) to find I liked it better there, a distance removed from the audience.

And *Candide* looked better in the Broadway (900 seats) than it did in Brooklyn (180 seats). Largely because of Art Carney's eminence in television, *Take Her, She's Mine* played almost a year, toured another season, and made a nice profit. It is the only play I have sold to the films before it opened. It had some grace and some charm, and it was what you'd call commercial, and I had a hit the first time out producing alone. Moreover, although Abbott had offered me free space again until I got on my feet, that hadn't been necessary. I could pay the rent.

Take Her, She's Mine could have been produced by anyone. A number of the shows that preceded it fit that category. Others, the best of them, the Abbott shows, had a texture which was his, but even he wasn't so much concerned with content as I was going to be.

REFLECTIONS ON CHAPTER 11
OF *CONTRADICTIONS*

When Bobby semiretired, he put all his considerable savings into a business building thirty-four foot cabin cruisers with sleeping accommodations for six, and he opened a shipyard in Boothbay Harbor, Maine. The boats were beautifully turned out in every detail. But they were priced so modestly that they did not sufficiently cover costs, and the business went bust. So the effort, which he anticipated as pure pleasure, became another traumatizing experience, adding stress and, ultimately, shortening his life.

Tommy Valando was responsible for publishing more of the scores of my shows than anyone else.

I was lucky to be invited by the Israeli government to represent a group of American Jews who would speak at Hebrew University in Jerusalem about their variety of Jewish experiences. Among the invited artists were Marc Blitzstein, Anna Sokolow, Meyer Levin, and me. It was an amazing experience. I arrived in Tel Aviv and was escorted immediately to the modest Jerusalem home of the president of Israel, Itzhak Ben-Zvi. There I met Prime Minister David Ben-Gurion, his wife, Paula, and Marc. The president, prime minister, and his wife reminisced about living in Brooklyn and sitting in Paula's kitchen around a table covered in oilcloth, planning the creation of Israel. Whenever we had any free time, I traveled to Nazareth, visited a kibbutz, Mount Sinai, and of course Yad Vashem (at that time there was no visiting the Old City).

One anecdote comes to mind: on our final night, as scheduled, we spoke to three thousand people in the auditorium at Hebrew University. Right before that session, Paula Ben-Gurion warned me that her husband would be raising hell with us for not living in Israel. He rose to speak, and true to her word he did precisely that, whereupon she leaned back, caught my eye, and clapping her hands on her face muttered, "Oy"!

❧

It was then Abbott told me that all those years he had been sending me on the road to maintain his companies was because he thought I might make a good director. The reports he'd received from the company managers substantiated that.

❧

I met Judy Chaplin in Paris the summer after Bobby Griffith died. We were introduced by Anthony Perkins, a good friend who was in Paris filming with Melina Mercouri. One night he invited me to dinner, where I met Judy. She had been living in Paris for some time. She had been a ballet dancer—a pupil of Carmelita Maracci's and a classmate of Allegra Kent's. In addition, she had studied as a concert pianist with Marguerite Long in Paris and Volya Lincoln in New York. My career put an end to her professional aspirations, and I regret that.

Anyway, we met in Paris and by sheer luck, the following fall she moved to New York, where we dated for over a year. We were married in October of 1962, Steve Sondheim was my best man, and we've been married almost fifty-five years.

❧

About my psychoanalysis: honestly, I didn't take to it. In fact, I recall sleeping during most sessions and the analyst waking me up to tell me the hour was over. However, I did learn one thing when I spoke of the grim summer when I was fourteen. He gave it a name—I'd had a nervous breakdown.

❧

The heroine in *Take Her, She's Mine* was Nora Ephron: THE Nora Ephron, who went on to write *When Harry Met Sally*, *Sleepless in Seattle*, *You've Got Mail*, and *Julie & Julia*.

CHAPTER
12

While we were working on *Tenderloin*, Steve Sondheim urged me to read the book of an original musical, *A Family Affair*, and subsequently arranged for me to hear the score. The music was John Kander's, and the book and lyrics were by James and William Goldman. It was a comedy about a middle-class Jewish wedding, from engagement to wedding march. The book was funny and the score superior. Though there were sufficient conflicts en route to the altar, there was also a certain predictability about them, and never a doubt where the show was going. For this reason, I did not want to do it.

Andrew Siff, a lawyer, optioned it in 1962, financed it, assigned Word Baker, who had done brilliantly with *The Fantasticks*, to direct it and Shelley Berman, Morris Carnovsky, Eileen Heckart, Rita Gardner, and Larry Kert to star. Berman was in his prime then, but was cast in a subordinate role, the uncle of the bride, unbalancing the project. His was the best material, the most flamboyant characterization.

I had seen the same thing happen years earlier when Abbott starred Shirley Booth in *A Tree Grows in Brooklyn* in what should have been a featured role. She triumphed, at the expense of the play.

A Family Affair opened in Philadelphia to a set of terrible reviews and was on the verge of closing without moving to New York. A call went out from Siff's office and from agents representing the authors to Robbins, to Abbott, to Gower Champion, none of whom was available and/or interested. Richard Seff, an actor's agent at the time and a cousin of the producers, suggested that I had expressed a desire publicly to direct and that I had plenty of experience as a producer. They invited me to Philly.

The show was a mess. The material that I liked so much on paper was impossible to see for the production that was imposed on it, a unit set that looked like a tiered wedding cake, with doughnut turntables that moved at a snail's pace, and a cyclorama of wedding lace, in front of which they played the entire show.

Instead of a realistic, old-fashioned musical with walls, and doors, and corners, they had gone chic with yards and yards of China silk and surrealistic costumes.

Still, I remembered the material, and if you could simply put back on the stage what I'd read, in focus so we could see *it*, that alone would have to make an enormous difference.

We could not extend the stay out of town. They had no audience. They could not meet the expenses, and we would have to open in New York in two and a half weeks as scheduled.

I asked for a midnight meeting at the Warwick Hotel in the authors' rooms with the three stars, one of whom, Eileen Heckart, urged closing the show in Philadelphia. I opened the meeting, acknowledging the obvious: I had never directed a musical, but I knew and admired the material. Further, I believed I could fix the show, at least make something respectable out of it, but there was no time left for collaboration. They would have to do exactly what I said, no questions asked. They took a vote. Heckart lost.

I worked with the authors the balance of that night, meeting the company at noon the next day. To establish confidence, turn the emotional tide of the company, we tackled the most cumbersome, least successful scene in the show, a passage-of-time sequence. Almost every musical in those days had such a section dominated by a real clock, or clock music from the orchestra pit, and people jostling each other in tempo in the streets, in department stores, or on the subway, simply to dramatize via mime and music that it was "later."

I had an idea and the Goldmans wrote it. It involved new dialogue for Shelley Berman, who instantly blew sky-high, refusing to do it. I offered to return to New York, no hard feelings—after all, it was only an hour and a half away. He backed down. I put the scene onstage, the cast applauded, Berman came to the edge of the stage and apologized, and we were in business. In a week's time, we substituted eighty new pages for the hundred ten which comprised the book, and moved on to New York.

Once I had decided to stay in Philadelphia, I remember, I phoned Abbott for advice. He approved, asking one question: If everything wrong with the show were fixed, did I think it would be a hit? I replied no. He warned me to remember that. No doubt I would do good work, the improvements would be real, but I must be careful not to be seduced by the experience into wishful-thinking a success, because that would turn an otherwise marvelous experience into a disappointment. Well, I was seduced, and it was disappointing.

Walter Kerr, who was the *Herald Tribune* critic, liked us. Howard Taubman on the *Times* didn't. The balance of the reviews were mixed, and the show ran a couple of months.

I know now we could not have accomplished what we had in ten days were it not for Baker's initial direction. The performers knew who they were. There has to be that solid a foundation for you to be able to upend it to the degree I did in such a short time without destroying it.

But Baker was married to the wrong material. He has a natural sense of fantasy, a light touch, but here he was working with a Jewish family comedy.

The scenery reflected his misconception. I lost my temper one night and started kicking it. More productively, I ordered the carpenter to paint out as many elements of the set as possible, to paint them black, so we couldn't see them. I would have preferred black velour drapes to that set—but then, I seem to prefer empty spaces to fussy sets.

I took billing on the show. Initially, I wasn't going to, but it seemed to me sheer cowardice to hide behind someone else's credit. Though the show was not a success, word got around that I had worked well, and I felt like a director—not to mention that, in an interview in the Sunday *New York Times* preceding our opening, Shelley Berman called me "ruthless."

I needed that in 1962.

REFLECTIONS ON CHAPTER 12
OF *CONTRADICTIONS*

To begin with, I would like to correct any impression that the designer, David Hays, was to blame for the scenery. He is a first-rate designer (credited, incidentally, with creating the successful National Theatre of the Deaf). What he was doing was at the pleasure of the show's director.

There are many reasons why I'm glad I directed *A Family Affair*. For one, I met John Kander, and that was the start of a happy collaboration. The same could be said for James Goldman, who wrote the book for *Follies*. And it introduced me to Linda Lavin, a member of the ensemble, but more on that in the *Superman* chapter.

CHAPTER
13

We had scheduled *A Funny Thing Happened on the Way to the Forum* for the fall of 1961, but Jerry Robbins decided the material wasn't ready, and that he wasn't going to wait for it to be ready, which left us without a director. We did *Take Her, She's Mine* instead.

Meanwhile, I arranged for George Abbott to hear *Forum* in his office; Gelbart and Shevelove to read their book aloud, and Sondheim to play the score. Much of that material depended on physical activity, so it did not seem that funny, and they were nervous, and it was very long. We started at eleven in the morning; at about one o'clock, they were still early in the second act when Abbott rose, announced a luncheon appointment, thanked everyone, and left. That happened on a Friday.

It was in the spring, and Abbott had begun spending his weekends in the Catskills, where he has a home. Later in the day over the phone, he called the show sophomoric. I told him he was mistaken, that he would live to regret that he hadn't done it. I asked whether I could send the script to him that day by special messenger (two and a half hours on the Short Line bus). Would he read it again as though he had never heard it before? And if on Monday he still said it was collegiate, that would be that.

He didn't wait until Monday. He phoned me that Saturday morning to say, "It is absolutely marvelous. I'll do it."

Abbott alone, in my experience, possesses the self-confidence to alter his opinion totally without getting involved with "losing face."

Since he was committed to *Take Her, She's Mine*, it took precedence, and *A Funny Thing* would have to wait till the spring of 1962.

During all this, I was negotiating with Nat Lefkowitz of the William Morris Agency, representing Milton Berle. Berle's demands were impractical. He wanted the world financially, and though I wasn't going to give anybody the world financially, that wasn't seriously at issue. More important, he was asserting his opinion with respect to casting, choice of choreographer, scenic and costume designers, even theatre. Stars have been encouraged to attempt such unqualified impositions.

I began to get depressed about the show. Instantly, we agreed to drop the negotiation; however, my depression evaporated. We were left without a star, but with a star role to fill.

The idea of interesting Zero Mostel was mine. I had seen him for years in clubs, and I loved his performance in *Rhinoceros*. In 1946 he had appeared in an Abbott-directed musical, *Beggar's Holiday*.

But he was an actor, and this had been written for a burlesque comic, a vaudevillian, for Silvers or Berle. We tried persuading the authors to accept Zero, but they refused. It got nasty. Meanwhile, it was December and we were aiming for a February rehearsal and a spring opening.

Tony Walton had designed the scenery and costumes. David Burns, John Carradine, and the rest of the company were signed.

I was in about $50,000, which I could ill afford to lose. I continued to negotiate with Mostel, while the authors, independent of me or Abbott, auditioned Red Buttons, among others, and enthusiastically. I warned them those auditions might make the newspapers and that there was a risk involved should Mostel hear about it. They did make the newspapers, but Mostel wisely ignored it and we made a deal.

At this point, the authors—invoking the Dramatists Guild contract, which gave them approval of casting—threatened to withdraw the play rather than accept Zero.

That, too, happened on a Friday. Again Abbott backed me up completely, saying if Zero weren't accepted, we would miss our rehearsal dates, and we could count him out. I sweated out the weekend. On Monday the authors' representative called and informed me that, reluctantly, they would go ahead with Zero Mostel.

(Apropos the Dramatists Guild contract, if you lived up to the letter of your contracts with any of the affiliated theatrical guilds and unions, you would never get a show on!)

And Zero was brilliant.

We had a run-through in New York before we left for New Haven. It was triumphant.

In New Haven the reviews were tempered—good, but not great. Something was wrong, but it was difficult to say what.

Jack Cole choreographed what little there was too slowly, so he wasn't ready. We had to replace both the ingenue and the juvenile. (Wonder what would have happened had Joel Grey and Barbara Harris, whom I'd wanted originally, been cast?) That sort of thing, but nothing really alarming.

The audience kept telling us it didn't quite know what to expect.

Recall Oscar Hammerstein's words about the first five minutes of a show: ours opened with a charming ballad called "Love Is in the Air." Burns sang it. It was well staged, and the audience seemed happy. Amend Hammerstein's dictum. It isn't enough to "grab them" in the first five minutes. You must also set the guidelines for the evening, and set the tone.

We moved on to Washington, opening with a benefit performance, an audience predominantly of government officials and Washington hostesses. A bad idea. They began to walk out on us soon after the curtain went up. By the bows we'd lost over 50 percent of them. The reviews reflected it. Richard Coe, perhaps the most influential and respected of the critics, suggested closing it.

Subsequent audiences, numbering fewer than a couple of hundred people a night, had a hard time enjoying it. Laughter needs company; not to mention, we needed their laughter. Try fixing a farce with silence from the house. Amazingly, the actors, led by Mostel, played the show, and there was no morale problem. But we needed an opening.

Jerry Robbins was in California, winning an Academy Award for *West Side Story*. I reached him there, and he agreed to come and help us for about ten days.

Though I knew how much we needed help, I paused before I called him. I didn't want to panic. It is difficult to distinguish between moving decisively and moving out of fear. If you know what to do, don't vacillate.

Theatre time is unnaturally brief. I mean, a week on the road is only thirty-two hours of rehearsal time. Immediately, Jerry polished numbers, in particular the second-act chase, which needed it. Primarily, he concentrated on the opening.

Prompted by Robbins, Steve wrote "Comedy Tonight." *That's* what the evening was about. Robbins staged it, but it didn't go into the show until we were in New York previewing, and the minute it did, the show worked. From the opening bar of that number, we had the laughter back, and we never lost it.

It occurs to me that Robbins could not have accomplished what he did in those ten days had he not prepared himself a year earlier to direct the play. As for Abbott and Robbins, they couldn't have been more compatible.

We opened in New York on May 8, 1962. Most of the reviews were excellent (John Chapman of the *News* loathed it). We had an advance of only $40,000, and it was late in the season. Something about even the ecstatic reviews suggested ours wasn't a show for everyone. We worried for the next eight weeks with summer approaching. By the end of June we were selling out.

Sondheim had his first success as a composer, though his music was barely acknowledged and, when it was, invariably suffered by comparison with his lyrics.

Ultimately, it won the Tony Award as best musical of 1962, though Sondheim was not even nominated for writing the score.

In 1972 Burt Shevelove directed it (finally) with Phil Silvers. But Sondheim became the star of it, the same critics forgetting their initial reviews. And though the reviews were marvelous (better than they had been originally), I believe it wasn't nearly as good. Phil Silvers was the vaudevillian Mostel hadn't been, and the year became AD 1972, instead of 200 BC.

I missed Walton's production, particularly the lighting scheme he and Richard Pilbrow designed for the show. To emphasize the dimensions of the set, they built two towers on either side of the stage, from which they projected on a cyclorama upstage dozens of changing abstract images, one enhancing a love song, another emphasizing the midday madness of scenes, tranquilizing, exhilarating, keeping pace with the busy moods of the show.

Walton had to hand-paint on glass slides, which were then distorted by Pilbrow in London so that as they were cast at an angle of forty-five degrees, the distortion compensated for the distance they covered. It was involved and expensive, and worth it. I didn't realize how worth it until we toured the show without them.

I hate to admit it, but the latest *Forum* rankled me, for another reason. There is a rule in the existing Dramatists Guild contract that provides that four and a half months after a first-class production of a Broadway or touring play closes, the first-class rights revert to the authors.

A Funny Thing was a particularly difficult show to make a hit of. There is no way to separate the contributions of the director and producer from the success of that show, particularly in view of how much trouble it was out of town. It is impossible to say who suggests what and when. The point is that neither Abbott nor I, nor the 150-odd original investors, participated in the revival, which followed us by only ten years.

Surely there is a fair solution in a sliding scale which provides that the longer a show runs, the longer the original production participates. I resent that my heirs won't share in perpetuity in the success of *West Side Story*. As for *Fiddler*, though it ran almost eight years, a first-class production could be mounted tomorrow without our receiving a dime.

And if the quality of that production were poor, it might devalue the subsidiary rights, in which we do participate.

REFLECTIONS ON CHAPTER 13
OF *CONTRADICTIONS*

Though *A Funny Thing Happened on the Way to the Forum* was awarded the Tony for best musical of the year, its composer was not even nominated. The book writers, the director, and the producers were, and won. All of us neglected to acknowledge Steve Sondheim's contribution as its composer. After fifty-seven years, I'm still guilty as hell.

CHAPTER
14

Early in 1962, Bock and Harnick came to me with a completed *Tevye and His Daughters*, and I told them that unless they could get Jerome Robbins to direct it, they mustn't do it. Robbins was unavailable, so they put it away.

They had another show ready, and it was *She Loves Me*, only then it was called *The Shop around the Corner*. I agreed to co-produce it with Lawrence Kasha and Philip McKenna, who owned it.

I asked them to see a production of *The Matchmaker* I had directed for the Phoenix, which was touring New York State. They did, and asked me to direct *She Loves Me*. That was the idea.

Gower Champion had been interested in *The Shop around the Corner* earlier and then had decided to do something else. The something else fell through while we were in the midst of rewriting *She Loves Me*. Gower became available and told them that he had reconsidered. I offered to step aside. How could I keep them from Champion, who had staged *Carnival* and *Bye Bye Birdie* by then?

They stayed with me, which loyalty I've always appreciated, because if Gower had done it, it might have been a big hit. But it wouldn't have been *She Loves Me*.

About the same time this was happening, David Merrick heard about *The Matchmaker* and asked me to do what was then called *Dolly! A Damned Exasperating Woman*. I turned it down. Among other reasons, I didn't care for the score, particularly the song "Hello, Dolly!" I couldn't for the life of me see why those waiters were singing how glad they were to have her back where she belonged, when she'd never been there in the first place.

If you look at the basic material of *The Matchmaker* and *The Shop around the Corner*, you can see certain obvious similarities. The Harmonia Gardens and the Café Imperiale in *She Loves Me* are the same place. Mistaken identity figures in both plots. The love relationships are naive, awkward.

She Loves Me is one of the best things this office has done, and as far as I'm concerned, it's as well directed as anything I've ever done.

If you want to analyze carefully why it ran only nine and a half months on Broadway, and as of this writing has never been made into a movie, I have given it more thought than I like to give projects after the fact.

It was a style piece, an unsentimental love story. It had irony and an edge to it. It was funny, but not hilarious. It was melodic, but not soaring. There were only two dances, and they were small. No one came to the edge of the footlights and gave it to you. It was soft-sell.

And in 1963, we were at the peak of the noisy, heavy-sell musical.

Joe Masteroff wrote a beautiful book, Jerry Bock and Sheldon Harnick a near-perfect score. It was orchestrated for strings. The cast included Barbara Cook, Barbara Baxley, Dan Massey, Jack Cassidy. It was a company of actors, expert actors.

I may be making more of *She Loves Me* than I should. It was my first solo directing-from-scratch assignment. It received six excellent reviews from the dailies. Only Walter Kerr, writing for the *Herald Tribune*, disliked it. He likes his musicals to punch, and this didn't. But the good reviews were unexciting. It was a "dear" show, long on sentiment, charm, nostalgia (bad word then: what if we had opened in 1974?), a valentine.

We knew in a few weeks that it would never make it. Generally you can. The trouble is facing it. There are those exceptions, *Abie's Irish Rose*, *Wish You Were Here*, to keep you hoping. But they are exceptions, and almost always the trajectory of a show's popularity is a descending curve. Eventually, we lost most of the $300,000 investment, but it took nine long suffering months.

Originally, Julie Andrews wanted to play the lead. She was filming *The Americanization of Emily* and requested we wait six months for her. I didn't. I was in a hurry to work. Good as Barbara Cook was in *She Loves Me*, Julie Andrews would have overridden the sugary reviews. Had I waited six months, the show might have run three years.

I had difficulties with actors on this show, the difficulties I would have had on *A Family Affair* had those actors not been so desperate for help. I am trusted now. I can be as scared on the first day of rehearsal as I was then, but it is different. My record gives them the confidence they need. Actors test directors, much as children do parents, to see how far they can go (often they don't know where they want to go), to see how protected they are.

Today I can go dry, waste a day working in the wrong direction. All I have to do is admit it. Invariably it works to my advantage, giving the relationship the mutuality rehearsing requires.

In 1963 I didn't know that. I knew only to stay strong and to keep my perspective of the total. The good director sees the whole play. Many people can direct good scenes. The problem is directing good plays. Abbott and Robbins know from beginning to end what the evening is going to be. They may not know details along the way, but they see the total.

Carol Haney choreographed *She Loves Me*. We'd been friends since *The Pajama Game*, and she had a witty and imaginative mind and a collaborator's desire for the total. She was modest about her work. It's a modest show; the stars, the director, the choreographer, nobody "took stage," nobody showed off. Unhappily, neither did the critics.

It opened late in April and ran until February the following year, meeting expenses, occasionally showing a small profit, all the while going gradually downhill. I should have closed it at the end of December. Had I, we would have returned $60,000 to the investors. Instead, I threw that sum away on an additional three weeks. All for the love of a show.

She Loves Me played the 1,046-seat Eugene O'Neill Theatre. Aesthetically, the ideal theatre, but to meet our expenses, totally impractical. There's a theory in this business that there are either hits or flops. It isn't true. Of the seventeen musicals I've produced, only five played to capacity for any length of time. In the case of *She Loves Me* (as in *Take Her, She's Mine*), I overestimated the importance of the size of the theatre on the play's effectiveness.

There's no question but that there is a kind of play that needs an intimate theatre, but that intimacy exists only Off-Broadway or in the Booth Theatre and is common to England and the Continent. Excepting the D. H. Lawrence plays at the Royal Court, I know of nothing that could not be transferred painlessly from a six-hundred-seat house to a twelve-hundred-seat house.

She Loves Me played wonderfully in the O'Neill, but it would have played equally well in a theatre half again as large, and we would have made up on Wednesday and Saturday matinees, on Friday and Saturday nights, what we lost on Mondays and Tuesdays, and doubled our run on Broadway.

In that extra year, I know we would have sold it to the movies and probably repaid the investment. Julie Andrews and Dick Van Dyke wanted to make a film of it. They had just finished *Mary Poppins* for Disney, but it had not been released. In the additional time *Mary Poppins* would have to become the success it did, they would have had their way, and we would have sold our musical.

Until recently, I tended to think of *She Loves Me* as a flop—because it lost money. But a work is not necessarily measured in its own time properly. Success is not measured at the box office. The chances are, if you work often enough, consistently enough, some of your best work will be underestimated, some of your poorer work will get by. If you work consistently enough, it balances out. But in 1963 there was no doubt about it: *She Loves Me* was a flop. I could not continue losing my investors' money. The next one would have to be a hit. Not just a good show, a hit. The Robbins–Abbott shows made a profit.

As for the good reviews *She Loves Me* received, I wasn't mentioned in them. Presumably it had directed itself. So if I wanted to continue directing on Broadway, not only did I have to return the investment, I would have to get reviewed.

It has been said that in the best direction you do not see the director's hand. That isn't necessarily true. Brecht was hardly unobtrusive. I was always aware of Kazan. There are projects that should not be "co-authored" by the director, but I felt I must find a project that begged for such authority my next time out.

However, I wasn't ready to grapple with that yet. Instead, I went back to familiar territory, to Robbins and to *Fiddler on the Roof*.

REFLECTIONS ON CHAPTER 14
OF *CONTRADICTIONS*

T. Edward Hambleton, co-producer of the Phoenix Theatre, knowing that I had ambitions to direct, invited me to join the board of the Phoenix and in 1961 offered me a production of *The Matchmaker*. It was to be financed by the New York State Arts Council and produced by the Phoenix for a tour of the state. I took the assignment, and we cast Sylvia Sidney, Sada Thompson, Ralph Dunn, Joe Ponazecki, and Ralph Williams in the leading roles. It opened in the theatre at Vassar College, and it was my first professional assignment as a director. It was so well received that it led to David Merrick offering me *Hello, Dolly!*, which I turned down in favor of Bock and Harnick's *She Loves Me*.

I always thought my *She Loves Me* was closer in mood and content to *The Matchmaker* than *Hello, Dolly!* was.

On the opening night of *She Loves Me*, the show was playing as it should—a romantic comedy enacted by four of the most skillful, witty, and charming performers I'd ever seen. All stars, all deserving of that accolade.

Halfway through act 2, the scrim traveler refused to open. Time marched on. Two minutes (a month), six minutes (six months). The audience watched as the show stopped dead in its tracks until a stagehand, risking his life, tightrope-walked across the batten above and finally untangled it from its lines.

The show recommenced and the cast redelivered, but its momentum, an especially delicate element, was shot. The next morning, the incident made the front page of the papers; and the reviews, which should have been triumphant (lesser revivals have received what we deserved), were soft. "A bonbon of a musical," said the *Times*. Well, if you fancy sweets.

The day after *She Loves Me* opened, Abbott called me into his office and told me what an excellent job I had done (I'd also heard that morning from Richard Rodgers and Leonard Bernstein, both of whom were extremely complimentary). Still, Abbott informed me that good as the show was, it would not run more than the balance of that season. Audiences wanted pizzazz and more bash from a musical. I hoped he was wrong, but he was right—again.

We ran only nine months. I decided from then on to parcel the press nights over several performances. The advantage was that the official opening night was made up of fewer press and your investors attended only when the major media had already seen the show.

Today this has become the norm, *except* that the press has asked to judge earlier and earlier previews (give 'em an inch, they'll take a mile).

I've come to admire the score of *Hello, Dolly!* greatly, and it's worth noting, *Hello, Dolly!* ran for seven years, 2,844 performances, sent out countless road companies, and has been revived this season starring the peerless Bette Midler.

CHAPTER
15

When I first read *Fiddler* in 1962, it was fascinating, but alien. My background is German Jewish—different from Russian Jewish. Joe Stein gave me the script, then called *Tevye*, and Bock and Harnick a book, *Life Is with People*, a sociological examination of communal life created by the Jews forced to live separately in shtetls.

The original script was realistic. It opened with Tevye and his family at Sabbath prayers, concerned less with the community and still less with the larger world outside. It lacked size.

I thought it primarily ethnic, and in that sense special. Great art transcends particular milieus. Marc Chagall, using the same shtetl, creates universal art. I reckoned Robbins would do the same. Unfortunately, at the time, Robbins was working on *Funny Girl* and was unavailable.

Bock and Harnick and I did *She Loves Me* instead.

A year later Fred Coe optioned *Tevye*. By then, Robbins had dropped *Funny Girl* and accepted *Tevye* on the condition that I be brought in as a co-producer. *She Loves Me* was floundering, so I jumped, providing that my office produce the show.

Fred Coe was directing his first film, *A Thousand Clowns*, and seemed happy to relinquish the burden.

Robbins set about giving *Tevye* its size. In a larger sense, what was the musical about? Or rather, what should it be about? The struggle of parents to preserve traditions against the pressures of changing times. Robbins began restructuring the story, postponing the introduction of Tevye's family at Sabbath prayers, opening instead with the community, the whole company in a number, sung and danced (stylization created size), entitled "Tradition."

Once this was established, the townspeople, including Tevye and his family, became individuals. In the case of *Fiddler*, each member of the company had a story, a vocation, a life.

There wasn't much dancing in *Fiddler*, excepting for the opening number and one in the second act for Tevye's wife and three daughters (it grew out of second-act problems and was expedient). Robbins wanted the dances to be naturalistic, informal, as they would have been in a tavern, at a wedding celebration.

The point was to separate sharply realism (the events) from the poetically abstract (the message).

I suppose no man is indispensable, but on *Fiddler* I think Robbins was.

Tom Bosley was Jerry's choice for Tevye, not mine. I opted for a presence, specifically, Zero Mostel's. I was still worrying that there might be resistance and wanted creative and economic insurance. It was expensive. Zero refused to sign for more than nine months. The short-term contract appealed to me because in an interesting way it gave me the advantage in our relationship. I knew Zero. After a play has opened, he tends to get bored, amuses himself onstage to keep things interesting. He refused to take notes from anyone for the run of his *Forum* contract, and that show quickly lost the element in his performance which made it extraordinary—the character of the slave. Ironically, the actor had abdicated to the performer, pursuing laughs and ingenious bits of business, obliterating the story.

More generally, if an actor is signed to a long-term contract in a starring role and becomes identified with the show, it's very possible and even likely he will be encouraged to make greater and greater demands on the management because he feels indispensable.

On the other hand, if the actor is on a short-term contract, he may reason that when the show is a smash, he can renegotiate an extension and do even better. Zero's lawyer had just that in mind.

I still think Zero was the best in the role when he was at his best, but had he left after three years instead of nine months, undoubtedly it would have cut down on our run.

Robbins chose Boris Aronson to design the scenery. I consider the day I met Boris second only to the day I met Abbott. Yet *Fiddler* did not tap the best of Aronson. He recently told me that if he had *Fiddler* to design again, he would do it differently, because it was too influenced by Chagall, which was what Jerry wanted at the time.

Subsequently, his designs for *Cabaret*, *Zorba*, *Company*, *Follies*, and even *Night Music* expressed him as *Fiddler* did not. Over the years Boris and I, mutually encouraging, moved further and further from naturalism, from props and doors and tables, and units, wagons with rooms on them, until with *Follies* there were no tables, no chairs, no doors, no windows.

Pat Zipprodt, straight from *She Loves Me*, designed the most expensive rags for the company to wear. It was *West Side Story* again. The colors of the peasants' clothes were beautifully controlled, the clothes beaten and aged in a vat of dye, then shown to Jerry, who would say take them back and age them, and they would be beaten some more and dipped in dye and returned for his approval, which came reluctantly.

Everything was expensive on that show, but not for the usual reasons. Robbins, directing and choreographing, insisted on eight weeks' rehearsal. The "chorus," middle-aged, cast to type, required considerable acting experience, representing a high weekly operating expense. In 1964 the payroll for the cast, including Zero, was $15,000 a week. We capitalized at $375,000, but we spent $450,000. Robbins is a difficult man to control financially while he is creating. I don't think I was a rubber stamp. Nevertheless, before the curtain went up in Detroit, I was out of pocket $75,000.

I wasn't worried. We opened in Detroit in the summer during a newspaper strike, so there were no reviews. Still, we were a smash from the first performance. You couldn't get near the theatre. Parenthetically, the only review was a pan in *Variety*, which called the show excessively commercial, mediocre.

I wrote my investors to disregard what they might read; they had a hit. I had felt that way from the first day of rehearsal. Getting into rehearsal seems to have been our only crisis.

Gun-shy as ever, with the actors signed, the scenery being built in the shop, and only ten days to go, Robbins decided we weren't ready, that we must postpone a month. That was impossible: we had theatre contracts, bookings on the road, actors to pay. He replied he wasn't ready. In my opinion he was. The conversation was replaced by a telegram obdurately refusing to go into rehearsal. I accepted his decision, providing he sent me a check for $55,000, covering my personal liability.

Then there were phone calls, and then there was a visit from his lawyer. He was heartsick that it had come to this and asked if I really meant that I would sue Jerry for those expenses if he was not there for the first day of rehearsals. I said he could bloody well bet I meant it. And he said, "How could our friendship have come to this?" I told him that my feelings were as hurt as Jerry's, and he went away convinced.

Rehearsals began on schedule.

They began with improvisations as they had in *West Side Story*. I remember two in particular. One took place in a white-owned bookstore in the South and involved the attempts of blacks to purchase books. A lesson in minority relations. The other took place in a concentration camp after the time covered by *Fiddler*. Again Robbins created respect in the actor for himself and for what the play was about. I borrowed liberally from the experience with *Fiddler* when I did *Cabaret*.

The title *Fiddler on the Roof* was suggested by Chagall's painting. Joe Stein then accommodated what we all thought was an intriguing title with a monologue at the beginning of the show.

Fiddler on the Roof was sold to United Artists for $2 million, which is less than was paid for *Man of La Mancha*, *My Fair Lady*, *Mame*; but the 25 percent of the distributor's gross after recoupment of costs will more than compensate for the discrepancy.

I don't think a show will run longer than *Fiddler*'s 3,242 performances on Broadway. It was like a rent-controlled apartment that you leased eight years ago. The economics were based on contracts drawn eight years earlier. Though our minimums adjusted with each new contract, our royalties remained what they were in 1964. We were able to break even on a weekly gross of $47,000. If *Fiddler* were to open today, it would take $75,000 to operate each week, and that would curtail the run by more than three years.

REFLECTIONS ON CHAPTER 15
OF *CONTRADICTIONS*

Apropos "Tradition," there were meetings with Robbins, Stein, Bock, Harnick, and me. Quite a few long nights, all ending with Robbins asking, "But what is the show about?" The answer from the show's authors, invariably, was, "Well, it's about this milkman marrying off his five daughters . . ." Robbins would persist. "No, what is it *about?*"

Next day the authors gave a different answer: "Well, it's about the tough life of a Jew in Christian Russia." Robbins: "But what's it really about?" Finally, one late evening, Sheldon exploded: "Forgodsakes, it's about *tradition!*" Robbins said, "*That's* what it's about. Write *that* song!"

They wrote it, and Joe Stein wrote the introductions of family, community, and a fiddler on the roof. I don't think Robbins knew the answer when he asked the question, but he sure as hell knew it when he heard it and it provided the metaphor that unlocked the show. Robbins staged the *world*— "Make a bigger circle"—and staged it on a turntable. And this gave the show its universality. In Japan, audiences regarded the show as being about their traditions, as did audiences in every country in which *Fiddler* was a success.

Regarding the casting of Zero Mostel, I should have said an "outsized, larger-than-life figure."

As of the end of 2016, *Fiddler* has realized a profit in excess of 3,920 percent. I was wrong when I said I didn't think a show would run longer than *Fiddler*'s 3,242 performances. As of June 18, 2017, *Phantom* has run for 12,230 performances, *The Lion King* has played 8,155 performances, and *Wicked* has played 5,689 performances.

Over the years, I have been accused of not casting stars. Of course stars can be good for business, but let's put it this way: I don't like depending on stars to keep the show going. I think the show has to be the star, and I want the public to want to come to see the show rather than the star.

Fiddler had become known as the Zero musical, and when Zero's contract was up, the Shuberts told me I had to renegotiate at any cost. "You're going to kill the goose that laid the golden egg if you don't," I was told. Because I was young and still new, I went to the office of Sidney Cohen, who was Zero's agent. We negotiated terms that, frankly, I thought were excessive; I was not happy. Yes, Zero could be wonderful as Tevye, but he was beginning to show traces of boredom: he would plop his arm into the milk can "by mistake" and then wring it out on the musicians in the pit. "Don't you have any pride?" I asked him. He blustered. But still we came to terms, and I was about to re-sign him. But then, as I was leaving the office, Sidney said, "Zero wants a car and chauffeur to drive him to and from the theatre." Instantly I replied, "The deal is off the table." And I left. The Shuberts were furious. I suppose my collaborators were a bit nervous, but almost instantly we cast Luther Adler of the famous Yiddish acting family to replace Zero. He was a star on Broadway and in film. His interpretation clearly would be totally different from Zero's, but he was prestigious and he broke the mold. The show continued to sell out, and subsequently Adler was replaced with Herschel Bernardi, Paul Lipson, and, in Las Vegas, Theodore Bikel.

Picture if you will *Fiddler on the Roof* at Caesars Palace, the hottest attraction in Las Vegas. The theatre was a showroom located right off the gaming tables, with booze being served. Every night a line of a thousand people would curl around the blackjack tables and the slot machines as they waited to see the show. It was not my first time working in Vegas—in fact, I had directed versions of *The Pajama Game* and *Damn Yankees* at the Riviera in the sixties and *Tenderloin* at the Dunes. But *Tevye and His Daughters* at Caesars Palace?! Believe it or not, the bidding for it was fierce, because Caesars was the newest, shiniest hotel on the Strip and paid handsomely for the production. I cut it to an hour and forty-five minutes (fifteen minutes longer than any previous Vegas/Broadway production), there was no intermission, and we sold out for over six years with Bikel in the starring role.

I didn't return to Vegas with a Broadway show for almost fifty years and then with *Phantom of the Opera*, which also ran six years.

CHAPTER
16

Jean Anouilh is largely unappreciated in this country, primarily because his plays are "French" in the particular sense that French theatre can be as remote from ours as the Kabuki. Wordy, static, adult fairy tales, they seem to possess too soft a center for American audiences.

I was in London directing *She Loves Me* and saw a production of Anouilh's *Poor Bitos* in a small theatre club. In this instance, at center the play was hard. Donald Pleasence, in the dual role of Bitos and Robespierre, gave an epic performance.

Bitos wasn't tempting to the New York importers of plays. They calculated, correctly, its dubious commercial prospects. Disregarding the obvious, I imported it because it was the most astonishing play I'd seen in too long, and I wanted even remotely to be joined to it.

In the case of *Bitos*, we rerehearsed in New York, bringing only Donald Pleasence and Charles Gray from the London company. We recreated to the last detail the London set, although the United Scenic Artists insisted that we credit an American designer who in fact did nothing more than supervise the building and the hanging of it in the theatre. I deplore anything which inhibits a free flow of creative talent between countries. Much has been said about protecting the American actor from the infiltration of the British, and vice versa; but not enough to convince me. There are periods Broadway is British and vice versa and over the years it comes out even.

The director was an American, Shirley Butler, who has since died. She duplicated the London production except for the costumes, which were designed by Donald Brooks. There was no fun in the doing of it for any of us. There rarely is in duplicating.

Pleasence, frustrated by the literalness of the original production, had hoped that when it transferred from London, it would be totally reconceived.

I was quite willing to *listen* to the play. My predilection for theatricality is not exclusive. Occasionally, I like the static verbosity of French theatre.

A year later, when I saw Andre Gregory's surrealistic production at the Theatre of the Living Arts in Philadelphia—with sets, costumes, performances outsized, and the ideas at the heart of the play moving—I knew for the first time what Pleasence meant.

In the intervening years, my work probably is best characterized by precisely that production Pleasence sought, but at the time I didn't know what he was talking about. It is worth mentioning that *Bitos* sold out its two preview weeks to cheering audiences. Then we opened, and the show was dismissed with faint praise by the critics, and Pleasence virtually ignored. (In *The Man in the Glass Booth* a few seasons later, they noticed.) Business stopped dead. This is partly explained by lower preview prices, making Broadway theatre available to a less-affluent, intellectual segment of the audience.

After the disappointing reviews, I reduced ticket prices so that we could run on a week-to-week basis, meeting expenses, with no possibility of profit, but no one came. Two weeks later we closed.

REFLECTIONS ON CHAPTER 16
OF *CONTRADICTIONS*

This was not the last of my negotiations with the great French playwright Anouilh, or more accurately his agent Van Loewen, but that is covered in the chapter about *A Little Night Music*.

CHAPTER
17

After *She Loves Me*, there were many offers to direct musicals from other producers. Joshua Logan had agreed to direct one for Alex Cohen based on the Sherlock Holmes stories. Wisely, he changed his mind, and Alex asked me to hear the score.

I had always figured that someday I would give up producing and direct exclusively for other managements. I would put behind me advertising campaigns and theatre terms and actors' agents and union negotiations; that would be my nirvana.

The score for *Baker Street* had been written by Ray Jessel and Marian Grudeff. An audition was arranged in Marian Grudeff's apartment. I should have known from that day what trouble I was getting into. All the while Jessel, the lyricist, played the score and auditioned the material for me; Grudeff, the composer, talked through the numbers, Jerome Coopersmith, the librettist, imploring her to shut up and permit me to listen.

I admired two of the songs, but little of the rest. The book, which I read that evening, was well constructed, nicely written, a small atmospheric show. In the script they'd cooked up an antiseptic love affair for Holmes. A bad idea. They'd cast Inga Swenson, who the previous season had knocked them dead in *110 in the Shade*, as the glamorous paramour. The lady and the love story were a part of the package. I should have known.

Baker Street could have been a one-set musical—sans love, sans chorus, the whole of it in Holmes's study with red flocked wallpaper, Victorian furniture, steaming beakers, and sliding panels.

I agreed to direct it, providing that if by Labor Day 1963 the new numbers weren't acceptable, Cohen would replace the composers with Bock and Harnick. Then I went to work with Grudeff and Jessel to try to get the score right.

In the course of a career, you are afraid to work because you are afraid to fail, and alternately, you get to thinking that if you are working, you can't fail. This time the latter applied.

It is calamitous to accept inferior material. And arrogant. There are so many surprises in the making of a show—unanticipated disappointments, problems—you cannot afford to make compromises up front. Again I went to work because I wanted to work. I was easier to work with in those days, stifling demands, deferring explosion until it was too late.

By Labor Day, we didn't have the required material. I asked that Bock and Harnick be brought in. I was told that Alex Cohen was committed to Grudeff and Jessel and that if I backed out now, it was too late to replace me and the rights would revert to the Conan Doyle Estate, forfeiting four years of work and massive out-of-pocket pre-production costs. Was it worth scuttling the show? I decided no, it was not worth it. I was wrong. My acquiescence at a point when we might have turned it all around instead sank it. The intimate show I was planning was for the Broad*hurst* Theatre (1,100); we got the Broad*way* Theatre (1,800). Bring on the dancing girls, bring on the sets and costumes.

I had one good idea. The second act called for Queen Victoria's jubilee procession along the Mall to Buckingham Palace. I asked Bil Baird to build a parade of animated wooden soldiers, followed by a tiny gold coach with Victoria inside, waving a lace handkerchief. Although we had added thirty-six dancers and singers, we retained our puppets in act 2, and they walked off with the show. They showed the multimillion-dollar musical "with a cast of thousands," on the biggest stage on Broadway, what it might have been.

In this instance *Variety*, from Boston, reported we were a combination of *Around the World in Eighty Days* and *My Fair Lady*. So by the time we opened, we had that responsibility riding our backs. I hold myself responsible for its outcome. I'd backed off when I should have persisted. I don't like to fight, and when I work for myself, I don't have to. I shortchanged Cohen in my misplaced effort to be congenial.

A lot of the responsibility has been taken off my shoulders by Ruth Mitchell, my associate producer; by Howard Haines, who succeeded Carl Fisher as general manager; and by Annette Meyers, my assistant; but I know it's being done my way. Their mistakes are my mistakes.

Add to that I have a terrible fear of being replaced on a show. Since most successful musicals are in some trouble on the road, if I were working for another producer, he might get jittery and fire me. I remember telling David Merrick when he asked me to direct *Hello, Dolly!*, "You'll fire me. I can see it now in the *New York Times*. You're hiring me so you can fire me." He replied that he had never fired a director in his life. On the other hand, there's always a first time.

And too, if I gave up producing, I would be at the mercy of job offers. On Broadway, unlike in the West End, there is simply not enough work, and able directors are forced to accept inferior material in order to work. As a producer, I create my opportunities.

After *Baker Street*, I was not offered another directing job for three years.

REFLECTIONS ON CHAPTER 17
OF *CONTRADICTIONS*

Although I closed the producing portion of my office after *Merrily We Roll Along*, I note that I did share producing credit on two subsequent shows: *Grind* and *Hollywood Arms*. In each instance, I did not actively participate or raise money. So why in hell did I accept billing? Beats me.

CHAPTER
18

Flora, the Red Menace was the last of the plays I produced that I didn't direct. It was based on Lester Atwell's book *Love Is Just around the Corner*, the story of an extroverted young girl, a commercial artist, looking for work in the post-Depression years and becoming involved with the Young Communist League.

I wanted to direct that show.

Of all the shows I have done which didn't work, I regret the failure of *Flora* most especially. What it could have been! And it was the perfect time for it. Joe McCarthy was dead.

I gave it to Kander and Ebb to read. I had known them for some time individually, not as a team. They agreed to compose some songs on spec.

I asked Garson Kanin to adapt it. Instead, he recommended Robert Russell, with whom he'd written one of the Tracy-Hepburn films. Russell had had personal experience with the Movement. He went to work writing with Barbra Streisand in mind.

Quite soon, I realized he needed help in the craft of constructing a musical. Also, there was an obduracy, an unwillingness to bend, an impracticality, difficult to analyze. I came to think he had an uneasy compact with failure on this one, the result perhaps of his experiences during those painful years. Eager to work on the one hand, but pessimistic about the outcome. The cynic had replaced the idealist.

Anyway, we argued often, and it didn't get written. Someone had to be found: a collaborator, experienced, who could take from him the best he had to give. Who better than Abbott?

Abbott liked the novel and some of Russell's dialogue, and while he found Kander and Ebb's songs brilliant, he quarreled with the best of them on the grounds that they were overemotional, even turgid.

The title, which was Russell's, perfectly set the tone of the show. *Flora, the Red Menace*. Affectionate, somehow rueful. "Workers and peasants of Sheepshead Bay unite for bread, peace, and land!"

Abbott felt the affection, but the quality of the emotion eluded him. He was born in 1886. He has lived through three wars, two police actions, the Crash, and Joe McCarthy. Just as he was about to be drafted in 1918, Armistice was declared. He predicted the Crash and was out of the market six months before it happened. He has been secure financially for over sixty years. He is essentially an apolitical man.

He brought to *Flora* no clear attitude about the Party. His Communists were cartoon characters, some of them farcical, others evil.

I wish I'd had the guts to tell him then that I wanted to direct it. He would have been surprised, but characteristically, after the surprise wore off, the idea might have appealed to him. And had we worked together, perhaps I could have created a consistent attitude toward that element in the material. Instead, I abdicated.

Abbott sent the first draft from Florida, using little of Russell's material. The best of the numbers no longer fit. So I flew down to Florida with my misgivings. He suggested that a good solution would be for Kander and Ebb to visit him there. I assumed they would stay about ten days, and during that time could persuade him to put the emotion back in the show. More specifically, to clarify our attitudes about radicals in that period.

They arrived in Florida one day; they were back in New York twenty-four hours later. Abbott had conducted his characteristic terse session: Had they understood what he wanted? Did they agree with him? (Apparently they gave him that impression.) They returned empty-handed but ecstatic, buoyed up by the assurance of the man.

Abbott's granitelike stability tranquilized them. More appropriately, they were intoxicated, and this pattern prevailed. Each time they would come to me justifiably worried about the material, I would send them to the telephone or to the typewriter to contact Abbott, and each time they would return in orbit.

As for Abbott, he wondered what all the ruckus was about. Abbott loves the life in Florida in the winter. He was willing to return in mid-February, a concession, but unwilling to spend the winter in New York with us. Clearly it was my responsibility to insist that he be here or that we postpone till the following season, which no one wanted to do. Again, what was the rush? Abbott spends his summers near New York. We could have worked the summer months together. As it was, we went into rehearsal with an incomplete script. In addition, Abbott left the supervision of the scenery and costumes to me.

Meantime, Russell was furious and verbal about it. He knew it was wrong, but he didn't know how to fix it. And because he didn't and he was the outsider, we closed ranks around Abbott. Sometimes protecting Abbott took precedence over protecting the play. The point is, we had momentum. An opening date in April, the Alvin Theatre, and Abbott. People in the theatre overrate momentum. They worry that if they stop the engine, they will never get it going again, and too, theatre people rarely know when a show is going to work. The lady who corners you at the cocktail party and says she could have told you, just might have, given her objectivity; but doing shows is a subjective process, and there is always an element of surprise for its creators when a show succeeds. Wishful thinking is built into the best of shows.

We didn't cast Barbra Streisand. She wasn't available. But Liza Minnelli was, having opened Off-Broadway in a tacky but energetic revival of *Best Foot Forward*. Just nineteen, she had a voice that reminded you of her mother, intelligence about character, and best of all for me, she moved wonderfully.

I counted *Flora* out before it opened in Boston, spending most of my time in the lobby of the Colonial Theatre. This was a step ahead of staying in bed as I did in Philadelphia with *A Swim in the Sea*. Astonishingly, it was well received in Boston, by both the critics and the public. Somewhat surprised, but happy, Abbott and his collaborators, excepting me, worked hard and well, and the show improved. So much so that by the time we previewed in New York, I began to believe we had a hit.

The reviews on Broadway were awful. They needn't have been. How often before you learn the lesson?

REFLECTIONS ON CHAPTER 18
OF *CONTRADICTIONS*

When George Abbott received the Kennedy Center's Lifetime Achievement Award in 1982, they had instituted a program of three-hour interviews with honorees. Bill Moyers was assigned to speak with Abbott, but he became unavailable. Roger Stevens, who had masterminded the building of the Kennedy Center and was running it at that point, asked me to take Moyers's place. We met at Stevens's apartment adjoining the Carlyle Hotel, where there were cameras fixed on Abbott's face and on mine. I used the interview to ask a great many questions I had never asked Abbott. Over the years he was very short on anecdotes, and the ones he did tell were humorous. About an hour and a half into the interview, I suddenly said, "Do you suppose you've lived so long [ninety-three years at the time; he lived until he was 107] because you've never lived at all?" His face went fierce, and he asked coldly, "What does *that* mean?" "Well," I said, "you've lived through three depressions and never went broke and three wars and never put on a uniform." Clearly I had hit a sore point. He didn't answer, and I dropped the subject.

I was drawn to artists dabbling in the Movement because I'd known some and they were idealistic to a fault. They posed no danger for democracy; they simply saw the social inequities surrounding them and objected. And they met and exchanged liberal views. These were the same people who joined the Abraham Lincoln Brigade and fought in the Spanish Civil War. I admired them.

My wife has said how lucky I was to have been born later than these people, and to have been so engrossed in building a career that I ignored politics. Subsequently I haven't, and I don't doubt that I would have gotten into a load of trouble at the time of the Dies Committee and, later, the McCarthy witch hunts.

It's interesting, is it not, that for well over a decade the word "liberal" was erased from the language. As recently as eight years ago, you could not refer to yourself as a liberal. That has changed, though the rupture between liberals and conservatives has widened, deepened, and become inflammatory. In any case, I grew to care about the subject and to develop affection for the writers and actors who found their names in *Red Channels*, as well as the writers who went underground in Hollywood. They were at worst naive idealists.

When we produced *The Pajama Game*, we hired Stanley Prager, who had been blacklisted on the coast. For *Fiorello!* we hired Howard Da Silva, also blacklisted. And of course Zero Mostel in *A Funny Thing* and *Fiddler*. It never seemed worth discussing, and it proved you could work on Broadway, if not in film and television, as a liberal.

Abbott felt similarly about these issues.

Fred Ebb remembered that the day before we opened in New York with *Flora*, I invited him and John Kander to my office for a meeting at 10:00 a.m. the next day. Abbott advised early in my career that I start work on a new project immediately after the opening of the previous one. If you have a hit, you may resent rising so early after the opening-night party. But if you have a flop, what a welcome morning it will be.

So I met with Kander and Ebb the morning after the *Flora* opening and presented them with Christopher Isherwood's *Goodbye to Berlin*. And *Cabaret* was born. *Flora, the Red Menace* closed after eighty-seven performances, and *Cabaret* opened the following year.

Apropos the idea of "momentum," it's not possible today. Now it takes too long for a musical to reach maturity. Clearly influenced by the cost of production, the extra time more often than not makes for jittery, inconclusive decisions. I have said before that doing a musical in one year in no way adversely affects its quality, because the collaboration within that period is so intense. With no distractions, you have a better chance of creating wonder.

In 1987 the Vineyard Theatre, at the time a small Off-Broadway venue, reimagined *Flora, the Red Menace*. The book was totally new, written by David Thompson; Scott Ellis directed, and Susan Stroman choreographed. In a word, it was brilliant. There's no way I can imagine how these talented people, who have gone on to great success in the commercial theatre, were able to come up with something so persuasive, honest, and compelling. It was a triumph, and I've always wished that they would revisit it one more time for a larger theatre. Its score was always wonderful, and it could have a Broadway future.

CHAPTER
19

In 1965 I was working with Kander, Ebb, and Masteroff on *Cabaret*, but it doesn't belong here in the book because we were stymied, and *this time* I postponed.

Instead, I picked up another of David Merrick's discards, *It's a Bird . . . It's a Plane . . . It's Superman*. It was an original, written by Robert Benton and David Newman (*Bonnie and Clyde*), with a score by Strouse and Adams (*Bye Bye Birdie*). The script I optioned had been completed a year earlier and anticipated the pop art craze. It was old-fashioned and funny, in a wisecracking way. Dressed up in 1940s wardrobe, it would have passed in a season of *Too Many Girls* and *Panama Hattie*. The jargon was the 1960s, but there was no attempt to comment on those times. It didn't even occur to me that we might have.

In fact, long after the play closed, Boris Aronson told me that *Superman* was the one show that he wished he'd been asked to design, because it could have been the definitive contemporary musical.

The presence of *Superman* in a realistic musical describing the quality of urban life in the 1960s with real villains instead of mad scientists might have helped us survive the pop art fad which overtook us. Written in 1964, *Superman* set the style. Produced in 1965, it followed it.

Superman opened badly in Philadelphia. The reviews were humiliating, and there was trouble with Jack Cassidy, who was starring in a flashy but subordinate role. Because of this, I expanded the role in rehearsal to accommodate his many talents. When we opened in Philadelphia, we were long, and I began to cut, the normal way of things. But he resented these cuts terribly. For each excision he had a suggested alternative. He would whip out a scrap of paper with a new line and read it aloud in front of the entire company. I was forced each time to reject it, which didn't discourage him. Each day brought new scraps of paper and new jokes; the process wore us both down. In this instance I won, or I think I did, but I realized how castrating an actor can be if he chooses. We are all familiar with the occasions in which a director can bully an actor into confusion, but there are just as many times when actors run off with the play. Stars do it all the time.

Though the *New York Times* called *Superman* the best musical of that year, we couldn't compete with *Batman* five nights weekly on television, "Zowie" sweatshirts, and Andy Warhol. The fad had peaked, and we closed in four months.

With *Superman* Ruth Mitchell, my right hand, became an associate producer, in charge of all technical elements of the productions, and I never worried about them again. Almost imperceptibly, she also moved into the role of an assistant director.

As in *Flora*, there was another show in *Superman*, but I had neither the self-confidence nor *comprehension* of what I might bring to the work of other people. The trouble is, everything the show might have been became clear after I'd done it. A concept, a point of view emerged after the work. That was because I had not yet begun to think of myself as a director. It was a costly way to learn.

REFLECTIONS ON CHAPTER 19 OF *CONTRADICTIONS*

On rereading *Contradictions*, I realize how remiss this chapter is because I neglected to mention Linda Lavin, with whom I worked on *A Family Affair*. She was almost an ensemble member when I took over the direction of that show, and I realized immediately what a star she could be. So I kept adding characters and lines during the rehearsal period. By the time we got to New York, people knew Linda Lavin. I cast her in one of the major roles in *It's a Bird . . . It's a Plane . . .* and she delivered. Her standout number was "You've Got Possibilities"—a tongue-in-cheek seduction of Clark Kent, Superman's alter ego. It was a showstopper.

In addition, I chose Patricia Marand as Lois Lane, and it was pluperfect casting. A mad scientist motivated the plot of *Superman*, and he was played by Michael O'Sullivan—a uniquely eccentric and dynamic force, such a creative figure. Unfortunately, his career was tragically cut short; he'd have cut such a figure in the theatre.

With regard to the contentious rehearsal relationship with Jack Cassidy: unprepared as I was to tangle with an old friend and collaborator who had delivered so brilliantly in *She Loves Me* (and ultimately in *Superman* as well), I recalled reading Gay Talese's piece "The Soft Psyche of Joshua Logan," which was published in *Esquire*. It documented the great director's experience with Claudia McNeil during the rehearsals for *Tiger Tiger Burning Bright*. McNeil had known of Logan's history as a patient of psychoanalysis—he had experienced some breakdowns during the course of a brilliant career, which included the direction of *South Pacific*, *Mr. Roberts*, and *Picnic*. McNeil took advantage of Logan's emotional fragility, and every day she confronted him, making mention of his bouts with depression, always denigrating him in front of the entire company. She destroyed the show and its direction.

In reading the article, I realized that a director cannot make an actor do something he chooses not to. When circumstances build to a confrontation between a director and an actor and that actor remains intransigent, the only course for the director is to fire him. Accepting that, when Cassidy came down to the edge of the stage and said in front of the entire company, "Is this really the Hal Prince I worked with on *She Loves Me?*" I replied from the house, "Yes, it is. And Jack, if you don't do what I'm asking, one of us has to go—and it won't be me." He stayed, and he delivered.

I haven't emphasized how remarkable I thought the score was for *Superman*. Charles Strouse and Lee Adams were at the top of their form, and Benton and Newman provided a really funny libretto. The show we presented was what it intended to be. After the show had closed, Boris Aronson suggested that I should have insisted on a more serious, perhaps political, plot. In other words, used *Superman* as a vehicle in keeping with my interests. He knew me, and he was right. His suggestion would have been a precursor of what Sondheim and I managed in the 1970s. I don't believe I was ready for that.

Ruth Mitchell had spent much of her career preparing scripts for publication. Samuel French, Tams-Witmark, and Music Theatre International license their musical libraries to professional theatres and to stock and amateur productions all over the world. Ruth resented that these published versions contained my director's notes, and about this time, unnoticed by me, she erased all my stage directions from the published editions of my shows. This precluded any carbon-copy productions for a while, but now in the age of YouTube, a patient and diligent director can reproduce the original staging.

Years later in his autobiography, Charles Strouse took issue with the fact that I had not returned from Europe for the closing of the show. He was right. I rarely do attend the closing of shows. I wish it were because of sadness, a sense of depletion, but it isn't; I've simply moved on.

CHAPTER
20

G wen Verdon and Tammy Grimes had both been mentioned for musical versions of *I Am a Camera*, John Van Druten's play based on Isherwood's *Berlin Stories*. Sandy Wilson (*The Boy Friend*) wrote the book, music, and lyrics for one to star Julie Andrews, and for a time she was interested.

What drew me to *Cabaret* had very little to do with Sally Bowles. I say *Cabaret* rather than *I Am a Camera* because ultimately we used Christopher Isherwood's *Berlin Stories* to step off from. What attracted the authors and me was the parallel between the spiritual bankruptcy of Germany in the 1920s and our country in the 1960s. The assassinations of Martin Luther King and Medgar Evers, the march on Selma, the murder of the three young men, Goodman, Chaney, and Schwerner.

To implement our point of view, on the first day of rehearsal, borrowing from Robbins's technique, I produced a centerfold from *Life* magazine of August 19, 1966, of a group of Aryan blonds in their late teens, stripped to the waist, wearing religious medals, snarling at the camera like a pack of hounds. I asked the cast to identify the time and place of the picture. It seemed obvious I'd lifted it from Munich in 1928. In fact, it was a photograph of a group of students in residential Chicago fighting the integration of a school.

I went so far in one draft of the show to end it with film of the march on Selma and the Little Rock riots, but that was a godawful idea, and I came to my senses.

Calling it *Cabaret* was Joe Masteroff's idea. The life of the cabaret, a metaphor for Germany. In his first draft, he and Kander and Ebb experimented with two scores running concurrently, one within the book for the personae; the other, pastiche for the entertainers. But who were to be the entertainers? A dancing chorus was predictable and difficult to give dimension to. Sally had been a lousy singer, so there was some question about how much lousy singing you wanted to impose on the show.

(When we got around to casting Sally Bowles, Kander and Ebb opted for Liza Minnelli, an idea I summarily rejected. She wasn't British—I'm not sure why that was important to me—and she sang too well; I still think that was a flaw in the film.)

Then I remembered that when I was stationed with the army near Stuttgart in 1951, there was a nightclub called Maxim's in the rubble of an old church basement. Whenever possible, I hung out in Maxim's. There was a dwarf MC, hair parted in the middle and lacquered down with brilliantine, his mouth made into a bright red cupid's bow, who wore heavy false eyelashes and sang, danced, goosed, tickled, and pawed four lumpen Valkyries waving diaphanous butterfly wings.

The show started naturalistically in the compartment of a train with the arrival of the leading man in Berlin. Immediately it was to be followed by a "turn," six or eight songs fragmented to introduce Berlin nightlife and to be performed by my MC from Maxim's, making quick changes from Lenya to Richard Tauber to Dietrich, and so on.

I arranged an audition for Joel Grey, who immediately caught the component courage, self-delusion, fear, and sadness of this mediocre MC. He didn't bother with the Germanness.

For a short time we had two shows. A predictable realistic telling of the writer's encounter with Sally, and Joel Grey's fifteen minutes. Instead, we took Joel's numbers and scattered them through the show in an ascending curve energetically and a descending curve morally. He opened effortfully, empty laughter to an empty house. He'd lost the war, his self-respect. He carried his money around in bushel baskets. With National Socialism he found his strength, misdirected and despotic, feeding off his moral corruption. In those eight numbers, the MC became the metaphor.

It was a good idea, but only half a concept. What would it look like? How would it happen? I had no idea. I postponed and did *Superman* instead. In the spring *Superman* opened and closed, and I went to Russia to get away from it and the insoluble problems of *Cabaret*.

In Moscow I attended the Taganka Theatre's *Ten Days That Shook the World*, a political revue suggested by John Reed's book. Foy Kohler, the American Ambassador to Russia, recommended it, and had ordered and paid for the tickets well in advance. When I went to pick them up, I was told the Young Communists had taken the entire theatre, and my money was refunded. I made an awful scene (in Russia, scenes are often the only means of getting things done, and upon advice, this one was coldly premeditated), saying I had come all the way to Russia to see that production, then enlisted help at the American Embassy, ultimately receiving two seats in the last row of the balcony. Luckily, it was a small theatre.

I mention this because had I not gone, I would have missed out on a theatrical experience I count as a turning point in my thinking as a director. Part cabaret theatre, Taganka borrows liberally from the Russian actor-director Vsevolod Mcyerhold, who began with Stanislavski at the Moscow Art Theatre and broke away on his own in protest of the extreme realism of that movement, exploring instead means of using theatre techniques to excite, creating an audience of participants in which subjective involvement was all.

I'd been raised in a fairly conventional musical theatre. Even *West Side Story*—which had the audacity to contain that much dance and to move that much ahead with each dance, without words—explosive as the whole concept was, was not something new. It was the pinnacle of a tradition.

In 1964 Joan Littlewood's *Oh, What a Lovely War!* had fractured the musical form into something resembling a revue, discarding central characters, a story line. A couple of seasons earlier, her *Fings Ain't Wot They Used t'Be* explored less successfully ways of shaking up an audience by taking the predictability out of the experience.

Still, until that night at the Taganka, I believed the most important element of a musical to be the book. The score was secondary. A rule and as such, no more valid than the reverse, which is subscribed to by most of my peers.

The text of *Ten Days* was absurd. Trenchant political satire in Moscow in 1966 exploited the villainy of Alexander Kerensky and Woodrow Wilson. But the techniques, the vitality, the imagination to make every minute surprising, *involving*, yet consistent with a concept are the stock-in-trade of this theatre.

Ten Days began in the lobby, spilled across the stage into the audience, shattering the fourth wall. Nothing new in that: musicals always break the wall. Actors step down, turn front, and sing. But there are ways and ways to break walls.

The Taganka was conventional in that there was the stage, the proscenium, the orchestra pit, the auditorium: nothing environmental about it. However, there were technical devices which knocked me out. An apron built out over the orchestra pit into which searchlights were sunk. These lights, slanted over the heads of the audience to the last row in the balcony, when lighted, instead of blinding, became a curtain of light behind which the scenery was changed. Paintings on the wall spoke, inanimate objects animated, disembodied hands, feet, and faces washed across the stage. There were puppets and projections, front and rear, and the source and colors of light were always a surprise. All of it made possible by the use of black velour drapes instead of painted canvas. I date my love affair with black velour from that performance.

Each of these ideas capitalized on the special relationship of live actors and live observers. It is that relationship which is exclusively ours in the theatre. Film and television cannot touch it. And properly appreciated, it gives us the chance to make connections, to string unseen emotional bands between actor and audience. The business of physical contact is the least of it.

Old techniques? Probably. But I had never seen them used so well. They affected me like a shot of adrenalin.

A few seasons later, the Taganka's production of *Hamlet* worked brilliantly. They used a length of fabric strung from guy wires, which, moving in any direction on the stage, suggested a wall, a piece of furniture, a door, the exterior of a castle, or Gertrude's closet. Ingmar Bergman used something of the sort in the National Theatre's production of *Hedda Gabler*. Effortlessly, the actors moved a blood-red screen, about the size of a door and mounted on casters, to divide rooms, to construct unseen walls, to isolate the interior workings of a character's mind from his external behavior.

I came home and called Jean Rosenthal, who was going to light the show, describing for her what I'd seen. I asked her to give me a curtain of light so we could change scenery behind it. She informed me that there's no equipment in the world powerful enough to accomplish what I wanted in a Broadway theatre. The throw from the source of the light to the back wall wouldn't be intense enough.

Scrap that idea. Come up with another.

I suggested splitting the stage in two: an area to represent the "real world," the vestibule in Sally's rooming house, her bedroom, the train, the cabaret; and an area to represent the "mind." Joel Grey's material was divided between realistic numbers performed in the cabaret for an audience onstage and meta-phorical numbers illustrating changes in the German mind. We called this the "limbo area."

Jean designed a light trough about six feet upstage of the edge of the apron. Covered with a wooden shield, it rose electronically and could be directed at an angle of forty-five degrees upstage to the rear wall (we danced a Tiller chorus of lumpen Valkyries across the stage, lighting only their legs). Downstage at forty-five degrees, we momentarily blinded the audience. And at ninety degrees straight up into the flies, we made a curtain of dust. Our trough served as footlights for the MC. Five waiters singing "Tomorrow Belongs to Me" stepped across it and disappeared upstage. At the climax of the show, Sally Bowles sang "Cabaret," lost track of her audience, broke down, and for the first time in the evening, stepped across the footlights into the limbo area, and the audience understood.

So much for the lighting.

Boris Aronson is a good talker. He has a quirky and penetrating vision of people, time, and place. His analysis of a news event, of conflict in fiction, invariably surprises. He possesses an extraordinary active vocabulary. (He has been writing a book for years. I wish he'd finish it so I can read it.)

Cabaret was the first of our collaborations. We talked for three months—rarely of things visual, mostly of the characters, false motivations, interpersonal behavior, people in different countries, ethnic peculiarities, emotional expression as affected by national or ethnic considerations. Of course, he collected thousands of photographs, but he never observed the predictable: never the leg of a table, the shape of a lamp post, the ironwork on the hotel balcony rail. Rather, he would call my attention to the expression of the shoppers on the street, to the quality of light in a room, the emotional content in the architecture of a section of the city.

Boris puts great store in his opinion of material. He's right. Also, he makes problems or unearths them and worries them to death. He's not negative; he is troublesome. When Boris talks, I hear and see things I neither heard nor saw before.

Just about when you've run out of talk and you think it's time he went to work, he presents you with a finished design. Apparently he has been working on versions of it all along. Though his renderings in watercolor and gouache

131

are beautiful works of art, he always does a quarter-inch scale model. From this we make whatever changes are necessary (in Boris's case, they are very few): differences in the relationship of furniture, the shape of a roof, the adjustment of doors and windows, that sort of thing. Nothing major. Once those details are taken care of, he constructs a half-inch scale model for the scenic builders and the stage managers and for me to live with and to show the actors on the first day of rehearsals. The pieces in this model are large enough to remove and hold in your hand, detailed, finely realized down to the texture of wallpaper, the design of a stained-glass window.

The model I saw of *Cabaret* was of a slightly raked stage with three black velour drapes, two on either side of the stage running slightly diagonally up-stage to the third, which formed the rear wall. The side velours were rigged to fly quickly, letting the scenery roll in on winch-operated trucks. Overhead there hung two strings of street lights, built in perspective, and the tangled lines of a trolley. The lighting equipment against the black drops made it possible for Jean Rosenthal to design subtle, realistic lighting for the book scenes and to give the cabaret and limbo numbers the hard, sinister edge of spotlights.

In addition, there was the *Cabaret* sign in neon—Joe Masteroff's idea—which opened and closed the show.

Boris designed an iron staircase typical of those backstage in nightclubs, and he put it in the limbo area of the stage. I had not asked for it, but it was there, and I placed ladies of the chorus on it, observing the realistic scenes of the play, and as they lit their cigarettes they cast empty eyes on the events of the play. Their indifference generated a curious dynamic in the scenes. They became the surrogate German population. This was the first time I played around with observers onstage.

In the scale model, Boris surprised me with a mirror—a trapezoid, corresponding to the shape of the stage floor—suspended above the center of the stage and slanted to reflect the audience. It cast an additional, uneasy metaphor over the evening.

Apropros surprises, there are always surprises from Boris. In *Company* it was the two elevators. In *Night Music*, the plastic trees.

Fred Ebb recommended Ron Field as choreographer. Although I had never seen his work, I had no other enthusiasms, so I agreed. I imagine that seems an unprofessional way to make such an important decision, but we had come by Bob Fosse on *Pajama Game* exactly the same way. The point is, Ron Field had the experience, and when we talked, he had the enthusiasm.

Cabaret was an enormous amount of work for him; each of the numbers required an idea, and he seemed to have good ideas to waste.

Later, we did *Zorba* together, and then he began to direct; he was especially successful with *Applause*, but he succumbed to the glamor and insistent pressures of Hollywood and moved there to choreograph films, television specials, and Las Vegas club acts. Apparently, it is impossible to resist those temptations.

I am happy to say that he has since moved back to New York, back to the theatre. Isn't it paradoxical that television and film stars visiting New York (to present Tony Awards?) seem awed by the stage, while Broadway people can't wait to drop everything and move to California?

Because the shape of *Cabaret* had taken an unconventional turn, because we were experimenting with alien theatrical devices, we determined to move away from Isherwood's material. *The Berlin Stories*, from which *I Am a Camera* was written, are about Sally Bowles's "scandalous" relationship with a homosexual writer. Plotless, really, there are events along the way, but essentially they are a pair of character studies with ominous presentiments of anti-Semitism just offstage in the wings. We persuaded ourselves that the musical comedy audience required a sentimental heterosexual love story with a beginning, middle, and end to make the concept palatable.

Not content with that, we added Lotte Lenya and Jack Gilford in a subordinate love story. The structure, indeed familiar: Ado Annie and Will Parker, Hineszie and Gladys, Adelaide and Nathan Detroit.

In my opinion, we were wrong. The plotless musical might not have worked, but had it, the whole project would have been consistent with its aspirations. If we had *Cabaret* to do all over again, I believe we would have made the audacious choice. In defense, it was 1966. A lot has happened since then, and so quickly that the film, in 1972, dealt explicitly with homosexuality. I liked that part of the film; I missed the metaphoric use of the MC.

Re the presence of sufficient conventional elements to make a show comfortable for its audience: *West Side Story*, *Company*, and *Follies* didn't sell out; *Cabaret* did.

Just before we left for Boston, I ran separate performances of *Cabaret*, one for George Abbott and one for Steve Sondheim. They are the two I most like to hear from at that stage. They never waste your time with the obvious; they figure you see it and you'll get around to it in good time.

Soon after we'd opened in Boston, one suggestion kept cropping up from friends, but also from strangers who write letters knowing you are fixing. I resisted it until everything else was in place and the show had found steady legs. I learned from Abbott and Robbins that you can do almost anything drastic when the show is cut, there are no more lines to learn, and the performances are secure.

In this case, the pressure was to take "Cabaret" from the end of the show and use it to introduce Sally Bowles. This meant replacing her first song, "Don't Tell Mama," with "Cabaret" and replacing "Cabaret" with a marvelous Kander and Ebb song, "I Don't Care Much," which had been written for the show and never used.

My instincts were against it, but because it had been suggested so many times, I was dying to see what would happen. Three days before the opening in New York, Goddard Lieberson, in charge of Columbia Records, begged me to try it. I asked Jill Haworth, who was playing Sally Bowles, whether she was willing to learn a brand-new song that close to the reviews. She agreed. It went in that night and destroyed the show. The climactic moment of *Cabaret* was half as effective with the new song. The song, coming at the top of the show, went by unnoticed; the giddiness of "Don't Tell Mama" was missing. It was as though we had leveled the emotions of the show across the board.

Something like this happened with *Pajama Game*. Jerry Robbins had always wanted "Seven and a Half Cents" to open the show. Acting on instinct, Abbott resisted until a New York preview and then tried it. The number, which had been affectionately humorous at the end of the show, was serious business in front. It scared the hell out of Abbott, and he refused to try it for a second performance.

Twelve years later, I put things back the way they were—fast.

In the second act of *Cabaret*, Joel Grey sang a love song to a gorilla wearing a pink tutu and carrying a purse. "If You Could See Her Through My Eyes" was sweet and funny, except for the final line, in which he looked at her and sang, "If you could see her through my eyes, she wouldn't look Jewish at all." Some laughed, most were shocked, many were offended. It was as we intended, but that didn't matter. We began receiving letters of protest from individuals in the audience, and in time from rabbis and entire congregations. After the first New York preview, the audience stayed to argue in the theatre, sizable segments on either side heatedly debating the propriety of it.

I introduced myself to them and after listening to both sides, called the authors together. We talked. A sleepless night later, I made Ebb change the last line in the lyric, and I emasculated the song.

The company was upset. So was I, but not as upset as they. Fred Ebb still hasn't forgotten it. Ebb: "I've never known you to pander to the public." But I was right. I didn't want the show closing over that.

When we did the show in London, we put the lyric back, and the letters followed. And we took the line out.

When the film was made, they put the line in but shot a number of alternatives that they showed at sneak previews. Finally, they took it out.

The success of *Cabaret* at the box office made the difference. I was offered plays to direct for other people.

REFLECTIONS ON CHAPTER 20 OF *CONTRADICTIONS*

The composer/playwright Sandy Wilson, who wrote *The Boy Friend*, also presented a version of the Sally Bowles story to me many years ago, but once again, it wasn't political.

Of course, I still attribute so much of the *Cabaret* experience to seeing *Ten Days That Shook the World* at Moscow's Taganka Theatre. Founded by Yuri Lyubimov, a disciple of Meyerhold, it still exists today.

Many years ago, Joshua Logan told me that he had studied with Stanislavski in Moscow at the time when Meyerhold broke with the master, moving away from realism to heightened theatricality. Logan told me my work reminded him of Meyerhold's, and soon after, I received a letter from Meyerhold's granddaughter, who has since died, telling me that she'd heard similarly about my direction and asking whether I would contribute to a proposed museum in her grandparents' apartment. Meyerhold has always been one of my theatre gods.

Theatre is of central importance to Russian culture, and despite the dominance of Communism from 1917 to 1989 and the interference of Stalin in particular, the Moscow Art Theatre, the Vakhtangov, the Taganka, the Bolshoi, and the Mariinsky flourished.

Ten Days That Shook the World began in the lobby of the theatre. Five musicians in various costumes standing on a platform greeted you. Two of them were dressed as sailors from the *Potemkin*; another, in Communist workers' clothes, was the singer Vladimir Vysotsky—who was fast becoming the avant-garde voice of young Russia. He was a national icon and died rather young. After a number of political songs, the doors were opened, and the audience moved into the theatre itself, where a musical revue ridiculed the League of Nations and the villainous Woodrow Wilson. Their targets were lame; the theatricality, thrilling.

A year ago, the American ambassador to Russia, John Tefft, and my friend Dmitry Bogachev at Stage Entertainment, who was presenting *Phantom of the Opera*, invited me back to Moscow.

During this visit, I mentioned that forty-nine years ago the only Moscow restaurant that we visited was a Georgian one called the Aragvi. I was surprised to learn that the Aragvi still existed and was in the process of being renovated. My host, Dmitry, surprised me and arranged a lunch at the Aragvi during its renovation. Early in the meal, I realized that there was a man sitting next to me and staring. He was one of the *Potemkin* sailors who had greeted us so many years ago in the lobby of the Taganka. Our reunion was heartwarming.

In the fifty years since *Cabaret* premiered, sadly I still believe "it *can* happen here." Maybe wherever human beings live, it can happen. We have to accept that possibility. If so, how damned sad.

There have been many productions of *Cabaret* in the not-for-profit theatre and one Academy Award–winning film directed by Bob Fosse. Many of them are first-rate, but common to all of them is a disregard for the original metaphor which fueled our *Cabaret*. None of them dramatize the trajectory of the emcee from a simple, down-at-heels, bad-taste entertainer during the depths of the German Depression into a Nazi who incarnates the rise of National Socialism.

The final image in Fosse's *Cabaret* disregards totally our original intent. The number "Cabaret" was written to dramatize Sally Bowles's knowledge that she is pregnant: I moved her out of the Kit Kat Klub to the limbo area, where she struggled with that knowledge. From the line, "I used to have a girlfriend known as Elsie," she is really singing about herself, making up her mind to have an abortion. She moves emotionally from panic to exhaustion to elation, and the number ends on a note of manic hysteria.

I should mention that Joel Grey's performance as the emcee was strongly influenced when Tony Richardson took me to see his production of *The Entertainer* with Laurence Olivier's miraculous performance.

A couple of years ago I ran into Joe Masteroff, who wrote the book for *Cabaret*, and out of the blue he asked whether I'd ever received a token piece of the show from Kander and Ebb. When I said no, he expressed regret. Why in hell didn't he include himself as one of the authors?

In truth, I harbor some resentment that I've never been credited with unlocking the concept of *Cabaret*. My name has never appeared in the billing for subsequent productions, nor have I shared in the authors' royalties. Since then, all my other collaborators have publicly acknowledged my contribution to their shows.

When Abbott saw *Cabaret*, it was in three acts. As he was leaving, he expressed approval of what he had seen and limited his comments to: "Two acts, Hal, put it in two acts." Exit Abbott.

I went home poleaxed. Two acts, fine. But how? Ruth Mitchell solved the problem easily. Put acts 1 and 2 together and act 3 would be our second act. We did that and it worked. However, the first act of *Cabaret* is long. And the second act is too *short*.

Weeks before *Cabaret* opened, I wrote Christopher Isherwood to warn him that ours was a musical and not a dramatization of his *Berlin Stories*. I told him how much I admired his material and hoped he would understand that our approach was for another medium and, particularly, to accommodate musical numbers. He never replied. However, I heard from many people that he hated our version. Nevertheless, I suspect his royalties from *Cabaret* exceeded the total for all his writings.

Were I to do *Cabaret* now, I would take the opportunity, as Fosse did in the film, to restore the original gay subplot. Cliff was gay and there was no future for him and Sally. But putting Nazis on the stage in a musical seemed like a big enough step at the time. Years later, when the film was made, audiences were accepting more and more controversial issues.

✌

Cabaret led to a number of flattering offers. Federico Fellini paid me a visit to suggest I make a musical of *8½*. Leo McCarey, who won multiple Academy Awards with sly, romantic, well crafted, and amusing films, offered me the choice of adapting one of them into a musical. Later, Toni Morrison, a Nobel laureate and someone I've grown to know and admire, suggested we work on a musical about Storyville, but my earlier experiences with similar subjects made me gun-shy—I still regret that decision. And then there was a visit from Alex Haley, who offered me *Roots*—what a modest and engaging person he was—but, of course, that assignment was too intimidating for me to accept.

CHAPTER
21

Herschel Bernardi had the idea to musicalize the Kazantzakis novel *Zorba the Greek*, and he and Joe Stein brought it to me. Michael Cacoyannis's recent film was filled with exciting music and dance, and I was attracted to it philosophically. The novel multiplied my enthusiasm. Kander and Ebb shared it.

Maria Karnilova was our instant choice for Bouboulina, the part that Lila Kedrova played so well on the screen.

It all fell into place.

The public wanted to see it. The benefit party ladies wanted to sell it. Our advance sale, sans advertising, reached $2 million.

It fell exactly into that category of shows I said I would never do, a show so anticipated that it must disappoint. And that's what happened to *Zorba*.

Even the concept came easily. We would translate the traditional Greek chorus into a group of musicians I had seen in a bouzouki restaurant near Piraeus. Thirty-eight men and women sitting in a semicircle, each holding a musical instrument, dressed in the gaudiest of makeshift costumes with spangles, smoking, talking, singing solos or in unison, interrupting each other with horseplay and laughter.

Our play began in the present, and the company took us back forty years to introduce Zorba in a similar café on the waterfront. Assuming all the roles, they used their chairs and props to imagine a waiting room on a dock, and their musical instruments to create the sounds of the wind and the sea, and scraps of material from the women's skirts suggested costumes.

Boris Aronson's basic unit was the classic Greek amphitheatre with levels in a semicircle. Onto these levels he introduced fragments of scenery—an olive tree, the entrance to a church, a restaurant, a store, a balcony—and by the third scene in the play we'd constructed a realistic village in Crete, made of molded Styrofoam, and climbing the side of a hill. By then the entire company was realistically costumed.

The trouble is that we had turned our backs on the imagination we had displayed in the opening and, by the second act, we were defeated by the degree of realism we had achieved in the first. There is a mine disaster, important to the plot of *Zorba*. In the film, it was elaborately enacted on a real mountain with tons of explosives and hundreds of extras. We attempted a similar effect with two smoke pots, a taped explosion, and thirty-eight people running here and there, simulating terror.

The mine disaster was endemic to the plot. Had we acknowledged the limitations of the stage, we might have made capital of the mine disaster. Dance might have worked, though I'm tired of it. There had to be something imaginative, but we were stuck with realism, and what was worse, we couldn't keep the events offstage.

As for the casting, it was one of those educated guesses. Beware of those. Bernardi and Karnilova had played Tevye and Golde a year earlier. Apparently, I was counting on the audience wanting to see "the Lunts" playing totally different characters. I was wrong. And the casting created unnecessary comparisons with *Fiddler*.

I think *Zorba* was a first-rate, if depressing, show. What exhilarated me evidently depressed others. The opening number was called "Life Is What You Do While You're Waiting to Die." Arthur Laurents said that sank us.

In *Zorba* Boris and I got to know a great deal more about each other again. We did more thinking about the space than we had before. The palette: the blacks, the grays, the whites, how to work with them. We did more experimentation: the business of having people stand around and observe and comment, be within the story and without it, touched on in *Cabaret*, amplified subsequently in *Company* and *Follies*.

There was a ballad in the second act of *Zorba* in which a young man sings to the woman he loves, and it becomes a trio as a lady representing the Greek chorus observes the scene and joins in. I never got it to work.

In *Follies* several years later, I had a man sing to an apparition of a young girl he'd been in love with thirty years earlier, while her counterpart, the woman she'd grown up to be, stood by and mistook his song as being sung to her. Two women and a man, essentially the staging quite the same. In *Follies* I knew how to make it work.

So you learn. Boris said *Follies* would not have happened had it not been for *Cabaret*, *Zorba*, and *Company*.

Zorba closed prematurely because Bernardi and Karnilova got to fighting. Personal difficulties in Bernardi's life contributed to physical problems, and he began to miss performances. It was catching: Karnilova matched him performance for performance, and soon both stars were out.

Zorba was a disappointment for all of us. Our New Haven notices were marvelous, and we all thought we had another *Fiddler*. The *New York Times* and *Daily News* reviews were excellent, but it never happened. Each day the advance diminished.

Sometimes it's easier to close a flop, harder to live with a borderline case. *Zorba* hung on without either joy or relief. By the summer, with both stars out, I had no stomach for replacing them. Instead, we closed *Zorba* and produced two new companies, one for the Civic Light Opera in Los Angeles with John Raitt and Barbara Baxley, the other to tour, starring Michael Kermoyan and the unlikely but appropriately cast Vivian Blaine.

Zorba went on to run over a year out of town, but it never paid off its investment. It still owes its investors 26 percent, which I think will dribble in slowly but surely, and if we all live long enough, the show will pay off.

It's interesting that *Zorba* has had rather more life in Europe than in this country, and that has to do with the prevailing blackness of its mood, its European acceptance of mortality. I loved it at the Theater an der Wien in Vienna. It was also a success in the Scandinavian countries, particularly Finland, where there were four companies playing simultaneously.

REFLECTIONS ON CHAPTER 21 OF *CONTRADICTIONS*

In 1983, *Zorba* was revived with Anthony Quinn recreating his starring role in the film. The production was inferior artistically to the original; however, the presence of a bona fide film star made it into a hit.

Further, Kander and Ebb were persuaded to soften the edges of the show; "Life is what you do while you're waiting to die" became "Life is what you do till the moment you die."

In rereading this chapter, I disagree with my appraisal of our "realistic" production. It wasn't. Boris's set, far from being realistic, delivered an entire Greek village on a mountainside. Amazing!

The show's opening, "Life Is," was performed by a bouzouki group in a semicircle with a traditional Greek chorus, in this case a woman, played by Lorraine Serabian. She represented Greece over millennia. Direct, harsh, vulgar, and confrontational. And for that performance, Serabian got the star reviews. Overnight, we seemed to have found another Streisand. However, in a matter of weeks the strain took a toll on her voice and her performance and, with them, our audience.

Over the years, I've come to realize *Zorba* was a pretty damn fine show. That Herschel Bernardi brought the idea to me with himself in mind for the title role of course made it mandatory to cast him. But definitively I know that excellent as Bernardi and Maria Karnilova (as Madame Hortense) were, it was the very presence of our *Fiddler* stars that eliminated the excitement that the show deserved.

CHAPTER
22

George Furth, the actor, had written eleven one-act plays. Under the title *Company*, they were to be presented by another management in New York, starring Kim Stanley, as an evening of straight plays. There was nothing connective about them except the presence of this one glorious lady.

Sondheim, a friend of Furth's, felt there was something wrong with the scheme and asked whether Furth would object to sending the plays to me for advice. I was knocked out by them, seeing a potential musical which could examine attitudes toward marriage, the influence upon it of life in the cities, and collateral problems of especial interest to those of us in our forties.

I suggested this much to Steve over the telephone, and he agreed to do it. Just like that.

He was working on a show, *The Girls Upstairs*, with James Goldman. Joe Hardy was set to direct it, and they had scheduled rehearsals for the fall of 1970. *Company* would follow in the spring of 1971. All this, assuming Furth liked the idea.

A meeting was set, and I outlined a kind of freewheeling, unconventional musical, borrowing from the revue form and lifting those of Furth's plays dealing with marriage. We needed a central character to catalyze the partners in the marriages and to connect the disparate episodes. We invented a single man, and Steve baptized him Robert, so that he could be referred to differently by each of his friends. In other words, "Bobby," "Bubbi," "Baby," "Robbie," "Rob," and so on.

If in fact it could be a musical, how to make it one? The real problem was the plays stood on their own. Interruptions by musical numbers would kill their pace. Thirteen love songs wouldn't do, nor would thirteen marriage songs. The problem in the theatre occasionally creates the marvelous solution.

In this instance, Sondheim left the plays intact and composed a score for those members of the company not involved in a specific episode. The observers.

Still we lacked a unifying concept. Just as Steve needed an excuse to write the score, I needed an excuse to move the people.

We retained three of the original short plays. Furth adapted a fourth and wrote a fifth. At this point we had five married couples and Robert. George invented three single girls to keep Robert happy—or confused—or single. Those fourteen people comprised the entire company, still another play on the title.

I suggested ours be an "acting" company, fourteen individuals to assume the roles of married people only when we needed them. They would move the furniture and props around the stage; they would be required to inhabit the stage for the length of the show. Each would have one costume with perhaps a few accessories.

It didn't turn out that way, but that is how we started.

From the first, Boris and I wanted as spare a production as possible: a couple of tables, half a dozen chairs, a bench, some pots and pans, cups and glasses, and a bed. We agreed that Boris would design a structure encompassing five separate rooms. These would be interchangeable. The bedroom for one couple became the kitchen for another; the nursery for one, the library for another. The couples would move from room to room in the course of living even the mundane moments of their lives. And the decor in each room would identify its married couple.

To focus our attention on a particular couple, we would reproduce their room—center and stage level. As if that weren't enough, company numbers ("What Would We Do without You?") would be performed on the entire unit without any scenery.

Complicated? So complicated that we abandoned it.

I was filming *Something for Everyone* in Germany that summer. Toward the end of July, Steve phoned from New York that there were problems with *The Girls Upstairs*, that the director wanted a good deal more rewriting, and the producer, Stuart Ostrow, was determined to postpone until the spring—in other words, *Company*'s dates.

The idea of being without a show the next season upset me. I'd worked quickly with Furth and Sondheim, Boris was in the throes of designing, I'd booked theatres in Boston and New York, and even cast Elaine Stritch—all of this in less than three months. I refused to postpone. We had a contract, and I was going to hold him to it.

Steve said he felt as if he were giving birth to a stillborn child. He and Goldman had worked five years on *The Girls Upstairs*, and he didn't see how he could write *Company* in his present state of depression.

I sympathized but refused the postponement, reasoning that any solutions which had eluded them for five years weren't going to appear miraculously with an additional six months. And if there was to be no *Company* in January, then there would be no *Girls Upstairs* either. Steve, who hadn't been heard on Broadway since *Do I Hear a Waltz?* and was looking forward to two shows in the one season, suddenly was faced with the probability of none. I knew of no other way to deal with it.

With the problem still up in the air, Steve appeared in Europe with three songs for *Company*. The first of them, "Company," is probably the best song in the score. Talk about setting the ground rules for the evening, the style—"Company" does it perfectly.

The second number, "The Little Things You Do Together," was written for Elaine Stritch and the company and established the technique of characters observing in song the nonmusical material.

The third, written for Robert at the end of the show, expressed the opinion that living with someone is hell, but living alone is impossible. "Marry Me a Little" was brilliant and harshly cynical. Robert had covered no distance, learned nothing in the course of the evening. He would marry someone and they would go their separate ways, which isn't exactly what we had set out to say about marriage.

Marry Me a Little

Marry me a little,
Love me just enough.
Cry, but not too often,
Play, but not too rough.
Keep a tender distance,
So we'll both be free.
That's the way it ought to be.
I'm ready!

Marry me a little,
Do it with a will.
Make a few demands
I'm able to fulfill.
Want me more than others,
Not exclusively.
That's the way it ought to be.
I'm ready!
I'm ready now!

You can be my best friend.
I can be your right arm.
We'll go through a fight or two,
No harm,
No harm.

We'll look not too deep,
We'll go not too far.
We won't have to give up a thing,
We'll stay who we are,
Right?
Okay, then,
I'm ready!
I'm ready now!

Someone,
Marry me a little,
Love me just enough.
Warm and sweet and easy,
Just the simple stuff.
Keep a tender distance
So we'll both be free.
That's the way it ought to be.
I'm ready!

Marry me a little,
Body, heart, and soul,

Passionate as hell,

But always in control.

Want me first and foremost,

Keep me company.

That's the way it ought to be.

I'm ready!

I'm ready now!

Oh, how gently we'll talk,

Oh, how softly we'll tread.

All the stings, the ugly things

We'll keep unsaid.

We'll build a cocoon of love and respect.

You promise whatever you like,

I'll never collect.

Right?

Okay, then, I'm ready!

I'm ready now!

Amy,

I'm ready!

There are those admirers of *Company* who refuse to believe we intended the show to be pro-marriage. I assure them not only was that our avowed purpose, but to this day we regard it as a fervent plea for interpersonal relationships.

For those who still consider it an indictment, I can only drag out the old defense that some people are simply afraid to acknowledge the manifest difficulties of living together. Anyway, if you have read the lyric above, you see why we jettisoned it. (Replacing that song remained the major musical problem, one we never entirely solved.)

What to do about *The Girls Upstairs* still faced us, so I agreed to do it (I had little idea how at the time), providing we postponed until Steve finished *Company*.

Company was the first musical I had done without conventional plot or subplot structure. The first without the hero and heroine, without the comic-relief couple. There are, of course, plots, but they are subtextual and grow out of subconscious behavior, psychological stresses, inadvertent revelations: the nature of the lie people accept to preserve their relationship.

We constructed a framework of gatherings for Robert's thirty-fifth birthday, each appearing to be the same, but dynamically different from the others. Pinteresque in feeling, the first was giddy, somewhat hysterical; the second (at the end of act 1), an abbreviated version of the first; the third, hostile and staccato; and the final one at the end of the show, warm, loving, mature. Since Robert never arrives for the final celebration, there was some question whether they represented one birthday or a succession of them. I am certain they were one. I wouldn't be surprised if George Furth believes there were four. It doesn't matter.

About this time, Michael Bennett agreed to stage the numbers and choreograph the dances. There was to be one professional dancer drawn from Robert's girl friends. As it turned out, there was one dance for one dancer.

Everyone in the company had to sing, after a fashion; everyone had to dance, after a fashion. But as they were to be real people, their footwork and voices were subordinated to their performances. Which is not to say some didn't sing well or move well. Some moved with agility just as some of your living-room friends move with agility, but others were klutzes and we wanted that.

We used four singers in the pit to augment the voices onstage, a technique borrowed from *Promises, Promises* and suggested by Michael Bennett and Jonathan Tunick, who orchestrated *Company*. Pit singers, serving as surrogate musical instruments, supplemented the orchestra some of the time, and some of the time the singers onstage.

Company was a heavy show, difficult to assemble. To create the illusion of spareness required six tons of steel, two electric SCR motorized elevators, and twenty-eight carousel projectors. Most of the front projections operated from the balcony rail and the balance from X-rays on the front light pipe behind the proscenium. These were abstractions designed to support the emotions of scenes. Occasionally they contradicted the apparent mood, illuminating instead the undercurrents. The remaining slides were projected from the rear. For the scenes, we used black-and-white photographs in some detail of locations in New York City; for the songs, we used reverse negatives of the photographs, painted in color. There were six hundred slides in all, and most people weren't aware of them, which is as it should be.

Our projections were designed by Robert Ornbo of Theatre Projects London, and I think up until *Company* opened, projections had never been used as well on Broadway.

Company was well cast. We made no replacements on the road, which is unusual. The material adapts to many different personalities—all excepting Stritch's role, which was written for her.

When we played our first public performance in Boston, following six weeks of rehearsal, *Company* was serious business. Our cast—predominantly actors who could sing—played the results, the motivations, the subtext, and let the dark, neurotic side of their characters dominate, overwhelming the comedy. The next day, I suggested they take everything they'd learned about their characters, turn it upside down, and let the comedy rise to the surface. At the next performance, everything was where it should be. Good material warrants that approach. It's difficult to direct comedy from the outside in. In addition, remember that material with that much subtext will vary greatly in terms of audience response. Occasionally, they didn't laugh at *Company*, but still it worked.

In rehearsal we'd replaced "Marry Me a Little" with "Happily Ever After." Steve had produced a lyric which intended to say that Robert was lying, that what we were observing was empty bravura, but the audience took him at face value, and the statement as defeatist.

Happily Ever After

Someone to hold you too close,
Someone to hurt you too deep,
Someone to love you too hard,
Happily ever after.

Someone to need you too much,
Someone to read you too well,
Someone to bleed you of all the things
You don't want to tell.
That's happily ever after,
Ever, ever, ever after—

In hell.
Somebody always there
Sitting in the chair
Where you want to sit,
Always, always.
Somebody always there
Wanting you to share
Just a little bit
Always, always.

Then see the pretty girls
Smiling everywhere
From the ads and the TV set,
And why should you sweat?
What do you get?
One day of grateful
For six of regret—
With
Someone to hold you too close,
Someone to hurt you too deep,
Someone to bore you to death,
Happily ever after.
Someone you have to know well,
Someone you have to show how,
Someone you have to allow
The things you'd never allow.
That's happily ever after,
Ever, ever, ever after,
Till now.

Quick! get a little car,
Take a little drive,
Make a little love,
See a little flick,
Do a little work,
Take a little walk,

Watch a little TV
And click!
Make a little love,
Do a little work,
Get a little drunk,
You've got one little trip,
Seventy years,
Spread it around,
Take your pick:
Buy a little here,
Spend a little there,
Smoke a little pot for a little kick,
Waste a little time,
Make a little love,
Show a little feeling
But why should you try?
Why not, sure,
Feel a little lonely but fly?
Why not fly
With

No one to hold you too close,
No one to hurt you too deep,
No one to love you too hard,
Happily ever after?
No one you have to know well,
No one you have to show how,
No one you have to allow
The things you'd never allow.
That's happily ever after,
Ever, ever, ever after
For now.

Ever, ever, ever after . . .
Ever, ever, ever, ever, ever after . . .
Ever, ever, ever after . . .

Steve wrote the third and final version of Robert's song our last week in Boston.

Being Alive

Someone to hold you too close,
Someone to hurt you too deep,
Someone to sit in your chair,
To ruin your sleep . . .

Someone to need you too much,
Someone to know you too well,
Someone to pull you up short,
And put you through hell . . .

Someone you have to let in,
Someone whose feelings you spare,
Someone who, like it or not, will want you to share
A little, a lot . . .

Someone to crowd you with love,
Someone to force you to care,
Someone to make you come through,
Who'll always be there, as frightened as you
Of being alive,
Being alive, being alive, being alive . . .

Somebody hold me too close,
Somebody hurt me too deep,
Somebody sit in my chair
And ruin my sleep and make me aware
Of being alive, being alive.

Somebody need me too much,
Somebody know me too well,
Somebody pull me up short
And put me through hell and give me support
For being alive, make me alive,
Make me alive,

Make me confused, mock me with praise,

Let me be used, vary my days.

But alone is alone, not alive.

Somebody crowd me with love,

Somebody force me to care,

Somebody let me come through,

I'll always be there as frightened as you,

To help us survive

Being alive, being alive, being alive.

I am afraid it imposed a happy ending on a play which should have remained ambiguous. A number of the musicals I have done (*She Loves Me*, *Company*, *Follies*) court ambiguity. "The Lady or the Tiger?" thrills me, but people who go to theatre are frustrated by it.

By and large, the reviews were excellent except for the *New York Times'*. Clive Barnes didn't like the show, didn't understand it, although he said he liked it better than *West Side Story* (a line we appropriated). Walter Kerr *admired* the show but didn't like it a hell of a lot. It was too cold for him. *I* think *Company* is warmhearted—not sentimental, but warmhearted.

The real impact came from the news magazines. *Time* and *Newsweek* loved it.

We had problems with our star, Dean Jones. He had been signed for a year and was increasingly unhappy in Boston. I hoped that success in New York would appease him, but as we approached Broadway, he became ill, and that illness I suspected was psychosomatic. I reasoned that the best way to ensure an opening night would be to offer to replace him after we opened. Would the knowledge that he was leaving free him to give a good performance? It would and he did. And I replaced him with Larry Kert two weeks later. Business was not affected by the change. I don't know whether I would have been so generous had I thought it would be.

Excepting its final moments, *Company* represents the first time I had worked without conscious compromise. It represents as total a collaboration of authors, director, choreographer, and actors as I can remember. *Cabaret* established me as commercially successful. *Company* established me in my own eyes.

155

Company never played a sold-out week, often played to only 60 percent of capacity, but it paid off and shows a profit. And that is what commercial theatre must ask of itself.

REFLECTIONS ON CHAPTER 22 OF *CONTRADICTIONS*

When Boris first presented his set design to me, it contained the usual surprise. This time, there was an elevator—big enough to cram in the entire company of fourteen. It traveled from the second floor to stage level and back.

❧

I never knew what I might say that would spark something in Steve, and that uncertainty was always stimulating. He writes in pencil—with an eraser. He doesn't want to commit. I write in ink: I always like to *think* "this is final!" Steve's instinct is to keep challenging, and my instinct is to hope I solved it right away. Steve is not a first-draft fellow; he's much too impeccable to lean or insist on his first draft.

Often, Steve would ask, "Is that number okay?" If I replied, as I sometimes did, "I'm not crazy about it," he'd say, "Okay, I'll reexamine it." He has the confidence to know that he can come up with something even better. Many composers do not.

There was a number in *Company* called "Barcelona" which I didn't "get." Steve assured me it was right, and Judy Prince thought it hilarious. So I staged it, and only during that process did I realize how right they were. It *was* hilarious and consistent with Bobby the bachelor and a beautiful, seductive flight attendant.

❧

Later in the show, Michael Bennett choreographed a number for Donna McKechnie, the only professional dancer in the company. "Tick Tock" was a solo turn dramatizing the lovemaking of Bobby and the airline stewardess. It began slowly, erotically, energetically, and ended in—what else?—a climax. It was sensational. And, predictably, there were many who advised me to take it out of the show. It stayed. However, Michael's singular achievement was taking thirteen actors with little dance experience and making capital of that.

Finally, although I may have implied it earlier, it bears repetition: married people use a third person, a single man, to get things off their chests that bother them about each other. And as soon as that man is out of sight, you see how solid their relationship is. Now that's interesting!

The morning after *Company* opened, the *Times* review was soft enough to shake me, and of course there was the memory of what happened with *Superman* at the box office. So I phoned the Alvin (now the Neil Simon) to ask if there was *any* business. They replied that there was a line around the block. I rushed down to the theatre to see it for myself, and everyone in the line was reading the *New York Times* review! Go figure.

CHAPTER
23

The Girls Upstairs was a totally realistic musical about two girls and the two fellows they had married thirty years earlier, meeting at a real party in a real theatre, with real decorations and real food and drink. It dealt with the loss of innocence in the United States, using the *Ziegfeld Follies* (a pretty girl is *no longer* like a melody) as its metaphor.

The extent of its realism diminished its size, reduced its four leading characters to selfish, overindulged pains in the neck, whereas they might have represented the misplaced American dream. (We never really licked that problem.)

I began looking for a concept. In *The Best Remaining Seats*, a history in photographs and text of the great movie palaces of the 1930s, there appeared a photograph, originally published in *Life* magazine, of Gloria Swanson standing in the rubble of what had been the Roxy Theatre. She had opened the Roxy in a silent film, and when they tore it down, Eliot Elisofon photographed her in a black chiffon dress against the gutted proscenium. A very glamorous photograph. Elisofon had captured the metaphor.

About the same time, I arranged a screening of *8½* for Michael Bennett and Ruth Mitchell. It was a first viewing for them, the ninth for me. Some years earlier, a representative of Fellini's had sought me out to ask whether I would be interested in musicalizing *8½*. The movie is a masterpiece, and I was flattered and tempted, but came to realize soon that it represented Fellini's autobiography and not mine.

The Girls Upstairs dealt with aspects of character and relationships which, while not autobiographical, were intensely familiar. Its hero, Ben Stone, is a hugely successful middle-aged businessman with a stunning wife and all the perks of a wealthy lifestyle—a palatial residence, country homes, and a world-class art collection. His marriage is faltering, and his obsession with career is threatening his emotional stability. Little wonder that I was reminded of *8½*.

The relationship with Michael Bennett on *Company* was so profitable creatively, and stimulating and easy for both of us, that I suggested he do *The Girls Upstairs* when we got around to it. He declined, feeling that he was at the point in his career when he should be directing. Soon it became more and more obvious that there was enough at least for two directors, and so I asked him whether he would like to share the assignment. A difficult arrangement for two giant egos. And there were conflicts, but never with respect to what we wanted the evening to be, to say, nor of the quality of its theatricality.

It was to be surrealistic, inspired by *8½*, and rubble became the key word. Metaphoric rubble became visual rubble. A theatre is being torn down. On its stage, a party in celebration of that. The celebrants for whom the theatre represents youth, dreams lost, a golden time, are to be orphaned. (Aronson: "There's no place for patina in the United States.") Is the theatre torn down? Will it be torn down tomorrow? Or was it torn down yesterday? Keep it ambiguous, a setting for the sort of introspection that reunions precipitate, a mood in which to lose sight of the present, to look back on the past.

Goldman and Sondheim were about just such business, but not in surrealistic terms. However, they approved of our scheme and agreed to adapt to it.

The title, *Follies*, suggested the *Ziegfeld Follies*, but also, in the British sense, foolishness, and in the French, *folie*, which is madness.

Once again Boris went to work, this time creating rubble: a construction of levels, culs-de-sac, planked paths connected by metal stairways, the whole looking very much like the superstructure from which buildings are torn down. It was cut into three large sections, which were motorized to move upstage and down and diagonally offstage. From the start we had to decide where we would put every scene and number, though most were yet to be written.

At this time, naively, we figured that Sondheim would be replacing three or four of the numbers in the score. Ultimately, we kept six of the original songs, and Steve wrote sixteen new ones.

In the new draft, we added four figures of the leading characters as they had existed thirty years earlier. So much ectoplasm, they were to wander as silent memories across the paths of their present selves.

It worked so well that Goldman gave them words to speak. They intruded more and more into the evening, taking stage, confusing time, confronting the present with the past until ultimately, in a sort of collective nervous breakdown, they took over.

Bennett suggested dressing them in black and white, and putting clown-white makeup and black lipstick on them. For a time we even considered having them cross into color in the follies section, with our four leads fading into black and white. In this show everything qualified for consideration, no matter how lunatic.

Bennett wanted a grouping of unearthly plaster mannequin-showgirls in period costumes spanning fifty years to be displayed in the structure and changed during the evening. As the four young characters were given dialogue, he replaced them with living statues, ghostly showgirls wandering slowly and silently through the evening, their costumes and makeup black and white.

Florence Klotz designed two hundred costumes over a period of nine months. It was a monumental job, exquisitely realized.

The show arced to a mini *Ziegfeld Follies*, giving the audience in the final twenty minutes what it had expected all along. The only difference was that the stars of our follies would confront in lavish production numbers the lies that had led them relentlessly to the brink of madness. Defenseless, they would lay waste the past, leave the rubble of the theatre behind them, and start to live. It was clear what we wanted to do. But how to do it? The rehearsal script was more a screenplay than a stage play, with our equivalents of pans and tracking shots and dissolves. You can even give the effect of a close-up by isolating a person onstage.

We went into rehearsal without the follies section, seventy pages of script culminating in a Goldman-inspired confrontation of eight people, the four principals and their young counterparts in a Laocoön tangle, screaming at one another on an empty stage and suddenly trapped in a Ziegfeld extravaganza.

The script quit abruptly with these words: "What follows is a capsule follies—costume parades, comedy routines, specialty acts—traditional and accurate in all ways but one. Sets, costumes, music, movement; all this is faithful to the past. What's different and unusual about it is the content, what it's all about."

This was the last page in our script for the first four weeks of a six-week rehearsal period. I wouldn't take that chance with anyone but Steve Sondheim. It was a maddening experience, particularly for Michael Bennett, as the nonexistent follies section was his responsibility to stage. Steve filtered material to him the beginning of the fifth week of rehearsal with the Boston opening staring us in the face.

There were to be five numbers. "Loveland," for the entire company, was finished first (in fact, Steve wrote in sequence). Then came a number for each of the young couples ("You're Gonna Love Tomorrow" and "Love Will See Us Through"). Then "Losing My Mind." Numbers were to be written for Dorothy Collins, Gene Nelson, and John McMartin. He was even contemplating one for Yvonne De Carlo, perhaps to be shared with the other supporting ladies.

"Losing My Mind" had been written as a duet for Dorothy (Sally) and Alexis (Phyllis), but at one point Alexis suggested that the song was dead wrong for her, following as it does "Could I Leave You?," her other solo, and giving her no opportunity to move.

We agreed, and for a time it left Steve with four songs to write in ten days.

Now every day's rehearsal—and the days rarely ended before midnight—included an additional hour or two of talk, with and for Steve, about each of the four characters and how best to explain what they had learned during the evening at the party, what insights into their conflict had been revealed. During these sessions, it became clear that Buddy (Gene Nelson) was a masochist, rejecting love, courting rejection. So Steve wrote "Buddy's Blues" and Michael Bennett staged it.

Dorothy Collins's Sally learned nothing from the evening. Stripped of her lie, she went mad. Steve had written her song. "Losing My Mind" gave her the chance, in follies terms, to be Helen Morgan. It worked. Michael's assistant, Bob Avian, staged that number.

Five down and two to go, entering our sixth week of rehearsal. Steve wrote an elegant schizoid number for the two sides of Alexis's character and called it "Uptown, Downtown." He had the right idea and replaced it with a better number, "The Story of Lucy and Jessie," in Boston.

We'd rehearsed the first month at the American Theatre Lab, which is Jerry Robbins's dance studio, on a mockup of the set with indicated elevations—one foot for every five. In the final two weeks, we moved to the Feller Scenic Studio in the Bronx and worked on the finished set. Aside from the elevations and the staircases, the great maw that we worked in was heavily raked, and it was a shock to our company to see the angle on which they were expected not only to walk, but to tap-dance. It saved a great deal of money adjusting there (instead of in Boston with stagehands and orchestra hanging around).

In the middle of the last week, we still lacked Ben's (John McMartin's) number, which was to include the company. "Live, Laugh, Love" arrived the last day of rehearsal, and while they were dismantling the set and loading the vans for Boston, Hal Hastings, our musical director, taught McMartin the lyric and melody, and Michael Bennett choreographed the dancers. He completed the work in the Bradford Hotel ballroom in Boston and on the set at the Colonial Theatre while the stagehands focused the lights and hung the drops.

Coming out of McMartin's number, we planned a Felliniesque kaleido-scope of impressions of the events of the evening. Jim Goldman improvised a scene, and I staged it, ending in chaos, using the fifty members of the company all over the set. Again, in Boston, at dress rehearsal—with Tharon Musser still lighting, the cast in costume, and the orchestra in the pit for the first time—the chaos was choreographed, adapted to the moving scenery, and something achieved acceptable to open with.

When you go to Boston, that's all you really try to do: tie up the loose ends and get the curtain up and down for your first public performance. We usually schedule it for a Saturday, which gives us Sunday without scenery and costumes for cutting and polishing. On Monday afternoon we schedule a full technical rehearsal, and by Monday night the show is beginning to look like something.

In the case of *Follies*, I decided not to open in Boston until the Wednesday, which gave us six full technical rehearsals before getting reviewed.

Michael Bennett had an interesting technique for implementing the en-semble singing during the tap-dancing sequences. He recorded the company in rehearsal and had them sing in sync with their own voices in performance; otherwise they would have been too winded to achieve any volume.

Movies have been using the click-track and prerecorded tapes for years.

Ordinarily, I abhor this sort of thing. We didn't even use microphones until *West Side Story*, and there were never any problems. But performers aren't trained to project their singing voices, and rarely do they know how to protect them. Audiences, meanwhile, aren't trained to listen. The advent of television and electronic instruments has pushed the audience back in its seats. I remember when I first went to the theatre, having to adjust for perhaps five minutes to the sounds of the actors. I would sit forward in my seat, and the connection that I made with the stage was an investment in the experience. Had I taken away the amplification at *A Little Night Music*, which is a show that could have survived without it, it would have made the audience reach out to the stage. I wish I'd had the courage to do it.

Do we not run the risk of mechanizing the theatre until it becomes so slick it loses its "liveness"? The American musical particularly has for the last fifteen years been overpackaged, overproduced, lacking in content. Content is the key word. Content must always dictate style, form, the use of machinery. As soon as the technical things precede the text, we are in trouble. The salvation of modern theatre rests not with multimedia experiences and hyped-up sound, but the reverse: a return to a less sophisticated, more visceral relationship between actor and audience.

It was characteristic of *Follies* that there was an inordinate number of potential distractions. Gene Nelson was quoted in a magazine interview as saying that the show went against everything he'd been taught about not moving on certain dialogue because the laughs would be lost, about not upstaging key scenes with activity. Throughout *Follies*, six-foot showgirls wandered around in incredible costumes, glittering and gleaming upstage of some very serious book scenes, the content of which was necessary to understanding the show. And they were not distracting. It was as though we set our own ground rules and lived by them. The audience knew what to listen to and where to look. We made them work in *Follies*, and some objected. For others, it was exhilarating.

And there was no intermission. *The Girls Upstairs*, without plot or suspense, was to be performed in one act. *Follies* was too long for that, so we lowered the curtain rather arbitrarily halfway into the evening. After the show had found its proper length (two hours and fifteen minutes), we interrupted our showstopping number ("Who's That Woman?") for the intermission. We brought the curtain down on a stage full of beautiful women tap-dancing in unison, raising it for the second act at the same place in the number. It was effective but cut the applause in half.

I'm not concerned with creating showstoppers. I sometimes think that in the name of perversity (integrity?) I frustrate an audience's desire to applaud, which is contradictory in view of how I feel about involvement.

It took *Follies* five minutes to regain its momentum no matter where we put the intermission. Three days before we opened, Bennett and I were still fighting it out in the lobby. We solved it by playing the show in one act.

The most agonizing time for all of us on *Follies* came when we were in our final week of previews in New York. We had scheduled performances Monday, Tuesday, and Wednesday, with Thursday a day off, and openings on Friday, Saturday, matinee and evening, and Sunday. The critics had been invited to choose which of those four performances they would attend. Tickets had been distributed. On the Monday after the performance, I received a call from Los Angeles telling me that Gene Nelson's son had been hit by a truck on his way home from school and was on the critical list at Cedars of Lebanon Hospital.

I found Gene at home with friends who had seen the preview that night and were quietly celebrating. I got him to a telephone. His wife told him to stay on in New York with the show, that things were encouraging. I spoke separately with Marilyn Nelson, who told me that the child was in a coma and at this point Gene was better off busy working in New York.

The following morning at rehearsal, I suggested to the authors and Michael Bennett that we open Wednesday and not run the risk of waiting till the end of the week. Nelson might not be there by then, and even if he were, the pressure of these days would surely affect his performance. Meanwhile, we put his understudy into rehearsal and I called Mary Bryant, our press representative, instructing her to tell the critics what had happened, to swear them to secrecy, and request that they come in that night if possible.

I then called the company together, and reminding them of my abhorrence of openings, announced that I had invited the critics that night. Then I put in a brand-new last scene for John McMartin and Alexis Smith, and McMartin, on whom most of the burden of the new dialogue lay, was letter-perfect.

(Nelson's son remained in a coma for six weeks. The story has a happy ending: he has since recovered completely.)

I made a mistake with the original-cast album. I neglected to stipulate in the contract with Capitol Records that the entire score be recorded. There were twenty-two songs, and it would have taken four sides. (That was not unprecedented. *She Loves Me* had required a double album, and only recently Columbia recorded the whole of *Candide*, dialogue and music.) Capitol refused on the grounds that it wouldn't sell. The contracts were signed, and there was nothing I could do. I warned them that there would be many letters of complaint, and there were hundreds. There was more mail for *Follies*, which was never a standing-room-only show, than for *Cabaret*, which was. There were *Follies* "freaks" who saw the show a dozen times or more, and they campaigned in the *Times* for a limited edition of the complete score. But they lost. Cast albums don't sell.

I cannot wait for show scores to come into their own again. It is inevitable. Meantime, the amount of wax (do they still use wax?) wasted on uneducated, lyrically illiterate popular music is discouraging.

Follies cost $800,000 to produce. There were fifty in the cast, thirty in the orchestra, and twenty-eight in the crew backstage. It cost $80,000 a week to break even. At capacity it would have taken approximately forty weeks to pay off. But it wasn't the sort of show that plays to capacity. It ran sixty-five weeks on Broadway with grosses ranging from $113,961 to $31,853. We won seven Tony Awards in April of 1972 and our grosses rose to $91,000 for several weeks, but the summer was coming, so we moved to California and inaugurated the Shubert, the newest theatre in the United States, with a show about tearing down a theatre.

All of the Los Angeles reviews were marvelous, but the show wasn't popular, and the grosses ranged from $102,376 in the beginning of the run to $55,615 in the final weeks.

I am happy I did *Follies*. I could not do it again, because I could not in all conscience raise the money for it. Perhaps it's best summed up by Frank Rich, who was the critic for the *Harvard Crimson* when we were trying out in Boston:

> It is easy to avoid *Follies* on the grounds that it is, after all, a Broadway musical— and, given what Broadway musicals have come to mean, such a bias is understandable. But that is precisely why you should see it, for *Follies* is a musical about the death of the musical and everything musicals represented for the people who saw and enjoyed them when such entertainment flourished in this country. If nothing else, *Follies* will make clear to you exactly why such a strange kind of theatre was such an important part of the American consciousness for so long. In the playbill for this show, the setting is described

as "a party on the stage of this theatre tonight." They are not kidding, and there is no getting around the fact that a large part of the chilling fascination of *Follies* is that its creators are in essence presenting their own funeral.

He titled his review "The Last Musical." An unanticipated metaphor.

REFLECTIONS ON CHAPTER 23
OF *CONTRADICTIONS*

In retrospect, and because I regard *Follies* as a watershed experience for all of us, I realize that these reflections on the earlier chapter contain more than most. And that is because that musical is still alive in me all these years later.

In addition to creating four alter egos—young people for our middle-aged principals—we decided to do the same for each character in the show and mirror them with their earlier youthful counterparts. Everyone had a doppelganger, and this led to one of its high points: the mirror number, in which Michael Bennett brilliantly choreographed the principals and wiped them away with their youthful selves dancing in the *Follies* in costumes covered in small mirrors. And all of this tap dancing on a raked stage (1–12"—whatever that means!—permitted by Actors Equity). It was a triumph of staging in my opinion, as stunning as any choreography I have ever seen.

There was one touchy period in rehearsal when Alexis Smith asked whether I would not stage "Could I Leave You?" because she preferred that Michael Bennett do it. Obviously, she thought it should be choreographed. I had my doubts. They went away and worked for a couple of days and then presented it to Steve and me. They had decided to have Phyllis (Alexis) break down and throw her arms around Ben's legs. He tried to get away and dragged her across the floor—an idea of Alexis, I suspect. Steve and I hated it because it was more silent film than our *Follies*. So, though I was co-director, I was also producer and I exercised that authority and took over the staging of the number. To put it mildly, it made things awkward and unsettling for a couple of days, but "Could I Leave You?" remained as I staged it. This illustrates the difference between choreography and staging in character. Undoubtedly, Michael Bennett knew how to do the latter—he certainly proved that in *A Chorus Line*. But before *Follies* and since, I have always carved out staging of character numbers to be my responsibility, avoiding choreography, which can cost character.

We cast *Follies* using the example of Billy Wilder's *Sunset Boulevard*. We wanted the leads to be close to the characters they were playing, because it would help us persuade the audience that the people onstage were reliving their earlier celebrity, which is gone for them. We cast three movie stars—Alexis Smith, Gene Nelson, and Yvonne De Carlo—and Dorothy Collins, who had been a TV star on *Your Hit Parade*. De Carlo, a former Hollywood star, was, after all, as her character sings, still here. Gene Nelson, who had been in Hollywood musicals but had not been as prominent as Gene Kelly or Fred Astaire, was playing close to himself also. Dorothy Collins and her character had much in common: she had been hurt by her childhood, and I used that. Her first husband, Raymond Scott, had presented her as an early teenager and later married her.

Only John McMartin was playing a character not connected to his history. He was one of my favorite actors (I've worked with him often), and I cast him because the central fulcrum of the show for me was his character's story, about facing the road you didn't take. The message of the piece, for me personally, was to keep two "roads" in some kind of balance: to pay more attention to my family, and at the same time protect my career. It was a difficult balancing act. (Was I using the Method on myself as a director without realizing it?)

The casting of Ethel Shutta (who performed "Broadway Baby") was a piece of good luck that also certified our authenticity. When I was eight, I went to the Franklin School in New York, now called the Dwight School. My grandfather had graduated from that school when it was called Dr. Sachs. One morning in 1937, as I was coming to school, I saw a long line of kids waiting to get an autograph from the mother of two of my classmates, the Olsen brothers, who were twins. Their mother had been a *Ziegfeld Follies* performer named Ethel Shutta. In 1970, when I was just beginning to work with Steve on *Follies*, I received a letter from Ethel Shutta, who said I wouldn't know who she was but she would like to audition for our show. I wrote her back to tell her of the incident I recalled and to assure her that of course she must have an audition. When she came in to audition and sang "Broadway Baby," she knocked us off our chairs: she was the real thing. No one will ever be able to touch her in that role.

In earlier days, orchestrations leaned heavily on string instruments, but today the introduction of heavy brass and amplification has made body microphones necessary for the entire company.

❧

Until that time, *Follies* was the most expensive musical ever produced. Today, you would be hard-pressed to produce a one-person play on Broadway for the $800,000 I capitalized on *Follies*. Today, *Follies* would cost somewhere around $20 million!

❧

When in interviews I'm asked what is my favorite musical, I'm reluctant to reply, because there are many and they're favorites for different reasons. *West Side Story* was a watershed experience, as was *Company*. And *Follies* and *Evita* were high points. But—what about *Sweeney Todd*? Or *Kiss of the Spider Woman*? Oh, forget it!!

CHAPTER
24

In 1957, right after *West Side Story* opened, Sondheim and I talked about doing a kind of court masque, a chamber opera: elegant, probably about sex, a gavotte in which couples interchange, suffering mightily in elegant country homes, wearing elegant clothes.

We hit upon the idea of adapting Jean Anouilh's *Ring Round the Moon*, and I contacted Jan Van Loewen, Anouilh's agent in London. Steve was not yet known as a composer, and I was solely a producer. Van Loewen informed us that Lerner and Loewe had inquired about the rights (Lord knows why they wanted it after *My Fair Lady*), as had Irene Selznick and Leland Hayward. So we shouldn't hold out much hope.

However, I offered to go to Paris to meet with Anouilh; I was told to come ahead, and an appointment was arranged. When I arrived in Paris, Anouilh had left that morning for his home in Switzerland. I'm not that kind of tenacious. Put down by his rudeness, I returned to New York, and we dropped the project.

Probably we were fortunate. I am convinced that in 1958, which was in the eye of the brash, brassy, give-'em-a-lot-of-whoop-up-noise musical, ours would have failed even if the reviews had been good. That's what contributed, I think, to *She Loves Me*'s failure.

The years that followed surfeited that appetite in people, and by 1973, *A Little Night Music* was a blessed relief.

In 1972, after *Follies*, I thought now was the time to do that chamber opera we'd talked about. Again we inquired about *Ring Round the Moon*. Van Loewen wrote back that the author was still reluctant to have it turned into a musical. Would we take *Thieves' Carnival* instead? I said no.

I asked Hugh Wheeler to join us. We talked endlessly about various source material, finally singling out Jean Renoir's *Rules of the Game* and Ingmar Bergman's *Smiles of a Summer Night*. We arranged a screening of both films and read both screenplays.

There are interesting similarities in *Rules of the Game*, *Smiles of a Summer Night*, and *Ring Round the Moon*. Each takes place in a summerhouse on a weekend. Each contains a party, each a play within a play. The characters are similar. There is the old lady in the wheelchair who is adjusted to death. There are the young people on the threshold of life. And there are the lovers in varying degrees of frustration.

I consider us very lucky that Van Loewen and Anouilh turned us down. *Ring Round the Moon* is a much colder piece than *Smiles of a Summer Night*. The characters in it are bloodless, more literary, less dimensional, less involving.

Rules of the Game was a disappointment to all of us, perhaps because it is a classic and so much has been written and said about it.

Smiles of a Summer Night had everything. It had darkness and humanity. It is constructed brilliantly. Bergman wrote the screenplay, and I consider Bergman the writer every bit the measure of Bergman the director.

We contacted him through his lawyer in Sweden. In less than a week, we received a wire, asking for further details. Hugh Wheeler wrote a one-page analysis in musical terms and I a covering letter. The purpose was to assure him that we did not intend a literal translation of his screenplay. It was to be "suggested by" rather than "adapted from." Apparently, this appealed to him because, again, in less than a week we received a wire giving us the go-ahead, wishing us luck, and asking us to contact his representative, Paul Kohner, in California.

Kohner, over the phone: "My client doesn't like a lot of complicated negotiations. Will you make an offer you consider fair?" I recommended the Christopher Isherwood (*Cabaret*)/Nikos Kazantzakis (*Zorba*) royalty arrangement, and it was accepted immediately over the telephone, which is extraordinary, and we went to work.

Some justice: I received a letter from Van Loewen when I arrived in Boston for the tryout of *Night Music*, saying that Anouilh had reconsidered and *Ring Round the Moon* was now available. I had the pleasure of answering that we were about to open *that* show in Boston and obviously I was no longer interested.

Our initial plan was to tell the story of a group of diverse people converging for a weekend in the country. The first act was to introduce the characters and many subplots and was to end with their arrival at an elegant country house. In the second, we were to see three different solutions to the tangled relationships: one melodramatic, the second farcical, and the third (the real one) consistent with the style of the first act.

A Little Night Music suggested a Magritte painting to me. Figures . . . anomalies in a landscape. A gentle greensward on which to play scenes in bedrooms, dressing rooms, dining rooms. I wanted the figures in the landscape out of context, for no more reason than Magritte puts them there.

Steve talked of waltzes. The entire score in three-quarter time. And in some ingenious musical way that I don't understand, everything is indeed in some form of triple time, though not all are waltzes. *Night Music* contains scherzos, minuets, polonaises, barcaroles, and a variety of waltzes.

We wanted to do a kind of Chekovian musical, realizing that would mean considerable exposition in the beginning, moving slowly, and no big opening number; but we hoped, in time, we would draw our audience into it.

Early on, Steve asked me to add a group of classical singers to replace the conventional chorus. He needed them musically and referred to them as our *Liebeslieder Waltzers* (referring to Brahm's Opus 52). He wrote the score to include them everywhere.

Then I got the idea that they might represent the positive spirits in a negative household. Everyone in *Night Music* is frustrated, humiliated by sexual role-playing. The five Liebeslieder people are secure. Perhaps they are operetta singers, optimistic, extroverted observers. Each is a personality, each has a response to the events of the evening. No two are alike. They make the piece accessible because they lead the audience into it.

One week before we went into rehearsal, Equity ruled that the Liebeslieder roles were chorus because they had only songs to sing—solos, mind you, but no dialogue. It threatened to make them sign chorus contracts.

It had been as difficult to cast those five Liebeslieder roles as any in the show. They required not only operatic voices, but also presence and acting experience *because* they had no lines in which to develop character. I know we could not have found acceptable replacements for them from the chorus rolls, and they refused to sign chorus contracts. So Equity was threatening the future of the show.

I refused to acquiesce. The artists and I decided instead to go ahead with rehearsals, despite daily harassment from the union, and face arbitration proceedings. Equity backed down. When it came time to cast the national company, they tried to enforce it all over again. And failed.

If Actors' Equity insists on shackling the creators of shows, if it legislates the hiring of either less experienced or less talented personnel for roles which I consider as individual and responsible as any of the roles in a play, it will discourage employment, because I will not make these compromises.

It occurs to me each time I come to a showdown with the unions that my position is backed up by twenty years of producing. I have some clout. No wonder there are so few new producers.

When *Night Music* was in Boston, Sondheim came to me concerned that too many people felt the show was slow starting and couldn't we do something about it. I reminded him that we had set out to do a Chekovian musical, that there was no way to be true to our objectives and satisfy the conventional demands of some of our audience.

Over the years, I have grown to know how little Sondheim concerns himself with popular tastes, how obstinately he eschews the familiar solution. So this was a unique request. The only thing we did consciously to relax our audience was introduce the Liebeslieder group at the top of the evening to perform the overture. It suggested a musical was to follow without affecting the introduction of the characters and early exposition, which were nonmusical.

Boris Aronson was reluctant to design *Night Music*. He kept reminding me that he is a Russian. I said I didn't know the difference between the landscape in Leningrad and the landscape in Helsinki: it's all birch trees as far as I am concerned. So he painted a forest of birch trees on clear plastic to look like Fabergé enamel on crystal. He carpeted the stage in a gently rolling green lawn. Again, the scenery was designed before the show was finished, just as in *Follies* and *Company*.

His first designs included sections of wall, real doors, and chandeliers encompassed in the woods. Quickly, I eliminated these, reducing the production to choice pieces of antique furniture isolated among the trees. That made Boris nervous up until rehearsals. Over the summer, without my knowledge, he designed a totally new scheme, which he showed me when I came back in September. I didn't care for it, and we went right back to the original designs.

The next problem was Hugh Wheeler's. Our extravagant plotting of the second act plus Boris's plans (involving beds on lawns in front of the houses they were supposed to be inside of!) inhibited him, and he couldn't write. The first draft was a big disappointment.

I suggested that he forget everything we'd talked about conceptually, that he write his play (not ours)—better still, a screenplay—and forget it was to be a musical. Within two weeks, he turned in a finished script.

Hugh Wheeler (*Big Fish, Little Fish* deserves a new production; I believe today it would succeed) is one of the few serious playwrights who can handle the stresses of musical collaboration. His peers shy away from writing libretti on the basis that the composer and director get all the credit. Hugh's experience with *Night Music* and later *Candide* surely has given the lie to that.

The last fifteen minutes of *Night Music* take place in a country house. There are long hallways, and much of the stage business has to do with doors opening and closing. I took a bed from Désirée's bedroom, a wicker armchair from her mother's sitting room, a bench from the corner of the park, a statue of a cupid at the entrance to a gazebo, an alcove in a child's room, and put them at once on the lawn in front of the country house. The audience supplied the hallways and the doors. Hugh Wheeler didn't have to rewrite a word.

I have always found Scandinavian theatre engrossing but a little alien. I understand Nora's slamming that door, but I have a hell of a lot of trouble empathizing on the way there.

Ingmar Bergman's work is always fascinating, but often it keeps me at arm's length. I am in the company of exotic strangers.

My wife and I observed that firsthand a year before I did *Night Music*. Sweden is primeval territory. The reactions of individuals are curious, unfamiliar—what causes them to laugh, what engages them. Perhaps it is the light, adjusting to unnaturally long days and endless nights, that does eerie things to their psyches. "Perpetual sunset is rather an unsettling thing . . ."

Steve immediately responded to the darker side, but Hugh and I felt uncomfortable with this tone in Bergman's material.

Pat Birch agreed to choreograph, although there were no dancers in the show and little opportunity for dances as such. But dances don't interest her half so much as character and movement and the total musical. *Night Music* tried to be seamless, and when we collaborate, it's difficult to know where she leaves off and I start.

With the show ready to go into rehearsal, Steve had completed only half the score. The balance came in slowly, but the actors were patient. Glynis Johns's "Send in the Clowns" arrived two days before we left for Boston.

I staged the book, and with Pat, Steve's eight numbers, in the first two weeks, and there was nothing to do but await the rest, while fussing with what we had, which is dangerous because you are still too close to it.

The final scene in act 1 was a sequence for the entire company, to be musicalized, a miniopera. I got tired of waiting, and one day with some ad libs from Hugh I began to move the actors around: "You go here and you hand this person an invitation and you say, 'Look what happened. We've been invited to a weekend at the Armfeldts' in the country,' and you say, 'Well, I don't want to go,' and you say, 'Oh, please,' and you say, 'Well, I'll reconsider,'" and so on.

I took the company through these little scenes, perhaps six of them. Each time I came to the end of one, I would say, "Now you sing" or "You two sing" or "All four of you sing." And catching the spirit, with vocalizing and appropriate gestures, they made a mock opera of it. Simultaneously, I choreographed the birch trees to go with the scene changes and dialogue.

I invited Steve to see what we'd done, and he went home that night and wrote a fifteen-minute sequence so specifically that Pat Birch was able to choreograph the company without altering the blocking. "A Weekend in the Country" is such an accomplishment that Steve was prompted to suggest that next time we should stage our libretto without any music, show it to him, and then let him go away for six months to write the score.

I had trouble raising money for *Night Music*, primarily because of *Follies*. Many of my investors counted on the return from a previous show to finance their next investment, so we were able to raise only a little more than half of what we needed. I was surprised.

I had no right to be surprised. I had always believed it one of Broadway's virtues that you can't ride on past successes. Nevertheless, I was upset. I was affronted! I raised the money, but it was difficult, and we were in rehearsal a week before we were capitalized.

I felt the pressure from rehearsals through the opening in New York. If this one didn't pay off, I would be back doing auditions. In 1953, when we hustled for the *Pajama Game* money, it was fun. I was a kid and it was all part of the game. It doesn't represent fun to me anymore. All that Frank Merriwell stuff is behind me.

I am constantly brought up short by the necessity of appearing a businessman in order to do what I want to do. There's nothing onerous about being a businessman; it's simply unfair that that should be a requirement for artistic continuity.

In addition, I spent the Boston opening worrying about capital running out, whether the reviews would be good enough to help us meet operating expenses, how much would be left in the event we couldn't. There's a sinking fund of $35,000 in each show. It has been that figure for twenty years; $35,000 doesn't last long if you're in trouble.

Additionally depressing: this time the record companies weren't anxious to audition the score. Columbia Records had put a great deal of money into the *Dude* recording, and only out of respect for Sondheim and my office agreed to hear *A Little Night Music*. Clive Davis, who has since left Columbia, sat distractedly checking his fingernails for the better part of forty minutes while I told the story and Sondheim played the music. A day or so later, Tom Shepard, then a producer of records at Columbia, phoned me to say that they were going to "pass on this one," that it was his feeling that though the work we were doing was beautiful, we were in fact "casting pearls before swine." Did he mean his compatriots or the theatregoing public?

Subsequently, Goddard Lieberson, who had semiretired from Columbia Records, came to see a preview in New York. At his insistence, Columbia negotiated for the recording.

In the interim, we played the score for RCA, with whom I had done *Fiddler on the Roof.* Fourteen executives arranged themselves in a studio on Sixth Avenue. Sondheim and I were five minutes into our audition when a secretary came in and appropriated one of the executives for a telephone conference. Soon another secretary came in with advertising copy for approval, a third with some letters to sign. There was steady traffic of executives and their secretaries, a hum in the background of phone conversations. In forty minutes, when we were finished, of the original fourteen people, only five remained.

I am told the *Night Music* cast album is the first non-rock theatre score to have paid back its expenses in many years. Encouraging.

We were a week away from the New York opening when Glynis Johns fell ill. She has a history of hypoglycemia, and she had been fading fast, until one night, three days before our opening, she collapsed and was taken to the hospital. We put her understudy, Barbara Lang, on in the role; and because there had been so much excitement about the show, people kept their seats, and Barbara did well. She's young for Désirée, and she's close to five feet ten, so the costumes, which had trailed on the floor for Glynis, were a few inches off it for Barbara.

That evening I postponed the opening indefinitely. It was too soon to know what shape Glynis was in, and we had thought of only one possible replacement—Tammy Grimes. She came to see it, and we talked about getting her up in the part and opening a week late. She agreed, but she also raised a number of questions respecting interpretation, attitudes, and, most specifically, the costumes. It was too late to make the kind of changes she was suggesting. For the show to open with a substitute star in seven days, it would have to be the one I had rehearsed, and any alterations, including to the costumes, would have to be just that—alterations.

I stayed up most of the night worrying, and I decided to continue the previews indefinitely while I flew to London to seek a replacement. The following morning, I went to see Glynis in the hospital. She looked marvelous.

I contacted the newspapers to say that we would be opening as originally scheduled. Glynis was back on the stage the following evening, and we opened the day after that.

The reviews were excellent. Clive Barnes called it an opera in his opening paragraph. I always thought operas closed on Saturday night. So much for rules.

I do not see the natural progression from *Company* to *Follies* to *Night Music* that some critics pointed out in their reviews, and I take perverse pleasure in the fact that *Night Music* has enough plot for two musicals and followed *Follies*, which had encouraged the critics to predict that we were moving inexorably in the direction of the plotless musical.

REFLECTIONS ON CHAPTER 24 OF *CONTRADICTIONS*

There's more to the story of *A Little Night Music*'s beginnings and, strangely, I'd forgotten it when I wrote *Contradictions*.

We scheduled a reading of Hugh's play with excellent actors and no score. Steve, Hugh, Judy Prince, and I attended the reading. It came off marvelously, so much so that Steve announced, at the end, that there was no need for it to be a musical. My wife immediately piped up, "Of course it's a musical." And good as it was as a play, she reasoned that it would be that much more with Steve's input. She was right, of course.

As I mentioned previously, Glynis Johns's second-act number, "Send in the Clowns," arrived two days before we left for Boston. We had been awaiting a number that Steve planned to write for Fredrik Egerman (Len Cariou), but it never came. On the morning of the invited run-through, which was to be held at 2:00 p.m. on an empty stage before we left, Steve phoned me to say that he had written a song for that spot in the show, but not for Len—rather for Glynis. We met in the theatre at eleven that morning. Steve played the song and Glynis adored it, of course. To our great surprise, she offered to sing it at the gypsy run-through as long as she could have a cheat sheet if she needed it. She and Steve went through it a few times, and when she had to sing it in the second act, she never looked at the lyrics. She has a beautiful speaking voice, and her rendition was more spoken than sung. It remains my favorite version of the song.

I suspect *A Little Night Music* doesn't get a lot of play today regionally because it's so difficult to perform for artists with contemporary training.

I learned a lot staging the dinner table scene with Pat Birch: an abstract, poetic style I hadn't quite tapped before that has served me well for many years. Steve's score and Hugh Wheeler's libretto—pure magic.

When Bergman came to see the show early in its run, I was informed by his agent that he did not want Mr. Sondheim or Mr. Prince to come to the theatre that night and he did not want the company to know he was there. So, Steve and I stayed away and, subsequently, I received an excited phone call. Bergman had asked at intermission if he could meet the cast after the show. He went backstage and kissed every single member of the company. The next day, Steve heard from him. As did I:

> A few days ago I had the great pleasure to see your *A Little Night Music*. . . . I found the performance excellent, beautiful and disciplined. . . . I think it would be marvelous to have "Send in the Clowns" played at my funeral. . . . Thank you once again for a generous, stimulating evening at the highest artistical level.

CHAPTER
25

When T. Edward Hambleton asked me to join the board of the Phoenix Theatre, it had merged with the APA, establishing our most prestigious repertory company. Its artistic director, Ellis Rabb, had shepherded a brilliant repertoire of revivals, including an impeccable production of Kaufman and Hart's *You Can't Take It with You*, Shaw's *Man and Superman*, Pirandello's *Right You Are If You Think You Are*, an adaptation of Tolstoy's *War and Peace*, and, of great influence to me in my career, Ghelderode's *Pantagleize*. When Rabb left the APA Phoenix, the company went through a period of treading water.

But that's not the point; the point is I couldn't define a credo for the Phoenix, and I said as much at a board meeting.

Once again the Phoenix redefined its objectives. I was asked to become an artistic director along with Stephen Porter, and since neither of us had the time and inclination for administration, we invited Michael Montel, who had been casting director for the Mark Taper Forum in Los Angeles and had directed there, to join us. He would reestablish the Side Show Program, producing five or six plays-in-progress while Porter and I directed one play each.

The New Phoenix Repertory Company would open in Philadelphia at the Annenberg Center on the campus of the University of Pennsylvania and would tour college cities. In Philadelphia, Boston, and New York, consortiums of universities and colleges would be created to build up subscription audiences. We would play one-nighters and split weeks in smaller college towns: Ann Arbor (University of Michigan), Storrs (University of Connecticut), Bloomington (Indiana University), and Princeton. New York would simply be another stop in the tour.

From the point of view of the National Endowment and the larger foundations, we would be supplying productions of classics of high quality, performed in repertory, and there is no other company in the United States doing that today.

I chose O'Neill's *The Great God Brown* and Porter chose Molière's *Don Juan* for the first season (1972–73). Our reviews were better than the size of our audiences, and every week was a losing week.

In the second season (1973–74), I directed Friedrich Dürrenmatt's *The Visit*, Porter did *Chemin de Fer*, and we added a third play, Philip Barry's *Holiday*, directed by Montel.

I chose *The Great God Brown* because I'd read it in college and I wondered how it worked. It is flawed and overwritten, but it is passionate. It is a much better play than I thought when I began directing it. Only in rehearsal did I realize how adroitly constructed it is, how motivated the characters. I think it is a clear and brilliant play but must acknowledge its inaccessibility to others.

The Visit is another matter. Also a well-made play, it is not an embarrassing play. It is depressing but curiously exhilarating. It can be done realistically, surrealistically, or expressionistically. I chose the last.

I visited Dürrenmatt in Switzerland. During the interview, in which I spoke French and he replied in German, he encouraged me to direct a more audacious—if that's the word—primitive, vulgar—that is the word—version of the play. He said he had recently seen the opera at Glyndebourne, and it was heavy and dark, and he liked that.

I had seen the Lunts in *The Visit*, and they were very grand, very adept, very glamorous. But I didn't remember the play or the other people in it. The original production, which Peter Brook directed, had about forty-five in the cast. The Phoenix can afford but eighteen.

I asked Ed Burbridge, the designer, for three flat panels, maybe eight feet high and five feet across, to be used throughout the evening. Made of shiny vinyl, in the first act they would be black, in the second blood red, and in the third white. These panels would be moved around the stage by the actors to represent trees, to enclose a room, to make a path.

Burbridge surprised me with three periaktoi—triangular-shaped units, eight feet tall, three feet six inches across, on casters, that could be turned easily by any one member of the company. He added a circular iron staircase, on top of which was a black tufted-leather banquette, the balcony of the Golden Apostle Inn. And he designed a drop with the name of the town, Gullen, made of bits of broken glass. The triangles were covered in wood, glass, and ceramic for the first two acts, and in the third act, mirror.

The production was so spare I used Clara Zachanassian's baggage to serve as furniture.

I had never seen a Bauhaus theatre production, but the Phoenix budget encouraged such a concept, and it produced unexpected advantages. The Brook production had eliminated certain sequences because they were too cumbersome. One in particular, an automobile ride through the village and surrounding forest, became my favorite scene in the play. Seated on a pile of luggage, Schill and his family were propelled around the stage on a baggage cart through a forest of slowly turning mirrored triangles.

There's a great deal of talk about the loss of an audience for serious theatre on Broadway. That was true in the 1950s and 1960s, when the Broadway audience represented a narrow spectrum of the public, when it opted exclusively for musicals and situation comedies. In those years, the less affluent, more intellectual audience visited Off-Broadway and Off-Off-Broadway, and the young audience was addicted to film.

By the 1960s the regional theatre was flourishing. Actors, directors, designers were getting the sort of theatrical training that had been denied them for more than thirty-five years. And young people discovered the theatre in the regions.

Predictably, during that period, competitive lines were drawn, separating Broadway from "the theatre." The important press had a great deal to do with promulgating that.

During the 1970s, perhaps we will come to accept the obvious: we're all in it together.

The run of a serious play today is no more a gauge of its success than ever. Shakespeare doesn't play a thousand performances. O'Neill didn't. The only difference between 1973 and 1923 is economics. Take a look at these performance figures of plays which have entered the rolls of permanent theatre literature.

A Moon for the Misbegotten	68	*Design for Living*	135
Amphitryon 38	153	*The Iceman Cometh*	136
Anna Christie	177	*Winterset*	195
The Circle	175	*Outward Bound*	144
The Crucible	197	*The Time of Your Life*	185
Ethan Frome	120	*The Petrified Forest*	197

The serious play today has to be subsidized by the foundations and presented by a nonprofit organization.

(Ironically, I wrote the above before *A Moon for the Misbegotten* became the most successful play on Broadway during the season of 1974. It is commercially presented and represents a windfall for its investors. At this writing, it has played 225 performances at capacity.)

In its second season, the New Phoenix Repertory Company increased its audience in Philadelphia by 25 percent, in Boston by a third, and in New York by 400 percent.

Doesn't it follow that whatever the public wants, the commercial producer supplies? That's not the best thing you can say about us, but it is a fact.

REFLECTIONS ON CHAPTER 25
OF *CONTRADICTIONS*

Obviously, this chapter appeared in my 1974 *Contradictions*, but it still applies today. Only more so because it is arguable that to produce a straight play in the commercial theatre without a star has become foolhardy. There are numerous excellent Off-Broadway theatres presenting serious dramas. Many of them operate on a shoestring; all of them are not-for-profit organizations depending on generous backers with no expectation for recoupment. Is there a downside in this? I believe so. Because of economics and propinquity, these productions are subject to compromise. To illustrate this: I have seen countless reproductions of *The Glass Menagerie*, *A Streetcar Named Desire*, and *Long Day's Journey into Night*, but none can touch the originals.

CHAPTER
26

I first heard of the Chelsea about ten years ago when Anthony Perkins asked me to lend my name to the advisory board for a new theatre group working out of a church in the Chelsea area of New York. I agreed, and forgot about it.

Years later, I was in Brooklyn to see the Chelsea Theatre Center's impressive production of Edward Bond's *Saved*. After the performance, Bob Kalfin, the artistic director of the company, introduced himself to me and pointed out that I was a member of their advisory board. Subsequently, I made a number of return visits to the Chelsea, and the work was always superior.

Kalfin called me one day to ask whether I would be interested in working with them, and I said I would indeed. He suggested a revival of the Bernstein-Hellman-Wilbur-Latouche-Voltaire *Candide*, which had been done in 1956 on Broadway.

I told him I didn't think a revival would work. I had seen the original and it was ponderous and a bore, and I remembered it well. The score was exciting, but the performance confusing. I tend to think the production failed at the top from that confusion. Half the show was politically and socially oriented, and the other half was oriented to the satirization of musical operetta, Bernstein's musical-theatre joke.

I think it's unfair to say, as some people have, that the book was the villain. Tyrone Guthrie takes second place to no one in recent theatre history, but he made his mistakes and *Candide* was one of them. The book, music, lyrics, and physical production were inappropriate to one another.

About six months later, Kalfin called again and said he had a young man working on it, reshaping Hellman's original material. I read it, didn't think it accomplished much, and forgot about *Candide* again.

Three months later, *Night Music* was open, and I was looking for something to do for the 1973–74 season. Obviously, I couldn't get a new musical ready, and I began to think about *Candide*.

The first thing I did was read Voltaire. I had never read *Candide*. I was surprised by how light and impulsive and irreverent and *unimportant* it is. Apparently, he wrote it quickly and denied having written it, putting it down as a schoolboy's prank. And that's the spirit of it.

The three hundred and some odd years that separated Voltaire's writing it and the Guthrie version of it had served only to make a classic of it and spoil the fun.

Our version would have to be as outrageous in contemporary terms and, curiously, as naive.

I started to think about the structure of it, and the problem that telling a picaresque story with an infinite number of highs and lows and no real crises presents in the theatre.

It becomes boring. The hero, beginning his odyssey, runs into negative forces and overcomes them or subverts them, and then runs into more negative forces and more negative forces, and then after a while, a pattern is achieved and the audience loses interest.

Therefore, it must be a short evening. Anything that followed an intermission would seem to reprise the first act. Arbitrarily, I decided an hour and forty-five minutes was the proper length for the show. And when it went into rehearsal, it ran an hour and forty-five minutes. (Today it runs an hour and fifty-seven minutes—with laughs.)

I have talked about using a painting, a piece of sculpture, something visual to synthesize a play for me. What was *Candide*? A cartoon, of course, but that came later. More specifically, how to illustrate a picaresque story in static terms? A triptych. But how do you animate a triptych?

I thought immediately of a sideshow at the circus, a series of elevated platforms: in one, the Fat Lady, in others, the Sword Swallower, the Tattooed Man, the Bearded Woman, the Siamese Twins, and so on.

Supposing you were guided by the barker (Voltaire?) on foot from one booth to the other along the route of Candide's odyssey. The booths would have little curtains, and behind one there would be Lisbon in the throes of a child's-eye version of an earthquake. Another booth would contain war, another a gambling casino in Venice. The booths would be of different sizes, as they are in the circus, and the painting would be primitive, garish, indicating events, leaving the better part of detail to the imagination; the less specific, the more participation from the bystanders.

Once I had gone that far, I realized even *it* was schematic and would defeat an hour-and-forty-five-minute piece.

Nevertheless, some version of it would work.

I called Kalfin and told him what was on my mind. He liked it. I suggested we approach Lillian Hellman and ask her whether she would be willing to write a new *Candide*. I told her our scheme, and she said that was what she had always wanted, but *Candide*? Never again! In that case, would she object to my asking someone else to work with me? Immediately, she agreed. (When subsequently I put it to Bernstein and Wilbur and they agreed, I figured all of them wanted to lay *Candide* to rest once and for all.) The only proviso she made was that none of her original dialogue be retained in the new version.

I then called Hugh Wheeler. We met and listened to the album. Each of us took the Voltaire and underlined choice bits, going over what particularly delighted us. He went away to write it *before* the lawyers and agents had met and contracts had been negotiated.

That was a complicated business from the Chelsea's point of view, because the original had not only Bernstein as composer and Hellman as author, but also Wilbur, Latouche, Hellman, Bernstein, and Dorothy Parker as lyricists.

Hugh and I paid Bernstein a visit and told him our plan (he said it was what he had always wanted) and discussed new numbers—in particular an opening. I did not want to open with "The Best of All Possible Worlds" because it is a statement of philosophy, the idea rather than an introduction of the characters, the emotion. The original version was cerebral, keeping the audience at arm's length. Ours must be visceral, must envelop the audience.

Once again, we had a show that needed an opening number to tell the audience who its main characters are and set the style.

Next, Hugh rejected Venice, rejected Paris (and along with them, some of our favorite numbers, "What's the Use?" and "The Paris Mazurka"; ultimately, we did use the theme of "The Mazurka," but the show never visited Paris). We were going to use episodes from Voltaire that hadn't taken place in the original musical—Constantinople, for one.

Bernstein produced a file of melodies, themes, full songs in some instances, of discarded material from 1955–56. There was enough musical material to accommodate the new version, but who was to write the new lyrics? Lenny had, in fact, written "I Am Easily Assimilated" in its entirety, and the "Auto da Fé" with John Latouche, which though discarded in 1956 became valuable to us. But he was scheduled for a series of lectures at Harvard. Given the short time we had to work, it seemed expeditious to ask Steve Sondheim to help us out, since I had never met Richard Wilbur.

Wheeler finished a first draft in two weeks. Although not the rehearsal version, it was hilarious.

Chelsea arranged interviews with designers, among them Eugene Lee. I had seen his environmental set for LeRoi Jones's *Slave Ship* at the Chelsea some seasons earlier. More recently, he had been working with Peter Brook. I went through the whole trajectory of my thinking process, arriving at the sideshow scheme, voicing concern about the schematicness of it. Immediately, he suggested limiting curtains to some stages and varying the levels as well as the sizes of them. This suggested to me the possibility of playing scenes simultaneously on stages in opposite ends of the theatre. For the first time, I remembered the extraordinary Italian production of *Orlando Furioso*, which I had seen in Bryant Park in 1970 and which clearly hovered somewhere in my subconscious.

I had a thought about "Glitter and Be Gay," Cunégonde's aria: there would be a pianist, the real thing, in eighteenth-century French dress, white-powdered wig, big bosom with beauty mark, her wig emblazoned with diamonds, appearing from a sort of trapdoor concealed in one of the stages. (Lee loved that.) During the song, Cunégonde would denude the powdered wig of its diamonds, covering herself with them.

So a trapdoor had entered the conversation, and we began breaking the sideshow pattern. Had I any objections to people *sitting* in places other than the center of the environment? Sitting? Well, you can hardly expect them to stand for two hours. Hardly. I had no objection. How about all over the set? Did I object to that? No objection.

Lee and his wife, Franne, live on a sailboat off Providence, Rhode Island, and he went home to work. In about a month, he was back with drawings,

190

elevations. I told him I can't read drawings; he would have to construct a model for me. He returned with a shoe box, inside which was a model for *Candide* as it would look in the Chelsea.

We were going to use a ballroom at the Brooklyn Academy of Music that Harvey Lichtenstein had converted into a theatre. It would have held five hundred people. It was long and narrow, high-ceilinged, and had a balcony about fifteen to eighteen feet up. Most of the thinking I did was based on that room. Soon after, I learned that Peter Brook had preempted it and we were switching to the Chelsea's regular theatre, which seats 180 people.

At this point, Pat Birch asked me what my plans were for the following season. I told her about Brooklyn and that I assumed with all her offers to choreograph on Broadway (it seemed to me she'd been offered everything the following season), she wouldn't be interested. On the contrary, Brooklyn was going to be fun, and she wanted to be there.

From mid-April I started to walk around with my shoe box. I took my shoe box to Europe, I looked at my shoe box on the mantelpiece in Spain all summer, and I returned to New York in the fall with my shoe box.

As rehearsals approached, Lee asked me what my adjustment to the shoe box was. Did I think of it as a small one or a big one? I realized that I was looking at it and seeing the Broadhurst Theatre, and he was looking at it and seeing the Chelsea, fourth floor of the Brooklyn Academy. I am jumping ahead, but in September, when I went to Brooklyn to see the space without seats in it, I went into shock.

Later, when we decided to bring *Candide* to Broadway, I had no worries about the adjustment from the Chelsea to the Broadway Theatre. If there was one thing that bothered me about the production in Brooklyn, it was that there were too few people watching it. The relationship of the people with the people, the audience with the audience, is what makes *Candide* exceptional. The relationship of audience with actor is fairly standard.

People are self-conscious about responding when they're alone, and 180 people in the Chelsea were, except in a few areas, very much alone. If they wanted to laugh, they were aware that they might just be laughing by them-selves. In Brooklyn, we found that sometimes we had celebrations with our audiences, but more often we had silence. Smiling, grinning, nudging each other, but self-consciously editing audibility out of their responses.

Of course, there's a certain amount of the Richard Schechner Performing Garage business of people coming near you and touching you, but that's kept to a minimum. I have my own problems with this. As a member of the audience, I don't really enjoy actors mauling me, kissing me, hugging me, or grabbing me.

I remember that when I saw *The Blacks* at the Negro Ensemble Company, I was sitting in the front row, and they put a crown in my lap. Later on, Roscoe Lee Browne ordered me to bring the crown back to the center of the stage. I was appalled that I had to rise and move into the play. The response, at least, was intended.

Not so when I went to see Jerzy Grotowski. I was hit in the leg with a loaf of bread. That did little to draw me into the experience. More predictably, it alienated me.

So in the case of *Candide*, I instructed the actors, who are never more than a foot away from some of the audience, to be extremely polite, mindful of their intrusion on the audience's privacy. I instructed them to say "Please" when they wanted something and "Excuse me" and "Pardon me" when they were crossing in front of someone. That "Excuse me" was mentioned in almost every review.

The original shoe box contained seven playing areas; and during the course of the next six months, before we went into rehearsal, we shuffled those areas, particularly the entrances and exits, the number of trapdoors, stairways. But the final set retained seven stages, two of which are proscenium, a connecting ramp, and two bridges.

Bernstein suggested we reorchestrate the show for everything from one to thirteen instruments, with the emphasis on smaller groups. Obviously, I left all that to him and Hershy Kay, who had originally orchestrated *Candide* and was eager to do a totally different shoestring version of it, and the musical director, John Mauceri.

Mauceri, regular conductor of the Yale Symphony, had conducted Bernstein's *Mass* in Vienna. He was in the process of signing as an assistant to Pierre Boulez at the New York Philharmonic.

So Bernstein, Kay, and Mauceri designed what has now been called a quadraphonic concept, simply: thirteen musicians parceled out in four separate areas of the theatre and surrounding the audience.

I wanted, before I left for my summer in Europe, to have the costume designs in work and a certain amount of casting done. Eugene Lee introduced me to his wife, who had designed the André Gregory *Alice in Wonderland*. Ours was an eccentric encounter.

She brought me a tattered black leather valise, in which she had crammed bits of fabric, remnants from old costumes, old clothes, a piece of a shawl, an antimacassar from the back of a Victorian chair, a codpiece, a comb, a flower, a swatch of mattress ticking. Everything in the show would be made out of something used (later, when I had a series of run-throughs, one friend spotted it: "You can't get those 'whites' in less than fifty years of washing"), and that would give it the feeling that we had emptied a closet, unlocked an attic trunk, a multiplicity of events, times, places.

She put three or four of these pieces on my desk and told me that they looked like the character of the Old Lady. Another collage, Cunégonde. If I put one next to another, against a third, I began to see the characters emerging. Something meshed, something seemed right about that kind of thinking. Now that I've seen how she executes her rather primitive sketches, I am surprised how sophisticated and detailed the work is. And witty.

Had I been doing a show for $600,000, I wouldn't have had the guts to go along with it. And therein lies one of the problems of the commercial theatre.

With *Candide* the risks were all artistic, and artistic risks must always be taken. You need never characterize whether you can afford them or not. The trouble too often in the commercial theatre is that artistic risks are disproportionately magnified.

There were to be six principal characters and six young men and six young girls, all of whom danced and sang, to play the rest of the roles. Hugh and I decided early, before the first writing of the script, that whereas in the original production Pangloss had played one additional character, in our version, aside from Voltaire, he must appear in every sequence as another character.

I talked to Jerry Orbach, not only a good friend but also an adept farceur, about playing Voltaire/Pangloss. He was interested, and I let it go at that.

The next most important parts to cast were Candide and Cunégonde. In 1956 they had been trapped by the requirements of the score into being legitimate opera singers, and excepting Barbara Cook, were too old for their roles. It was characteristic of that production that the performers seemed to watch from outside themselves and comment on the text.

We must have children this time, or as close as we could come to them. Our casting call at the Chelsea was for actors between the ages of sixteen and twenty. (Eventually, we decided to look for our musicians from the rolls of newly graduated Juilliard students. On Broadway, even our ushers are young.)

I don't know how many Cunégondes we saw. An awful lot of girls can sing the "jewel song," but almost all of them kid the character. It seems irresistible to satirize Cunégonde.

Mark Baker and Maureen Brennan auditioned early on. They read beautifully, but the music department raised objections. So instead of signing Maureen and Mark in May, I agreed that the Chelsea and the music department would continue to look during the summer for other people, that Maureen and Mark would work on the score, and, come Labor Day, we would make a decision.

Meantime, I asked Nancy Walker to play the Old Lady (she wasn't interested) and Julie Newmar to play Paquette, the maid (she was).

Hugh was to arrive in the middle of the summer, which meant that I had about six weeks to forget the project. I had the designs and a script, the original *Candide* recording—I could play it occasionally when I felt like it—but I didn't have to concentrate, I didn't have any deadlines to meet. So I accepted and rejected the imminence of it as the spirit moved me. If I was a little bit bored and sunlogged, I began to think of *Candide* and ideas came. Simple ideas: perhaps the notion that the two kids undress each other during the song "Oh, Happy We," playing against the materialism in the lyrics.

My scripts are a mess by the first day of rehearsal. Covered in squiggles, they document better than anything the changes in tone and detail that inform a project. I note not only specific staging ideas, but also characteristics that I think are quirky or perverse, inconsistent. I'll write down Gertrude Stein's observation "When you get there, there's no there there," and what caused me to think of it. Perhaps I'll see someone in a restaurant, and I'll draw a picture of the hat she wore or tear out an illustration from a magazine. Collecting things on the way to rehearsal, and more and more striking them out with a red pencil, or writing "No!" meaning awful idea, inconsistent, or no longer valid. I don't have the self-discipline to cram for a play, cram atmosphere, cram character, delve microscopically into each speech to see what the subtext is. Instead, I take my time, and everything collects inside, where I can call on it instinctively.

At one point in the summer, Jerry Orbach wrote, saying he had been offered the lead in *Mack and Mabel*, a David Merrick musical, and if by any chance *Candide* should extend its run in Brooklyn, he would not be available.

So Orbach was out. At the suggestion of friends at the Mark Taper, I asked Roscoe Lee Browne whether he would be interested. His agent in New York turned it down. And then I thought of Lewis Stadlen, who had been brilliant as Groucho Marx in *Minnie's Boys*. We made him an offer, but that remained unresolved until the fall.

Because I couldn't think of anybody to replace Nancy Walker, and because Lewis Stadlen was in his twenties, I thought we should be consistent and cast young. Which made a problem with Julie Newmar.

We signed Mark Baker and Maureen Brennan. Then Lewis Stadlen turned us down on the basis that a stage direction in the script said, "Voltaire plays this role in the fashion of Groucho Marx." I invited Stadlen to substitute another harmless, lecherous vaudevillian for Groucho, and he came up with Irwin Corey.

In other places in the script, I characterized the governor as Errol Flynn, and so Stadlen wears an Errol Flynn wig and a tatty Errol Flynn uniform. I arranged a reading of the play with a provisional cast, which included Mark and Maureen, Sam Freed, whom I'd picked for Maximilian, and June Gable, whom I had asked to read the Old Lady. It went even better than our fondest dreams, with Stadlen, adding an impersonation of Mel Brooks's Oldest Man in the World, as the Tibetan monk.

In the meantime, unbeknownst to me, Julie Newmar signed to do a play for Joseph Papp. Problem solved.

Soon after we had signed Lewis Stadlen, Roscoe Lee Browne called to ask what was happening with *Candide*. He had no knowledge of his agent's refusal on his behalf. That is not unusual.

At this point, I sat down with Steve Sondheim to discuss new lyrics. We needed an opening number to introduce four of the leading characters of the play in a humorous way, to set a lightly cynical, informal tone for the show, and to establish the sensuality and the innocence of the people.

Hugh wrote a monologue for Voltaire designed to orient the audience to the time and place, and four vignettes, some of which Steve set to Bernstein's music from the Venice "Gavotte" and called "Life Is Happiness Indeed."

The first quatrain is Candide's and illustrates how to tell an audience quickly where it's going.

> (*Candide is discovered on a hillock, an angry falcon perched on his left wrist.*)
> Life is happiness indeed:
> Mares to ride and books to read.
> Though of noble birth I'm not,
> I'm delighted with my lot.
>
> Though I've no distinctive features
> And I've no official mother
> I love all my fellow creatures
> And the creatures love each other.
> (*He releases the falcon, which is jerked clumsily from his wrist and shoots upward stiffly to disappear. A second later a large stuffed swan clunks down on the stage.*)

Cunégonde sings about the beautiful rosebush she's tending:

> Life is happiness indeed:
> I have everything I need.
> I am rich and unattached
> And my beauty is unmatched.
>
> With the rose my only rival
> I admit to some frustration;
> What a pity its survival
> Is of limited duration.
> (*In a fit of jealousy, she tears one of the roses from its branch.*)

And so on. In each instance, an aftertaste.

In addition to the opening, we resurrected the *Fons Pietatis*, which Bernstein had written for the original.

Latouche and Bernstein had written "What a Lovely Day for an Auto da Fé," which became one of our "big" production numbers. We needed some solo lyrics in the middle section for spectators, and Sondheim provided those.

Sondheim also wrote a lament for Candide, using the Paris "Mazurka." We had to find a substitution for the song "Eldorado," something funny, something for two pink sheep and a lion to sing. Eldorado figures importantly in the novel, describing a perfect society where human beings wilt from boredom. There was nothing wrong with the original "Eldorado," except that they had chosen to bypass Eldorado and we had chosen to visit it. Bernstein had written a lovely melody in 1956, "Fernando's Lullaby," and Steve set a lyric to it.

When we reexamined the script, in our efforts to keep everything moving, the sameness of pace was boring. We had to find places to stop for breath. The need to slow things down prompted a series of questions by Candide of a disembodied Voltaire. These questions and Voltaire's replies anchor the evening.

So much for the new material.

We went into rehearsal on October 21. I cautioned the young company not to turn our set into a gymnasium. This was not to be an evening with a stopwatch, not to be about racing and jumping and shouting and sweating, mindless aiming to please. If ever there was a show to which "less is more" applied, *Candide* would be it.

And subsequently, the few problems we had with performance involved effort—or rather, effort showing. I predicted that the environment, which was the show, was as off-putting as it was engaging. Just as many people were going to label it avant-garde hijinks on wooden boards. To counter that, we must respect the content, the structure, the rhythms, that Hugh had carefully provided. Vitality would follow effortlessly.

To protect myself, I scheduled six and a half weeks of rehearsals before the first preview. Pat Birch and I staged the show in eight days. Still, it had its advantages. If we had a sluggish day, we let it go. If things were going well, we worked a full five hours and quit. We rarely bothered to break for lunch—and so avoided coming back logy and distracted. If someone's voice was bothering him, he saved it.

I began to appreciate the privileges of socialized theatre, the seven months that Dr. Walter Felsenstein required to direct *Fiddler on the Roof* in East Berlin. (I'm only kidding; given that time, I would go nuts.)

Also, we had the luxury of four weeks to try it on small groups of friends. Based on their responses, we kept filling and building. *Candide* evolved.

One of the things that made it all so much fun was that I was not worrying about returning an investment. I was not worrying about it running indefinitely. I was doing a show for five weeks in Brooklyn.

We opened over a ten-day period with critics at every performance. We were sold out beforehand, and the Brooklyn run was extended two weeks. The reviews were marvelous, many suggesting a move to Broadway, the *Times* concerned that we might lose something in the course of it.

Now let's talk about how not to produce a show. Let's talk about how I ignored everything I'd learned, or should have learned.

Kalfin and his partners (Michael David and Burl Hash) and my team—Howard Haines, Ruth Mitchell, and I—set out in search of space in Manhattan, preferably a ballroom. The available ballrooms were in old hotels and too small to contain us. The set in Brooklyn required a room at least sixty by forty feet. In order to increase the capacity of the audience, we needed more than that. The larger hotels weren't interested. We couldn't compete with conventions.

Haines, my general manager, canvassed the City Center basement, an abandoned bowling alley, and for a time seemed to be doing business with the Waldorf Astoria for the Sert Room.

Always in the back of my mind was the possibility of the Broadway or Winter Garden Theatres. I would strip them of their seats and utilize the space on their vast stages for a portion of our audience. Both theatres were available.

The Winter Garden would have been easier because its balcony is small, wasting less of the usable space on the orchestra floor, but it is a more sought-after theatre, and I reasoned that the Shuberts would not give us a contract to ensure an indefinite run.

The Broadway, something of a white elephant, is a good theatre. Not as handsome as the Winter Garden, and a couple of blocks farther up on Broadway, it is abutted by a rather ugly parking lot and surrounded by steadily declining real estate. Paradoxically, that was an advantage to us. I did not underestimate the ambiance of the Brooklyn Academy of Music, of its faded elegant lobby, or even more, of the fourth floor, where the Chelsea is. I coveted the ingratiating informality, the earnestness of its tatty peeling walls and threadbare carpets. I joked that there was even an additional thrill getting from the Atlantic Avenue subway station to the Academy of Music alive! Perhaps we would simulate that on Broadway and Fifty-Third Street.

The economics of the production in Brooklyn were such that at capacity the Chelsea Theatre Center lost $4,000 a week. When they extended the run two weeks, that represented a sacrifice of $8,000. However, in order to move to Broadway (where they might realize some profits), we had to keep the weeks between the closing in Brooklyn and the opening on Broadway to a minimum.

What did moving quickly incur? Kalfin and I told the cast the good news, which was met with a great whoop of joy, and then the negotiating began. Billing, never a factor before, and television "out clauses" tended to give the lie to the original concept, which is that it was a group effort. All these things I understand. I understand how hazardous and frustrating an actor's life can be. The irony is simply that within minutes of the decision, the air surrounding the project was changing.

That was just the beginning, and the actors were the least of it.

Next we met with the architects, as well as Eugene Lee, to determine how to preserve the structure and increase the size of the audience observing the show. We figured the move to cost a couple of hundred thousand dollars, including building, advertising, and one week's rehearsal. The new structure had to qualify from the point of view of Fire and Building Department regulations, more rigorous in a Broadway theatre than they would have been in a ballroom.

We started to blueprint a production which would accommodate, we hoped, one thousand people against the 180 in Brooklyn, and at the same time preserve the original playing areas. We succeeded with the latter. The Broadway playing area is twenty feet longer than the one in Brooklyn, but the stages are identical.

To add capacity, we created a bleachers section, on a first-come, first-served basis, and I moved the show into the bleachers whenever possible.

Instead of one thousand seats, we settled for nine hundred.

Simultaneously, we petitioned the Musicians Local 802. Ordinarily, the Broadway (capacity 1,800) by contract must carry a minimum of twenty-five musicians. With *Candide* at the Broadway (capacity nine hundred), we requested an adjustment to reflect the new capacity. At a hearing before the union's executive board, I pointed out that in Brooklyn, according to that contract, we might have done the show with one pianist, but instead we had chosen to use thirteen musicians.

The score had been orchestrated for thirteen musicians, and we hoped to transfer them to New York. With a capacity of nine hundred, *Candide* was a risky proposition. It would take a minimum of forty weeks to return its investment, but once it had, it would represent a chance for the Chelsea to see some money. Twenty-five musicians and necessary reorchestrations would delay that.

They rejected our petition.

It was too late to turn back. We had closed in Brooklyn on January 20, and in order to reopen without losing momentum, we were obliged to sign the Broadway Theatre contract, move ahead with the architects, and spend money advertising our plan while awaiting the union's decision. It never occurred to me they would turn us down.

We requested a second hearing, this time before the Musical Theatre Committee of the union. It was pointed out by Gerald Schoenfeld of the Shubert Organization that the Broadway Theatre had been empty for thirteen months (excepting one night for the Miss USA pageant), that we were bringing in a hit musical which might run there indefinitely, providing we could keep the operating expenses within sensible limits. Ruth Mitchell informed them that there would be other productions, if the show succeeded on Broadway—in Los Angeles, Boston, and so on—giving jobs to musicians (of course, from other locals!).

The union turned *them* down.

It is interesting that when the musicians' union turned us down the second time, the stagehands' union called and offered to intervene. They did and it didn't work.

There was a third hearing, at which time the musicians' union ruled that while twenty-five musicians were mandatory, we would not have to pay them extra for wearing funny hats and vests while playing (ordinarily they get about sixty-eight dollars a week more for that).

Three weeks had gone by, and it was too late to cancel the show. We decided we could not afford to reorchestrate; consequently, there are twenty-five musicians on the payroll, eighteen of whom play, while seven sit in the basement.

I wrote the union.

January 28, 1974
Mr. Max Arons, PresidentAmerican Federation of Musicians
Local 802
261 West 52nd Street
New York City 10019

Gentlemen:

I can't repress the desire to tell you how insulting I thought the behavior accorded me at the meeting I was invited to attend before the executive board of Local 802.

It is unprecedented in my twenty years as an active producer of musicals to have met with so little knowledge of not only what I do in the theatre, but what is done by my peers.

We approached you to aid us in making a production viable on Broadway so that it can relight a theatre which has been closed for over a year and perhaps give employment to musicians, actors, stagehands, wardrobe women, etc., here and across the country. The rudeness, the outright suspicion, with which our request for practical help was met prompts me to make the following statement.

Personally, I have made my first and last appearance before your august board. Also whenever possible—and I think it will be possible more often than not—I will seek to design my future productions for the smaller theatres. The lack of logic that motivated your final decision to force us to use twenty-five musicians in a theatre with a seating capacity of nine hundred bears out my worst fears, that the theatre is not dying: rather, it is being systematically killed.

Sincerely,
Harold Prince
HP:am
CC: Gerald Schoenfeld

(How can I feel this way about people who play the violin!)

Isn't it possible that we are reaching a time when unions must assume a responsibility for the future of the theatre? Is it too much to suggest that a committee of last resort be established from among the producers, the artists, the craft unions to deal expeditiously with problems that affect the entire industry? This committee should be headed by an impartial figure with some political and public-relations experience, but more important, someone whose stature would command respect from the individual guilds and unions.

Surely the collaboration of artists to create a play is an impossible concept, but it works. Why, then, cannot groups of the same artists collaborate to the benefit of all?

I had problems with Equity as well. In the Broadway, we found that because of the choreography, the actors could not be heard singing Sondheim's solo lines in the "Auto da Fé." I phoned Equity the day before we opened and asked for permission to tape those eight lines during a performance without paying each of the actors a week's salary. (At this point we were $100,000 over budget.) I was informed that the Equity council was not meeting until the following week. By that time we would be open. I urged them to make an exception. They turned me down. I went back to the theatre and cut the two quatrains, and Pat Birch pieced the number together.

The move to Broadway became the responsibility, more than anyone else, of Howard Haines, working with the architect (Leslie Armstrong of Armstrong, Childs and Associates, who had supervised the musical *Dude* a year earlier in the same theatre), a consulting engineer (Henry M. Garsson), and the builder (Peter Feller). I never saw *Dude*, but we benefited from the experience of that production in money, time, and, one hopes, wear and tear on the nerves, but I can't imagine being *more* apprehensive than I was in the seven-week period during which we reconstructed the interior of the Broadway to the specifications of the city agencies.

No sooner had we accommodated their rules than I would come into the theatre and eliminate seats. One day, I took out 121 in the bleacher section because of sightlines. The point is, with *Candide*, no one in the audience sees everything, but everyone must see almost everything.

There's no question but that we couldn't have gotten *Candide* on without Peter Feller's help. Over those seven weeks, he would no sooner get the structure up when he would have to change it. Raise this row, take out these seats, raise that stage, put backs on those benches, guardrails along that aisle, and so on.

By the time we were ready for Tharon Musser, she had two and a half days to light the show.

At the Chelsea, there was no amplification. On Broadway the problems were critical. We brought Jack Mann over from *Night Music* to solve them. Five minutes before we opened the doors for our first performance, Tharon was adjusting specials, Jack was concealing shotgun microphones (a patron refused to sit next to one of them, explaining that she likes to talk during a show), Howard Haines was still numbering seats, and I was rehearsing the ushers.

Adjusting *Candide* to the Broadway was more like opening a new hotel than a play (Are the elevators working? How is room service?).

I had anticipated some problems acclimating the audience to an unfamiliar environment, but it was far worse than I imagined. Coming in off Broadway, under a conventional marquee, into a conventional lobby, they were frightened by the structure. There is a book, *The Hidden Dimension*, by Edward Hall, which deals in detail with the amount of space an individual requires in order to feel secure. It differs with the individual. It is an instinct shared by animals. There is a Spanish word, *querencia*, which defines the space around the bull which he needs to remain passive. When the bullfighter violates that space, the bull charges.

Our audience charged, some refusing seat locations, complaining about sightlines, maximizing the discomforts of grandstand seating. An environment which would have been acceptable to them in a ballpark offended them in a theatre.

So the Chelsea redecorated the lobby, covered the marble floor with un-finished plywood, set up hot-dog-and-beer stands, hung balloons and streamers and the canvas drops from the Chelsea production to obliterate the crystal chandeliers and the gold leaf. Then Michael David designed an advertising campaign defining the *Candide* person. The *Candide* person buys a can of beer and fills his pockets with free peanuts on the way in. He sits on a wooden bench with a back or in the pit on a padded stool. If he can't see something, he rises in his seat. If he's in the pit, he turns 360 degrees to catch the action. It worked.

Now that you *can* see from the seats and there are pads on them, and backs on all but those in the pit (and the bleachers), I assumed the complaint letters would stop coming in. They haven't. Not entirely. And that is because so much of the Broadway audience today is corrupt, concerned with creature comforts, rejecting the experience. If you gave those people beds, they could come in and sleep, and we wouldn't have to worry about what we put up on the stage.

Part of the blame is ours for desensitizing them, but if the theatre is to be a collaboration of living beings on either side of the proscenium, then they are derelict in their responsibilities.

Earlier I have said that each play seeds the next. Nowhere is it more apparent than with the success of *Candide*.

I have known for years that content dictates form, but in *Baker Street* I didn't have the courage to go full distance with the form, and in *Zorba* I tried to twist the content to fit the form. In *Candide* form and content merged easily.

It occurs to me that I loved working on *Candide* in Brooklyn and I hated bringing it to Broadway. I must conclude from this that I am growing older, the wear and tear on the nerves is more difficult to take. Is it possible that explains why so many theatre artists seem to retire in their forties or move away from directing or writing for the theatre into a more solitary creative experience?

Or, and this is just as likely, maybe I simply don't enjoy producing.

REFLECTIONS ON CHAPTER 26
OF *CONTRADICTIONS*

Lillian Hellman, whom I had met through Lenny, voiced no objection to the new project. Clearly, she wanted to bury the entire *Candide* experience. When the *Times* published a piece that implied conflict between the original creative team and the proposed new one, I wrote a letter correcting that impression. There was no conflict. I received a charming handwritten note from Hellman.

> . . . I haven't seen *Candide* but will on my return. I am sure we should and are grateful to you for taking us out of the years of pain and fights into pleasantness.

In 1982, when *Candide* transferred from BAM to Broadway for a two-and-a-half-year run, Hugh Wheeler and I heard from Hellman again. Not so charming this time:

> I am accepting the check from Amberson Enterprises. . . . But I want you to know that I will have no part of the money for what has become a piece of trash. . . .

In 1981 Beverly Sills, a good friend, told me that I had to put *Candide* onstage at the New York State Theater for the New York City Opera. I said it was an impossible task, but Beverly, being Beverly, insisted and made it happen. We restored much of the material and put it in two acts. The Chelsea Theatre production was entirely influenced by Voltaire's denial of authorship (he said it must be some schoolboy's jape), and we had cast it with actors in their twenties or younger. Now we were moving into an opera environment. Instead of Eugene Lee's environmental production, I asked Clarke Dunham, who also had designed *Madame Butterfly* for me at the Chicago Lyric Opera, to reconceive an opera house version. This one would accommodate opera singers from Beverly's company and elsewhere. John Lankston would be Voltaire/Pangloss, Erie Mills our Cunégonde, and David Eisler our Candide—all of them older, more experienced, and opera rather than Broadway performers. Pat Birch and I fleshed out the original material with an assist from Arthur Masella, and Lenny's additional numbers enriched the score.

Of course, we went from thirteen instruments at the Broadway to over fifty at the New York State Theater.

Candide's invited dress was the same day as its scheduled opening. The house was full, and we made it only through the first act. Nevertheless, the audience was ecstatic. However, you can imagine the anxiety shared by its director, cast, music director John Mauceri, orchestra, and crew as we approached the premiere.

Miracle of miracles, the opening night was spectacular, and the *New York Times* headline said something like, "Triumph at City Opera, Disaster at the Met" (naturally, I would remember that!). It continued at City Opera as its most popular attraction, and when City Opera announced its closing, the final performance was a matinee of *Candide*. It received a huge and lengthy ovation.

I had never been sadder to see an organization close shop. City Opera had been the idea of Mayor Fiorello La Guardia and had opened at City Center, which now houses Alvin Ailey American Dance Theater and Encores. One of its earliest artistic directors was Erich Leinsdorf, who was followed by the enormously talented Julius Rudel. Both served as conductors and administrators. Many years later, Julius was responsible for inviting me to direct operas. I had observed my British colleagues moving freely among musicals, dramas, and operas, but there was little precedence for that in the United States. During an interview with the *New York Times*, I mentioned that fact and my desire to do operas. Julius called immediately with an offer of Josef Tal's Israeli opera *Ashmedai*. Simultaneously, I received a telegram from Carol Fox of the Chicago Lyric offering me the opening night of Puccini's *La Fanciulla del West*. I accepted both offers. I staged Tal's opera with John Lankston in the leading role (which is how I thought of him for Pangloss some years later).

In the interim, I've directed Kurt Weill's *Silver Lake* at City Opera with Joel Grey starring, and ultimately, after Beverly Sills took over as general manager, Mozart's *Don Giovanni*, which stayed in the repertoire for sixteen seasons. I've directed productions at the Teatro Colón in Buenos Aires (ably assisted by Vincent Liotta), the San Francisco Opera, the Staatsoper in Vienna, and the Metropolitan in New York. The latter was an unhappy experience, probably because of an interim general manager who lasted only one year and my decision to accept *Faust* as my assignment. I don't much care for that opera—is it French or is it German? Or is it just too damned old-fashioned?

There can be an advantage to directing opera: its composers and librettists are long gone. There are operas so brilliantly structured (Puccini's, for example) that they provide every note of music and every note of silence that a director requires to tell a story, whereas so many other operas are structured exclusively to be sung. Significantly, Puccini's *Madame Butterfly* and *Fanciulla del West* (Girl of Golden West) are the basis for successful plays directed by David Belasco on Broadway.

Finally—because I'm often asked how directing operas is different from directing musicals—for me, there should be no difference, as long as the libretto accommodates the music and vice versa, and your cast of opera singers are excellent actors, which today has become more and more the case.

As I write this, I'm planning to revisit *Candide* for the reconstituted New York City Opera, based now at the Rose Theater in the Time Warner Center at Columbus Circle. I'm participating because I want so much for that organization to be reborn and to thrive in the hands of Michael Capasso. This version will be significantly different.

It will be darker than previous versions. I've asked Ken Billington, our original lighting designer, to switch from stage lighting to fluorescent lighting for Lenny's glorious anthem "Make Our Garden Grow." In earlier versions this has been performed earnestly, optimistically, and with a touch of humor. But now for the change: elements of the set will disappear, to be replaced by a stained white muslin. Fluorescence will drain vibrant color from the stage, replacing it with acidity. At this point, the company will abandon their characters, move downstage unrelated to each other, and lock eyes with the audience, in Brechtian fashion; I will urge them to think Donald Trump.

Now, during the process of editing this book, I find myself three months later having opened and closed the production to welcoming reviews. Though it was celebrated over forty years ago, I guess I've been working on it ever since because this, far and away, was the best. It was not only funny but serious; perhaps Lillian Hellman would have been happy finally. Gregg Edelman's Pangloss, Jay Armstrong Johnson's Candide, Meghan Picerno's Cunégonde, and Linda Lavin's Old Lady were just about perfect. Chip Zien, Brooks Ashmanskas, Jessica Wright, and Keith Phares rounded out the principal team. A dream cast and an ensemble to match them.

Note: it is here that *Contradictions* ended. This new book has given me the opportunity to revisit those years and flesh them out or, yet again, contradict myself.

But now, what follows is new. Each chapter discusses new productions from 1974 to the present, and there will be no reflections.

CHAPTER
27

I first encountered John Weidman when working with his father, Jerome, who co-authored the musical *Fiorello!* and won a Pulitzer Prize for it. I say "encountered" because I'm not certain I actually met him. He was this kid on a bicycle moving from room to room in the Weidmans' Upper East Side apartment.

Years later, the adult John Weidman came to my office with a play about Commodore Perry's incursion into Japanese waters off Edo (now Tokyo) after hundreds of years of Japan's self-imposed isolation. Perry's job was to open trade negotiations between the United States and the empire of Japan.

The play, extremely well written, covered meetings on Perry's flagship between him and his officers and a "delegation" of Japanese composed of a lonely sailor, Manjiro, sent out to beg the Americans to turn back and go home. The story continued with additional meetings, which Japanese officials attended as Perry refused to leave. John Weidman's play predicted the inevitable acculturation of Japan.

What Weidman proposed was the stuff of potent theatrical storytelling, and I thought there might be a musical in it. A musical sans a conventional love story. A musical all about American hegemony and careless, aggressive bullying, which may well have greased the way to Pearl Harbor and the Americanization of one of the most profoundly beautiful cultures on earth.

I proposed a meeting with Steve Sondheim and John Weidman and persuaded the two of them to consider writing a musical, which I would direct in the Kabuki style. They went away to ponder, and when they returned, we were in business.

After we agreed to do the show, Steve, Judy, and I flew to Tokyo, where we were generously greeted and entertained by the Toho Company and by Keita Asari of the Shiki Theatre Company. (In Japan, I went on to work for Asari directing *Phantom* and, through my friend Yasushi Abe, a production of

Kiss of the Spider Woman.) We attended the Grand Kabuki and the Noh Theatre. Our Japanese hosts expected us to be bored, and how wrong they were! At the Grand Kabuki, they offered us the chance to leave early, but we stayed an extra hour. We arrived at the Noh an hour late, not knowing there was an entourage to greet us. Incidentally, we were enthralled by the Noh and remained for almost three hours. Our hosts were flabbergasted.

One evening, we were taken backstage at the Grand Kabuki and introduced to a man who was preparing to be made up, his costumes hanging on a rack in the corner. We stayed only a few minutes because curtain time was approaching. We left, but our guide kept us outside his dressing room. Within twenty minutes he reappeared, perhaps two-thirds the size of the man we had met, and was transformed into an onnagata, a lovely Japanese creature in full kimono and obi. She had a fan in her hand and bowed ceremoniously to us, completely in character, and with small steps she made her way to the wings for her entrance.

The Kabuki concept suggested we cast the musical with an all-male, all-Asian company, which was unprecedented on Broadway. Asian actors were rarely seen on Broadway, much less comprising an entire cast. I should mention also that we did cheat—there were ladies in the company who served as koken, covered in black, which in Japanese theatre rendered them invisible to the audience as they moved props and scenery.

It was arrogant of this American director to pursue a Kabuki staging, particularly in view of the fact that there's a three-thousand-year traditional foundation to those performances. However, our work was to be an American's interpretation, as well as an homage to Japanese culture. And once again, with Boris Aronson designing the scenery, we had a master on board. Then Florence Klotz made magic with her costumes, authentic to the Japanese tradition. Finally, Patricia Birch staged her version of traditional Kabuki movement. The team was as excited as it was inspired.

For the end of Act One, Weidman wrote a scene where the Japanese built a small teahouse in which to meet the American delegation. They covered its floor with tatami mats made of straw, and when the Americans departed, they took up the mats, destroyed the teahouse, and confirmed that the United States had never set foot on Japanese soil. Sondheim wrote the most complex and satisfying account of this episode: "Someone in a Tree" told the story through the eyes of a young man perched in a tree outside the house, reporting events unseen by the audience, while another Japanese samurai hiding under the floorboards of the house reported the negotiations he heard. Their observations relayed to the audience what happened in the meeting—amazing! Quintessential Sondheim.

Another episode in act 2 was entitled "A Bowler Hat." Encapsulated in that number were two figures. Kayama (played by Isao Sato), a traditionalist, transformed from a small, insignificant man sitting on a pillow practicing calligraphy and working an abacus into a Victorian gentleman of great wealth, owner of a bowler hat and a Bonnard masterpiece. Meanwhile, Manjiro (played by Sab Shimono), on the other side of the stage, ceremonially and with great detail slowly—ever so slowly—performed a traditional tea ceremony, at the end of which he rose transformed into a traditional samurai fixing a ferocious sword to his waist.

There were other equally rewarding watershed moments: Pat Birch choreographed our opening, "The Advantages of Floating in the Middle of the Sea," a history lesson on three hundred years of Japanese isolation. "Four Black Dragons" was a thunderous number dramatizing the arrival of Perry's warships and the hysteria that created in the Japanese population.

And Steve composed a musical haiku, a duet for both leading characters.

The finale, "Next!," detailed the influence of Western culture on Japanese tradition. In song, Steve turned the almost bucolic serenity of their nation-building from curiosity to invention to invasion, while Weidman provided the details. For example:

[First voice] There are 223 Japan Airlines ticket offices in 153 cities throughout the world.

[All] Next!

[Second voice] There are eight Toyota dealerships in the city of Detroit, and Seiko watch is the third best-selling watch in Switzerland.

[All] Next!

[Third voice] Fifty-seven percent of the bicentennial souvenirs sold in Washington, D.C., in 1975 were made in Japan.

[All] Next!

[Fourth voice] This year Japan will export sixteen billion kilograms of monosodium glutamate and four hundred thousand tons of polyvinyl chloride resin.

We'll let it go at that.

We previewed in Boston at the exquisite Colonial Theatre. Judy Prince decided it was time for our children to see what "Daddy does," so the family gathered in Boston to watch tech rehearsals, and they attended their first opening night. The reviews were brutal. My family observed Steve, John, and me reading the reviews, reacting to them, and then returning to work. It's worth mentioning that Bernard Jacobs and Gerald Schoenfeld—"the Shuberts"—who were awaiting our occupancy at the Winter Garden Theatre on Broadway were in Boston for the awful reviews. They generously reconfirmed their allegiance to us, urged us on, and supported us through the trauma.

I regard *Pacific Overtures* as a major accomplishment. The cast, headed by Mako—the great Japanese actor in the role of the reciter, a tradition in Japanese theatre—remained focused, dedicated, and optimistic, not least because of his influence. I also want to mention the performance by the Korean star Soon-Tek Oh playing an onnagata, a female role—it was lovely to watch, perfectly nuanced, and fragile.

In New York, the show ran 193 performances and lost its entire capitalization. Of course, that was no surprise to most of our investors, but I believe they were proud to have been part of it. Many of our colleagues in the theatre count it among the best of our musicals.

The original production was filmed by the Coca-Cola Company as a present from the United States to Japan to commemorate our bicentennial in 1976. It can still be accessed on YouTube.

CHAPTER
28

After *Pacific Overtures* in 1976, I had nothing planned. No new productions, and I was itching to work. Betty Comden and Adolph Green—good friends for many years and the brilliant authors of *On the Town* and *Wonderful Town* (for which I'd been a stage manager) as well as the epic film *Singin' in the Rain*—approached me with *On the Twentieth Century*. They had written it with Cy Coleman, a sensational composer and popular performer. I can't recall whether they had lost a previous director or if I was the first they came to.

Nevertheless, I was eager and intrigued, not least of all because it was a musical version of *Twentieth Century*, one of George Abbott's great successes. For me the primary challenge was to see whether I could direct farce—pratfalls, double takes. Whether I had the capacity to make things outrageously funny and still honest. In other words, replicate Abbott's rules for farce. Also, I wondered how to confine a musical to two compartments on a train from New York to Chicago. I found that I could, thanks in large part to Robin Wagner's handsome art deco sets. Florence Klotz provided the costumes in Necco Wafer colors, complementing Robin's work. And Larry Fuller staged the dances.

The authors opened up the book so, in fact, it was not totally confined to a train: there was an arrival at Grand Central Station, a musical comedy excerpt, a shiny steel show curtain in front of which four Pullman porters presented the entr'acte, and finally, a montage covering many areas, including the front of the Twentieth Century train with the lights beaming into the audience's eyes. Cy Coleman and his lyricist partners chose to write an operetta score, which lifted the entire project to a higher level and made it more inviting to me and more unusual for the audience.

The producers should be mentioned, because they were uncommonly obliging. They were Robert Fryer, who had produced *Wonderful Town* and whom I knew well; Martin Richards and his wife, Mary Lea Johnson; and

James Cresson. Mary Lea took charge of the logo and delivered a handsome advertising campaign in keeping with the production.

The cast was unparalleled. John Cullum, who played his version of John Barrymore, was all ego and bluster: articulate, persuasive, and phony. The other male lead was Kevin Kline, who was not yet *the* Kevin Kline. He delivered a youthful variation of Errol Flynn—sort of a walking profile, flamboyant, egotistical, and always as near as possible to a mirror. The two gentlemen delivered such creative imagination and vitality to their roles; they shone. The leading lady was Madeline Kahn, who had been cast before I joined the show. This may be difficult to believe, because of course I knew and admired her films and earlier stage performances, but it was only on the first day of rehearsal I realized we were not using Bernadette Peters. Of course, I was not discouraged. The fourth of our stars was the great Imogene Coca, one of the pillars of TV's *Your Show of Shows* with Sid Caesar.

Rehearsals went extremely well. To say the cast was inventive would be an understatement. In particular, Cullum and Kline—it was amazing how they came up with comic business. I think on this assignment I acted more as an editor and stimulator than anything else. It was thrilling to collaborate with them. Working with Madeline was a different matter. She seemed unable to retain a performance. For a while I blamed it on her enormous success in film, which I imagined contributed to her improvisational magic. However, in the theatre you mustn't improvise past rehearsals; after all, you're working with other actors, and they're depending on your timing being substantially the same at each performance. Obviously, I know that no two performances are identical, but operating independently on the stage is a bad idea.

After almost every performance in Boston and every preview in New York, I would go backstage to remind Madeline that there were other people on the stage. Some nights her energy level flagged to a degree that she disappeared, and other nights she was so manic that her co-stars couldn't deliver their performances as rehearsed. She seemed unable, or likely unwilling, to give the same performance every night, and certainly she never reached the heights I knew she was capable of. That is, until opening night, when she delivered 100 percent. When the curtain came down on our success I rushed backstage to her dressing room. I could not have been more enthusiastic as I told her, "That's it! That's the performance! And you gave it on the right night!!" Whereupon she looked in the dressing room mirror and said, "I hope you don't think I can do that every night." I died. And she was as right as her word—she rarely gave that performance again, at least never two nights in a row.

In a couple of months she left the show, and Judy Kaye, her understudy, took over. Judy was fantastic. Her interpretation was hers alone. It was authentic, so crisp, and funny—everything the doctor ordered. (Parenthetically, Judy's place in the company was taken by Christine Ebersole. I believe it was one of her first jobs.)

On the Twentieth Century won Tony Awards for Comden and Green, for Cy Coleman, and for John Cullum and Kevin Kline. But as Judy Kaye was not eligible, and Madeline Kahn was nominated but not in the show, we lost that one. The musical ran for 449 performances. Had Judy Kaye opened in it, I believe it would have run for twice as many.

One day Scott Ellis, who was going to direct the Roundabout Theatre's 2015 revival of *On the Twentieth Century*, came to my office to discuss the material. When it opened and received excellent reviews, I thought I'd pay it a visit—alone. Scott Ellis regretted that he could not be there that night, as he would be out of town. The production was splendid, and during the bows suddenly Scott appeared onstage, quieted the standing ovation, and said that every revival was a representation of an original production and the director of the original production was sitting in the house. He asked me to take a bow. How 'bout that for generosity?

I suppose here is an apt moment for me to comment on revivals of my own shows. Generally, I don't go to see them. Excellent as I'm sure so many of them are, I retain an impression of the original, and often I miss the metaphor which informed the original production. Many authors I've worked with go regularly to see revivals of their shows, and I understand that: as authors they want to see their work still living. They are right to want that. I am a director, and that's different.

CHAPTER
29

J udy and I and our kids spent about twenty summers in a lovely old
house at the top of El Calvario (the Calvary) in Pollença on the island of
Majorca, Spain. There one day, I received a letter from Andrew Lloyd Webber
saying that he and Tim Rice had written a musical on the life of Eva Perón.
A rags-to-riches story ending with her as first lady of Argentina. She died in
the Casa Rosada, the Argentinian White House, at the age of thirty-four.
The story had everything I could wish for.

Judy and I invited Andrew to visit the summer of 1976. He brought a tape
of *Evita*'s score, which had already been recorded by the London Symphony
Orchestra and was being edited for release late that year. The first band he
played was a mammoth musical depiction of Eva Perón's funeral in front of
the Casa Rosada, a gathering of two hundred thousand mourning their
queen. It was stunning. And irresistible.

A political musical describing the rise and fall of a fascist couple with
unbridled ambition—what more could I ask for? As common, vulgar, even
ordinary as they were in real life, they became mythological figures not just
in Argentina but on the world's stage—the Macbeths for their time.

I had to direct it. After I heard the entire score, Andrew returned to
London, and I wrote a three-thousand-word letter to him and Tim with
suggestions for cuts. There was a third character in the musical to triangu-
late the relationships, Che, whom I took to be Che Guevara. I urged them
to excise a number that dealt with his being an insecticide salesman. I
thought this was a red herring—irrelevant and oddly diminishing. Of
course, I did not know at that time that Tim had named him Che because it
was a popular Argentinian name and had never thought of him as Guevara.
I mailed my letter, and I didn't hear from either of them for some time until
there was a rather meek, apologetic reply telling me that they were writing a
concept album and perhaps had been ill advised to have approached me at

this time. They thanked me, and that was that. I did not expect to hear from them again.

One day, almost a year later, the receptionist in my office buzzed me to say there were two gentlemen in the waiting room who had come bearing a gift and would like to see me. I stepped out of my office to see Andrew and Tim holding a copy of a record—a handsome white sleeve and, inside, six pages on slick paper of Tim's lyrics. Their concept record, entitled *Evita*, had been released in London and had traveled through Europe like wildfire. A success of spectacular proportions, it had not made it to the United States, because few in our country had heard of Eva Perón.

The recording had been produced by Robert Stigwood, discoverer of the Bee Gees, and David Land, discoverer of Lloyd Webber and Rice. Both gentlemen were to produce the show in London. That morning we became a team. However, I had a scheduling conflict directing *On the Twentieth Century*, and I couldn't begin working on *Evita* for six months. It took a year and a half to get the show ready.

My first disagreement was with Tim. Having assumed that Che was Che Guevara, I then insisted that was who he must be. As a student, Che had been politicized by the Peróns and left Argentina, settling in Mexico City where he made a living as a street photographer in front of the Chapultepec Palace. And there, ironically, he eventually met Raúl Castro—an enticing subject for another musical! Ultimately, Tim came around, and that insecticide number disappeared.

To begin with, as I was starting with such a popular score, but was limited to the shiny pages accompanying the recording, I needed a proper script. So, using the locations and the lyrics of the numbers, I dictated scenes to Arthur Masella, my assistant, adding a brief description of what each contained and ideas for staging. The script took the form of a political revue, not unlike the work of Meyerhold and Lyubimov. It was twenty-five pages long.

As I've said before, I like to bring on designers as soon as possible, because they are intrinsic to the motor of a musical. I had admired the work of the designers Tim O'Brien and Tazeena Firth, and we invited them to join the team.

At the same time I asked Larry Fuller, who was staging the musical numbers in *On the Twentieth Century*, to do the same for *Evita*. I consider

Larry Fuller's staging in *Evita* up there with Bob Fosse's in our early shows, Ron Field's in *Cabaret*, and Michael Bennett's in *Follies*—imaginative A+.

In New York, we began to dissect Tim's story line. It was remarkably precise. Each number was an episode in its entirety. Tim's lyrics, brief and punchy, invited details and activity—nuggets to be translated into stage business. Now for *the metaphor*. Clearly, this was a show about flashbulbs, microphones, and film, dramatizing how much the media can distort our vision of ordinary humans and create icons of them.

Eva was the illegitimate daughter of the well-to-do head of the Duarte family. The show began in a cheap movie house in Junín, the dirt-poor town in which she was born. On a huge movie screen downstage, we saw a segment of an early Western B picture starring Eva Duarte. Beneath the screen and ranging upstage were lines of seats occupied by down-at-heels men and women. The film broke down, causing the audience to hoot until there appeared in silhouette a man announcing to the audience the death of Eva Perón. This was followed by an audible gasp, a woman screaming, and much sobbing. The screen then made its way diagonally upstage, lighting the rows of faces as it found its place on the upstage wall. The company rose, moved chairs into the wings, and replaced them with a coffin—Eva's. There were lights embedded in the raked stage which circled the open coffin and reached up to the flies. The setting was little more than a simple black box. Che would then appear, and the company assumed the roles of two hundred thousand mourners.

Within this black box, we moved back in time, introducing Eva, in the company of her family, seducing or being seduced by Carlos Gardel, the famous Argentinian tango singer. Once the setting moved to Buenos Aires, a revolving door took its place onstage, through which Eva discarded her lovers, replacing them with more and more influential politicians and military officers. In the original text, we moved to a meeting in Luna Park between Eva and Juan Perón, who was there to make a political speech to a crowd of thousands. It was here that I thought we had jumped too quickly and robbed Perón of a proper entrance. So I suggested that Tim and Andrew write a number for five officers—lieutenants, generals, colonels. Perhaps they were sitting in oversized rocking chairs and we would play musical chairs with them, eliminating one at a time until only Perón was left rocking and blowing smoke rings into the air. This entire episode was punctuated by appearances of Eva on the side of the stage observing the rise of Perón. Then we moved on to the Luna Park sequence. Each of the episodes was delivered with a minimum of scenery—a chair, a microphone, a door on an empty black stage with strong lights spiking it. It was powerful stuff.

All of this was transferred to a half-inch model of the stage, one on which we worked out every bit of business before going into rehearsal. As I examined it, something seemed to be missing, but what? We were months away from rehearsal, and Judy and I took a week's vacation in Mexico city. We visited Chapultepec Palace, which houses many of the great political murals of Diego Rivera and David Alfaro Siqueiros that chart Mexico's tumultuous history, pitting peasants in revolt against the oligarchs in control. In the murals I found what was missing in our design. I went to London with a huge book of Siqueiros plates and asked O'Brien and Firth to design a proscenium depicting political revolution: the peasants and the oligarchs, the people in the street and the people in palaces. They framed the black box exactly as I wanted, and their proscenium provided an electricity to the space. It's worth mentioning that it was then that I discovered what a proscenium can do to power an empty black box. This is something I've used again and again—the best example is the elaborately carved figures surrounding the black box that houses *The Phantom of the Opera*.

Then we began the casting process. Originally, I thought that Eva should be played by three ladies, one for each phase of her ascendency. Bad idea. There were literally hundreds of auditions until we saw Elaine Paige, who nailed it perfectly. Experienced in the West End, most recently playing a substantial role in *Billy*, Elaine had and still has one of the best voices in the British theatre. She's a tiny woman, as was Eva, but she cast a towering shadow—all grit and determination and, ultimately, glamor. As Juan Perón we cast Joss Ackland, who had had great success playing Fredrik opposite Jean Simmons in the West End production of *A Little Night Music*. David Essex, a rock-and-roll star, auditioned for the role of Che. He had a huge following and played the part with charm and even poetry. It worked.

As we approached our opening night, the press was hysterical. They had been checking the stage door during auditions, photographing actors coming and going, and building excitement each day as previews approached. I asked for nine previews, but though the critics were not in the house, at the first of them the tabloid gossip columnists were, and the morning after, the front pages of those papers were rave reviews. For the next nine years, there were long lines waiting at the box office for any cancellations.

A year after the London opening, we took *Evita* to Broadway, where we cast Mandy Patinkin as Che, Patti LuPone as Eva, and Bob Gunton as Perón. Mandy's performance, rather than poetic and soulful, was fierce, and we knew that was right for an American audience. *Evita* opened to mixed reviews, but it was a box office success from the start. I recall putting those reviews in permanent picture frames in the lobby of the Broadway Theatre, where we played for a little under five years.

Simultaneously, there was a national company that played for over two years in Los Angeles before touring the rest of the states. It starred Loni Ackerman, who made a terrific Eva, and the show was as successful as it had been on Broadway. In the intervening years, there have been two first-rate tours staged by Larry Fuller and Kim Jordan.

On opening night on Broadway, I was sitting in the last row of the theatre with my wife when someone tapped me on the shoulder to tell me there was a bomb threat. Now, let me interrupt myself to say that during that period on Broadway, I had made unexpected appearances in two musicals. I walked right down center stage in a scene during *Company* to tell the audience there was a bomb threat and to please file out to the street and we would have them return when it was safe. That occurred again at *Pacific Overtures*. And here we were at opening night, and I was being asked to stop the show five minutes before the curtain on the first act, during a celebration of the Peróns by members of labor unions and political clubs carrying bold signs and torches of fire, while the Peróns in contrast occupied a huge bed, having just made love and plotting their next Macbethian plan. To stop all of this was too much for me. So I gulped, and decided (albeit nervously) to play to the end of the act. No bombs went off, and during intermission, sniffing police dogs came and went, moving through the empty theatre, and the audience appeared oblivious. *Whew!*

CHAPTER
30

S teve Sondheim saw a production of *Sweeney Todd: The Demon Barber of Fleet Street* at Theatre Royal Stratford East (Joan Littlewood's home for years). I assumed from Steve's description that it was a lighter-hearted work and that didn't tempt me. So I dismissed it as a *revengical*. Steve, however, was on to more serious business, and so I was interested. *Sweeney* is about cannibalism, about a man's revenge for the loss of his wife and daughter. It isn't remotely campy, and meat pies would be out of order for the production we finally came up with. I'd like to say here that revenge is not in my nature, but perhaps that's what scares me: perhaps it *is* in my nature.

We invited Hugh Wheeler to write the book—a perfect choice—and Eugene and Franne Lee to design the set and costumes. Larry Fuller signed on to stage numbers. Now to search for the metaphor, which would make it more political than perhaps my colleagues wanted. Eugene and I found it easily in the time the play takes place: the industrial age. The collective slavery of sweatshops, assembly lines, the blocking out of nature, sunshine lost to the filthy fog spewing from the smokestacks of factories.

Eugene Lee located a factory in New England that was abandoned and for sale. The producers paid $25,000 for it—its iron exterior, its gates, and a mess of machinery. The only theatre available on Broadway at that time was the Uris, now the Gershwin. It has two thousand seats—enormous by 1980 standards. Today, thanks mostly to the road, theatres sometimes twice as large as the Gershwin house Broadway musicals. In those days I wouldn't have believed it, but I've come to accept it, as have contemporary audiences. For example, *The Phantom of the Opera* plays at Her Majesty's in London to 1,200 seats, while there are over 1,600 in the Majestic Theatre in New York.

I proposed the factory setting to the authors, who immediately asked if they would have to rewrite to accommodate that information. My answer was "Absolutely no!"

Sweeney Todd's principal cast includes the title role and Mrs. Lovett, the owner of a pie shop, who is bankrupt until she and Sweeney discover they can murder people and make meat pies of their cadavers. In addition, there are two young lovers, a crazy old lady, and very importantly, a villainous judge. The story also calls for a community of dirt-poor people of all ages—where better to set such a collective than the jail of a factory?

The stage of the Uris stretches over fifty feet across, but with a smaller area depending on the proscenium opening. It was a huge space, which we didn't need. Our show needed to be confined, and so the factory became a picture frame with a vaulted glass roof covered in soot, so filthy that the sun could not make its way to the "slaves" below.

We put a cube in the middle of the factory. From the stage level, stairs led to Sweeney Todd's barbershop at the top of the cube, and each side of it presented a different venue: Mrs. Lovett's pie shop, her parlor, the cellar of Sweeney's barbershop (where he dispatched his victims), and the fourth side was the stairs. Strewn almost randomly over the stage were machines and parts of machines. Some pieces were disguised platforms, which could be manually pushed into place anywhere on the stage to accommodate a scene. When anyone asked what they made in that factory, the best I could offer was a musical called *Sweeney Todd*!

When the book was completed and Steve had written sequentially most of the material for Act I, but none for Act 2, we decided to have a reading with Angela Lansbury and Len Cariou. Steve would play the few songs he had written, and our stars would read the entire text. We learned a great deal from that; we must lighten up the mood for variety and leaven the tension for the audience. Both authors addressed the issue of highs and lows. Steve then wrote "A Little Priest" for Mrs. Lovett and Sweeney at the end of the first act. He finished the score—not overnight, but brilliantly—and we began casting. Angela and Len stayed as our leads; Ed Lyndeck played Judge Turpin, the villain and *deus ex machina* of the plot. The young lovers were played by Victor Garber and Sarah Rice. Merle Louise was the old lady, who we discover late in the evening was Sweeney's wife, who had been driven mad.

The musical began with a silk banner illustrating the British class system in the nineteenth century. As the houselights darkened, two workers entered and tore down the banner, simultaneously triggering a factory whistle. It shrieked again during the show every time Sweeney cut someone's throat. Now, a bit about that factory whistle: I suggested it and auditioned levels of sound until it was almost unbearable. Audiences found it excruciating, but we loved to torture them. Parenthetically, none of the revivals of *Sweeney Todd* have taken place in a factory, but all have found the factory whistle irresistible.

I worried about how to deal with the ensemble. I knew I needed to give them something to elevate their contribution, so I encouraged each one to create a character. "You are prisoners in a factory and collectively driven to cannibalism," I told them. "You never see the sun because of the soot that covers the roof of the factory. You must decide, individually, whether or not you are married, whether you have any children. Make up a history for your character. You don't have to tell me what you have decided, but you have to make specific choices for yourselves." One of the ensemble said she had seen an illustration of a young woman wearing a heavy iron brace from thigh to ankle and asked me if I would mind if she wore one. It was exactly the kind of thinking I wanted to stimulate in each member of the ensemble. The entire chorus created lives for their characters, backstories that enriched what was onstage throughout the show.

Sweeney opened cold on Broadway with a minimum number of previews. I had had such a successful experience with *Evita* in London that I persuaded everyone to take that chance. It worked again this time.

On the afternoon of the first preview, I had yet to stage the bows, so I took the company upstairs to a rehearsal room and started the conventional way with the cast peeling off into the wings, leaving Sweeney and Lovett downstage. Lovett then crossed the stage like a dead puppet while Sweeney moved upstage center and exited through an iron factory door: *Slam!* Blackout. Perfect!

The only changes after the first preview were the elimination of a tooth-pulling sequence and one number in which Judge Turpin, peeking through a keyhole at our ingenue, flagellated himself into an orgasm. However, it has been restored in all subsequent productions.

The show played to capacity for the length of Angela Lansbury's contract. When she and Len Cariou left, despite excellent star replacements (Dorothy Loudon and George Hearn), business dropped precipitously, and the show ran only another four months. I've come to believe that it wasn't so much the new cast—as good as the show was, there was an audience that refused to see a show about cannibalism. After it closed on Broadway, it toured the country with Angela Lansbury and George Hearn in the leading roles. Happily, there is an excellent TV taping of a performance from the stage, filmed in Los Angeles.

Sweeney's producers—Richard Barr, Charles Woodward, Robert Fryer, Mary Lea Johnson, and Martin Richards—had financed the show for $3.5 million. Someone told me it took eleven years to recoup. Since it closed, there have been countless productions in Europe and the United States, as well as opera house and concert versions. Recently in London, a production took place in a specially constructed pie shop. And by the time this book is published, this production will have played in New York.

CHAPTER
31

Judy Prince suggested that Steve and I should do a musical with young people. After all, we had two young people living with us: Charley and Daisy Prince. Both were musical, and as I write this, both are making their careers in music—Charley is a maestro, and Daisy is a director as well as a teacher in musical theatre for Syracuse University. Musicals featuring young people have been something of a tradition in the theatre—*Babes in Arms*, *Best Foot Forward*, *Bye Bye Birdie*, *Annie*, and of course *Grease*.

Responding to Judy's idea was easy. I had always loved a play of Kaufman and Hart's called *Merrily We Roll Along*. I mentioned that to Steve, who shared my enthusiasm for it. Of course neither of us had seen it; it did not enjoy success, running only five months in 1934, but we had both read it and were attracted to its structure. It followed the lives of a group of middle-aged people: most of them wealthy, some powerful, and some theatrical celebrities. And it told their stories in many short scenes, each going back in time so when you'd gotten to the finale, you were at the beginning of all of their lives, when they were naive and innocent, simon-pure and full of dreams of the future.

To write the libretto, we interested George Furth, whom we regarded as our J. D. Salinger. (I'm serious about this. What a pity that George didn't write more. He enjoyed a career as a supporting player in films, and he bifurcated his choices.) Ron Field, who had done brilliantly by *Cabaret*, signed on for musical staging. Martin Starger, who had produced a number of plays and musicals on Broadway as well as films, assumed the producing slot.

George and Steve went to work. We made such headway with the book that we began casting from hundreds of young actors, singers, and dancers. I believe we came up with a terrific cast, among them my daughter Daisy, who was sixteen at the time. There were three leads. Lonny Price, who was a protean performer, signed on as Charley Kringas, the lyricist; James Weissenbach was cast as the composer, Franklin Shepard; and the woman in their lives, Mary Flynn, was played by Ann Morrison.

Steve wasn't ready for our schedule. So we had to break the news to the youngsters that there would be a lengthy postponement—almost a year. And they hung on. It was worth it, waiting for Steve. I still believe his score for *Merrily* is one of his best. Amazingly smart, funny, loving, and ultimately heartbreaking—brilliant on all counts.

For me, there was a huge problem: I could not visualize the production. I depend so much on scenery to pace a show; often, for me the scenery is the essence of a show's movement. I don't need much, but I do need that metaphor. I was lost, and surprisingly enough, so was Eugene Lee. We decided on a gymnasium for the basic set. Bad idea. And we went from bad to worse.

I called a meeting of my office gang and confessed that the only thing I could come up with that remotely resonated was to offer the audience an empty stage with a work light in place when they entered the theatre. As the houselights dimmed, a cast of kids would rush onstage, some pushing pipes of costumes that would line up across the rear of the stage and come down on both sides. I suggested that during the storytelling they would pull from the racks bits and pieces of clothing for each sequence. I thought this would have the appropriate energy: kids telling their story, getting together to make a musical. I knew that though it would add rehearsal time, it would certainly save production costs. Plus, it was the only thing I could think of.

I asked the office to react, and predictably, all of them urged me to go ahead with that scheme. But I didn't have the nerve. I remember mentioning the cost of theatre tickets and how disappointed the audience would be in getting so little for their money. In hindsight it's easy, of course: I was wrong, and very likely had I followed my instinct, it would have added substance to the production that it needed.

The two musicals which preceded *Merrily* (*Evita* and *Sweeney Todd*) had opened cold with a minimum of previews and no out-of-town tryouts. Apparently, I had made a cost-saving discovery? Well, apparently not!

As Kaufman and Hart's play had depended on middle-aged people over the course of an evening assuming the roles of twenty-year-olds, I hoped it would be as easy to start with twenty-year-olds playing middle-aged people and reverse the process. I believed it would be particularly touching to see how over the course of a lifetime we lose the glister and optimism of youthful ambition. I was wrong. It was too damn complicated.

Still, I cannot remember being happier waking up each day and going to rehearsal. And each evening I would return home filled with the pleasure of working with that cast. There was so much enthusiasm, so much creativity, and collectively it was a party.

Early in techs at the Alvin Theatre, Ron Field had what could best be described as a temper tantrum. I threw him out of the theatre. It was the first and only time in my career I've ever done that to a collaborator. I did not know at the time that Ron was seriously ill. In fact, I did not know until he died of AIDS. Larry Fuller finished up the job.

I believe the history of our production was greatly influenced by its cold opening on Broadway. In addition, *Time* magazine had featured a photo of Steve and me representing the promise of Broadway's future. Expectations were so high that though the first preview was not attended by the critics, there was plenty of press the next morning—and all of it negative.

I'm proud of the preview period because Steve, George, and I soldiered on with extensive rehearsals every day. We were restaging and changing much of the book. We even threw out Judy Dolan's beautiful costumes because they were precisely that: costumes. We replaced them with sweatshirts on which we printed each character's relationship to the story. For example, Daisy Prince's read, "Next Mrs. Shepard." My original notion of choosing bits and pieces of secondhand wardrobe would have been more appropriate. The show really benefited from this period. However, audiences would not journey with us—they came to see a flop, and that was that. For the five weeks of previews, a few performances of which I didn't attend, I recall my daughter coming home from the show to report that for the first act the theatre was full and when the second-act curtain went up, it was half empty. I went to bed night after night bathed in flop sweat.

The show ran for two weeks after its opening, when of course it received bad reviews. Steve and I believe that had it not been so anticipated, it would have run as a flawed but engrossing musical. But that was not the case.

I've had many failures, but this one was the most painful. It was heartbreaking. I loved all the kids we had cast, and I knew they were having the time of their lives. And all during rehearsals, I had been convinced that it was great. I set them up as sitting ducks. And to this day, I feel personally responsible for letting them down. Surely the book was too complicated, surely the original play on which it was based had not been a success, but I bear the burden of most of its failure because I couldn't see it. In falling in love with a cast, you lose your objectivity.

As a result of *Merrily*, both Steve and I, after more than a decade of successful collaboration, thought it would be advisable to sever our partnership. Had *Merrily* been a hit, our partnership would have been sustained. But it flopped, and we both moved on. Of course, I still miss the creative sessions, which were deeply probing of character and incident, always fun, and so damned stimulating. We both went on alternate routes successfully; still . . .

After Steve and I had split up, I remember sitting in a theatre downtown, the Sheridan Square Playhouse, with Judy, where I overheard the manager of the company say, "Well, we got Sondheim away from Prince." Of course, it upset me. I felt that the body of our work together was being erased or minimized. Steve went on to collaborate with James Lapine on *Sunday in the Park with George* and *Into the Woods*—wonderful shows. And now more recently, a light has begun to be focused on the years that Steve and I worked together.

Surprisingly, Steve doesn't care about whether or not he's remembered the day after he dies; I do. Yet he's done more than anybody for the contemporary musical theatre. People forget that it did take a while for him to be recognized—and that was not because, as the conventional wisdom has it, he was too pessimistic. It was the size and the uniqueness of his talent. It took time for audiences, much less critics, to see that he was bringing to the table something new and dangerous. He was changing the musical theatre as Kern and Hammerstein had done seventy years earlier, and as Richard Rodgers did when he teamed with Oscar Hammerstein. But Sondheim is Sondheim.

And one thing for certain—we remain best friends, and the triumvirate of Steve, Judy, and Hal is as solid as ever.

Merrily has been resurrected any number of times with casts of different ages—older people, middle-aged people—but never the young cast we assembled. Some of the productions after ours were well received, but I don't think any of them have successfully dealt with the show's structural complications. As for me and my relationship to the cast, I'm still guilty, so much so that when Lonny Price put together a reunion in 2002 at the John Jay auditorium, at which the entire cast reproduced the entire show, I had no intention of attending, until Judy and Steve, thankfully, forced me. I reluctantly arrived at the reunion, and I could not have been happier that I had. It was a celebration—of *Merrily* enthusiasts in the audience and of an ecstatic cast onstage. Steve, Judy, and I sat together, and after the show Steve and I went to the stage. You would have believed that *Merrily* was the revival of a smash hit.

Most recently, Lonny Price directed a documentary of the creation of *Merrily* entitled *The Best Worst Thing That Ever Could Have Happened*. The film premiered in October 2016 at the New York Film Festival, and I regard it as a masterpiece. However, I didn't have the nerve to attend the premiere, at which many of the original cast members were present and Steve answered questions from a moderator in front of an audience of superfans.

I watched the film on my own, and I owe a huge debt to Lonny Price for his documentary, which made me finally know I had gotten it all wrong. Most of the *Merrily* kids have gone on to have excellent and productive lives, some even in the arts. And the show had represented a high point in all of their lives. Again—*whew*!

CHAPTER
32

Not every show is going to work, and in a long career you have to expect disappointments. If you have a bunch of years where everything suc- ceeds—I had five hits in a row—then sure as night follows day, there is going to be a disaster. Well, from *Merrily* in 1981 through *Grind* in 1985, I had five Broadway flops in a row. I picked them. Are you steeled when disaster strikes? I was bummed out the morning after a flop had opened, but I went back to work on a new project, not knowing at the time that I would be working on my next flop. And that uncertainty is the nature of the work, the *adventure* of the work: not even after decades in the theatre do you know how your new show will be received. Over a long career, there are lessons to be learned, and sometimes they are never learned.

I took a break from the theatre when in 1981, David Gockley, the artistic director and general manager of the Houston Grand Opera, offered me *Willie Stark*, the eminent composer Carlisle Floyd's adaptation of Robert Penn Warren's *All the King's Men*. The material follows loosely the career of Huey Long, governor of Louisiana, a dynamic and ruthless politician. I liked the material and jumped at the opportunity to work at an opera house in a city I'd never visited.

Our Willie was Timothy Nolen, a singer with first-rate acting chops. The set, designed by Eugene Lee, was a permanent structure of stairs leading to the state capitol. Embedded in the stairs at various points were old console radios, different but large, and capable of serving as pedestals for speeches and as benches for citizens to sit on to listen to Willie's voice. They were the only props on the stage. The material was terrific. Floyd, the composer of the classic *Susannah*, had delivered a complex and beautifully realized score. I thought it might work on Broadway, and I invited the Shuberts to come down to see it. And here's something I never learned: when I direct a new opera, I tend to think it can make it to Broadway. That's not why I take it on, but undoubtedly I blur what belongs on an opera stage with what is right for Broadway.

Memorably, I got to meet Robert Penn Warren and in fact hold his hand onstage during the opening-night bow. The show went well in Houston, and then even better at the Kennedy Center.

Then followed *A Doll's Life*. Betty Comden and Adolph Green offered me many suggestions for musicals. Wouldn't you know that the one that grabbed me was the idea of following Nora Helmer after she slammed the door on her husband Torvald and child at the end of Ibsen's *A Doll's House*? We observed a terrified but resolute woman leaving her overbearing husband and going into the world by herself to find work, to make a single home for herself, and ultimately to find friends and even a lover. Of course, it was a feminist tract, and that element appealed to all of us. Larry Grossman wrote the music, which was varied and excellent, as were Comden and Green's lyrics. I asked Tim O'Brien and Tazeena Firth to design it, which they did with great imagination. The show began with a rehearsal of Ibsen's play on an empty stage with a ground cloth on which tape indicated entrances, exits, tables, chairs—the usual process when rehearsing a play. At the end of Ibsen's play, when Nora slammed the door leaving her family, the ground cloth slowly moved upstage and flew along the back wall. It was stunning to observe as the show shifted into reality. Appropriately, I thought, I'd used Munch's famous paintings of the three women on a bridge (and even provided a bridge) to enhance our vision of Norway. It was an abstract element that remained unexplained, as did other Munch references.

We rehearsed in New York but opened at the Music Center in Los Angeles for a long run. Audience response was good, but reviews were mixed. We moved to New York, where they savaged us. There is a temptation when you work on a flop not only to criticize the material but also to find a reason for its failure with the critics and the public. In this case, I was certain that at that time feminism was a controversial subject and the critics took issue with it. And also I believed that they would not accept such a serious musical from Comden and Green. At one point, Nora went to work in a herring factory, and while I thought that was appropriate, there is something about the authors' reputation for lighthearted and exuberant comedy that made that incident seem ludicrous. We ran on Broadway for only eighteen previews and less than a week after the opening.

Briefly, a word about critics. I learned a long time ago not to write to a critic or to protest a negative review. You cannot win that battle. While we were out of town with *A Doll's Life*, Michiko Kakutani, a reporter and subsequent literary critic for the *New York Times*, came up to see the show and to talk with some of us. This was unusual, as in those days newspapers did not generally report on out-of-town tryouts because of the gentleman's agreement, a perfectly correct one, that you let people alone while they are working on a show. She watched some rehearsals and interviewed us; she seemed friendly, but she definitely was not. She did a hatchet job on us, writing that the show was in deep trouble. We had gotten killed by the *New York Times* before we even came to New York. Lesson: no matter how enticing an offer is proffered to visit you in advance of your opening (press agent: "It will be good for business!"), don't believe it.

In 1984 I directed Joanna Glass's *Play Memory*, a troubled-family story centering around an alcoholic father and his wife and daughter. I had a marvelous cast—Donald Moffat, Jo Henderson, and Valerie Mahaffey. You could not ask for better actors. We opened at the McCarter Theatre in Princeton where we received marvelous reviews. Alexander Cohen and his wife, Hildy Parks Cohen, immediately picked it up and took it to Broadway. The notices were mixed. The show was Tony-nominated (for best play), as were some of its performers. Nevertheless, it closed after five performances. This time I explained our failure as diminution of interest in serious theatre on Broadway. Actually, that has come to be true, but at that time it was premature.

Now I was approached by Steve Martin (another Steve Martin) for advice. He and his colleagues wanted to produce *Diamonds*, a revue celebrating baseball—our national obsession. I encouraged them. In fact, I asked them why they hadn't asked me to direct it. It had not occurred to them that I'd be interested, but I was.

There is a lot of existent material about baseball that would fit into the revue form. For example, Bud Abbott and Lou Costello's "Who's on First?" Among their friends was Alan Zweibel, a first-rate writer of comedy and a baseball fanatic. There were others—Harry Stein, Joe Stein's son; John Lahr, the longtime theatre critic for the *New Yorker*; and Roy Blount Jr., a staff writer and editor for *Sports Illustrated*. I also invited some of my friends who I thought might be interested in contributing material to the project.

All in all we had fourteen book writers, eleven composers, and eleven lyricists, including Alan Menken, John Kander, Cy Coleman, Gerard Alessandrini, Craig Carnelia, Larry Grossman, and Jonathan Sheffer. Among the lyricists were Howard Ashman, Betty Comden and Adolph Green, Fred Ebb, Ellen Fitzhugh, and David Zippel.

There was a cast of ten protean performers, including Loni Ackerman, who had just come from playing Eva Perón for years; Jackée Harry, who went on to TV stardom in *Sister, Sister*; Dick Latessa, with whom I worked in *Follies* and who won a Tony Award for *Hairspray*; and Chip Zien, with whom I'm working on *Candide* as I write this.

We gathered the material and looked for an offbeat space, settling at Circle in the Square on Bleecker Street. I used an environmental staging for the show, seating the audience on three sides; there was a baseball diamond in the middle and a small stage on the fourth wall. Tony Straiges, who designed *Sunday in the Park with George* beautifully, took on our show and delivered a happy setting for a happy revue. My old standby Judy Dolan designed the costumes and Ken Billington the lighting. Paul Gemignani was our musical director, and Ted Pappas choreographed with humor and exuberance (he went on to an estimable career as artistic director of the Pittsburgh Public Theater).

Everything was in place, and once again I had a sensational time. No metaphor for this one, just a whole lot of laughs. I couldn't imagine it being anything less than a success, which it was not. I have absolutely no idea why. End of chapter . . . well, almost.

In 1984 Fay Kanin, a celebrated film writer who had a hit on Broadway years earlier with *Goodbye, My Fancy*, sent me a film script which had gone begging and which I found fascinating. It was about a burlesque house in Chicago with black and white performers who socialize backstage but never perform together onstage. There are dangerous confrontations at the theatre and in the city. I decided that script could be shaped into a musical about violence, which had been on my mind for some time.

More and more I was witnessing acts of violence in our society.—not only on the streets, where road rage was an escalating factor, but also in the proliferation of domestic violence. And this is the lesson I never seemed to have learned: you cannot take a piece of material which dramatizes one event and warp it into something else.

The musical that evolved from this was called *Grind*. It had a fine score by Larry Grossman and Ellen Fitzhugh, containing one of the best opening numbers of any musical I've ever directed: "This Must Be the Place." But I wasn't focused on Fay Kanin's screenplay, which presented an interesting story in an even more interesting setting; I was focused on the epidemic of violence in our society. It remained for Sondheim and Weidman to succeed brilliantly with that subject in *Assassins*. Once again I was maneuvering to jam a round peg into a square hole. *Grind* closed after seventy-one performances on Broadway.

CHAPTER
33

It began ordinarily enough, while I finished dinner at Le Caprice in London. I don't recall what I was doing in that city at the time; I might've been checking up on *Evita*. In any case, across the room at dinner were Andrew Lloyd Webber and his then wife, Sarah Brightman. They invited me to take my coffee with them, and I moved to their table. In passing, Andrew said that he'd been thinking of doing a musical based on Gaston Leroux's *Phantom of the Opera* and asked if I would be interested. It is uncharacteristic of me to say yes without thinking of some reasons not to take on a project. In this case, no hesitation whatsoever: "Yes, indeed!"

Andrew and I share a great affection for Rodgers and Hammerstein's *South Pacific*. It represents one of the few great romantic musicals of our time. It's interesting about romance and musicals—you would think that most musicals would be romantic, whereas very few actually are. I think of *My Fair Lady*, which works its way to its most romantic moment: "Eliza, where the devil are my slippers?" Or *The King and I*, where the leading couple never gets any further than a gorgeous waltz. Of course, *She Loves Me* was romantic, and there are other examples, but far fewer than one would imagine. I mention romantic musicals here because *Phantom* is unabashedly romantic, which I believe is a key reason for its great and continuing success.

Phantom's metaphor was omnipresent for me. I'd always wondered why in the presence of deformity our atavistic response is to pull back, perhaps not in horror, but instinctively. And then, if we are sentient human beings, we quickly realize how irrational that response is. Years ago, when I was in the Casbah in Algiers, a leper shook my hand, and I recoiled. Then I was with George Abbott in Havana when he told me that the manager of the Tropicana was a leper who was missing fingers, and I shook his hand timidly. I shared these memories with the company on the first day of rehearsal, and I have continued to say it to new companies ever since. It is for me the reigning metaphor of the show, the concept that gives the show its human focus and along with the romantic theme supplies a good part of the power it continues to have for audiences.

Andrew invited Richard Stilgoe onto the team as lyricist. He and Andrew had had a considerable success with *Starlight Express*, and I knew him as an excellent writer, a prescient commentator who delivered much of his material on radio. Andrew had written some themes for the show, but we were pretty much at the starting gate. At one point, when Andrew felt he needed an additional writing partner, he chose Charles Hart, who had recently graduated from the Guildhall School of Music and Drama. Andrew's producing partner in the venture was Cameron Mackintosh. They had come fresh from a huge success with *Cats*, and Cameron independently had opened *Les Misérables*. Gillian Lynne (also from *Cats*) joined as choreographer. I had known her for years; she had had a long and celebrated career, first as a corps dancer and then featured in the Royal Ballet.

It was the summer of 1984; I went to Majorca for a brief spell and Andrew to his country home. Cameron Mackintosh sent me photos of the work of various designers, one of whom was Maria Björnson. The photos of her set from a production for an Ibsen play persuaded me. The set was spare, and yet it contained such atmosphere—nothing tricky, but in its simplicity there was great beauty. I chose her. We brought on Andrew Bridge for lighting design and Mick Potter for sound design. Both were standouts.

I decided I should pay a visit to the Palais Garnier, the opera house in which much of *Phantom* takes place. I contacted the management, who offered me the grand tour. There are five floors from the stage to the roof, and another five to the lake below—and I covered all that ground. It isn't actually a lake; much of Paris is built on sand, so architecturally the theatre is supported by a mixture of water and sand. It's a huge edifice, and of course I don't understand what I'm explaining, but I took them at their word. At the time I dropped a coin down a grate in the basement and heard it *plunk* into the water. I was informed that occasionally they drain much of the water and have taken publicity photos of ballerinas in rowboats.

Rising above the cellar is a series of dungeon-like staircases leading to workrooms, shops, and finally the dressing rooms. The dressing rooms are especially interesting because they have extremely high ceilings and are more commodious than what we're used to in New York. When you reach the stage, it is large, and there is some stage machinery still in the house, but mostly everything is quite modern. Upstage of the playing area behind the rear wall is a beautiful fin de siècle red damask room with small tables and chairs, in which the ballerinas of the company historically entertained their gentlemen friends, I was told, sometimes even during performances! All of this supports the relationship of our leading character, Christine, with the juvenile *vicomte*, Raoul de Chagny.

There are five floors before you reach the magnificent roof of the Garnier. There's a walking path around the lower part of the roof and gold angels mounted on the four corners of the roof, and rising from this is a dome. I was invited to walk to the top of the dome and straddle its peak. I did so, and there was a fierce wind. The fellow who took me on the tour stayed below—I'm sure it was safe, but it felt precipitous. Once at its peak, I viewed a panorama of the Place de l'Opéra and, behind it, the Galeries Lafayette—Paris's largest and probably most famous department store. The whole experience was that currently overused word—awesome. Oh yes, the management offered me a directing job: any opera of my choice. I never took them up on it. Damn!

I left Paris and returned to New York, where Andrew and I exchanged notes about progress and agreed to meet in London fairly soon. Then I received a letter from Mackintosh informing me that he would be in New York and asking if we could arrange a breakfast meeting at the Ritz-Carlton on Central Park South. I arrived for breakfast with all my documentation, which by now was pretty impressive. Photos, books relating to the subject, ideas of my own in notebooks, correspondence from Andrew: a great deal. Before I could say anything, Cameron interrupted to tell me that he'd had second thoughts—this was an English show and should be directed by an Englishman. Obviously stunned into silence, I rose from the table, gathered my materials, blurted out the f-word, and left.

I walked back to my office and told my secretary to keep all this material near at hand because "they'll be back." I've always thought it was thanks to Andrew that they were. In about three weeks I received a call and I was back on the team.

In discussing the structure of the show, we all agreed that it should open without music at an auction on the stage of the opera house—an abstract, dreamlike sequence. When directing it, I've always told the actors that they are working underwater. As the auction progresses, they applaud ritually with gloved hands in a disjointed tempo that I feel adds unease to the sequence. All of the voices at the auction are deadly, unemotional, as at a funeral. The music is introduced during the sequence, notably, by the juvenile love interest, who when we meet him is a man in his nineties in a wheelchair—fragile and more attentive to memory than to the present. Eerie. Perhaps everyone on the stage has died?

From that prologue through all of *Phantom*, which has many settings in its storytelling, each sequence must deliver a surprise, often a shock. The lighting is timed so that in some scenes the stage goes dark before the dialogue has finished, and in others the dialogue precedes the lighting.

As I had with *Evita*, I insisted on "doing" the entire show on a half-inch model. When the model had been completed, I remarked to Björnson that there were no costumes designed and we would be presenting the show to the producers in ten days. "Not to worry," she assured me—she would design fifty costumes every day, and by God she did! Five hundred costumes exquisitely designed in ten days! Maria and I showed it to Andrew and Cameron that way, and then again the first day of rehearsal to the entire company.

Maria Björnson's set designs were minimalist. Tell that to any of our audiences and they won't believe it. But it's true: *Phantom* is staged in a shiny black enamel box in which choice props are revealed. Yes, there's one huge sequence with a staircase representing the lobby of the Garnier; there are some canvas drops rendered in the style of nineteenth-century scenery; and of course, there is the roof of the Paris Opera that I climbed. There's the travelator which delivers the Phantom and Christine to his underground lair. But otherwise, there is a small dressing room, a desk, a table, no doors, *but* many beautifully designed hand-painted drapes that were by a family that Björnson had located in France. All of the drapes, like some of the scenery, are delivered from the floor rather than the flies.

Of course, there is the *chandelier*. Andrew always envisioned it in dust covers on the stage when the audience entered the theatre. The dust covers were removed, and it rose over the audience's heads to the ceiling. And it has—for thirty years. So often the show is referred to as a spectacle—it isn't. I would maintain that once again the proscenium design—the picture frame—is the key to the show. Its magnificently carved gilt figures erotically entwined. And when it is revealed after the prologue, I don't believe the audience examines it, but I'm certain that it casts a heavy erotic atmosphere over the entire show.

Speaking of the proscenium, I recall taking one trip early by Concorde to London to meet with Björnson in a warehouse where a segment of the proscenium had been mocked up in plaster. We approved it, and I caught the afternoon Concorde back to New York. Which brings up traveling, doesn't it? I took about ten trips to London to meet with the authors as the material was being written. Simultaneously, I met with Björnson to refine the scenery.

Andrew came up with the title song, and with "Music of the Night," as well as "All I Ask of You," my favorite in the show. When I first heard "Music of the Night," I thought it was such a long number that staging it would be a hell of a task. After all, for two people to simply stand onstage with one singing and the other listening seemed to beg for old-fashioned opera staging. However, when I realized that the Phantom was Svengali and Christine his Trilby, I discovered that the words in the lyrics were commands and that not only was he hypnotizing Christine, he was seducing her. That solved it.

"Masquerade," Gillian Lynne's act 2 opener, reveals about eighty figures—forty of them our cast, and the other forty dummies fully costumed and on springs. As the dancers move among them, they move as well. Early in the show's run, it fooled a lot of experts: "How can you afford such a huge company?"

For me, a major accomplishment is the three cod operas. The first is a faux Verdi *Aida*, the second a Mozart commedia dell'arte, and the third a twelve-tone Schoenberg. I'm still amazed that such a popular show features material of that nature, and that the audience seems to get it and is entertained by it . . . twelve-tone and all.

The show developed well and on schedule, and so it was time for casting. Andrew had fashioned the leading lady for Sarah Brightman, who did audition for it and seemed the personification of a nineteenth-century leading lady. Her voice and acting fit that bill perfectly. We then looked for a Raoul and our Phantom. Steve Barton, an American who was living with his wife in Germany and starring in the Theater des Westens, flew to London, and the role of Raoul was his. Parenthetically, his wife, Denny Berry, came on to assist Gillian Lynne as dance supervisor, and thirty years later she is still on the team.

As for the Phantom, we had little luck during the London auditions. I returned to New York having cast all the supporting roles and the chorus, but still no leading man. Andrew phoned about a week later to say that he believed that he had solved it: "What about Michael Crawford?" Well, I had seen Michael Crawford as a farceur; he played in Peter Shaffer's *Black Comedy* and was currently starring in a very successful production of *Barnum*, in which he was called on not only to sing but also to exhibit astonishing gymnastic prowess. But as the Phantom? Andrew supplied the missing information: Michael had been a star boy soprano and also had trained in opera. I flew to London the next day, and we met in Andrew's office. Michael sang perhaps eight bars and we'd found our Phantom.

Before the first day of rehearsal, I flew from Spain to London to meet with the prosthetic expert, Christopher Tucker, where we decided on the design of the Phantom's mask. I wanted a mask which bisected his face from forehead to chin, because it would free half of his face to express everything he was feeling. It was molded of clear thermo plastic. For each performance, the false deformity beneath the mask would be applied to his face, along with a bald pate. All of this would be discarded after each performance and replaced.

We went into rehearsal on schedule in a gymnasium in Lambeth for five weeks. I wish I had stories to tell about difficulties and surprises—there were none. I stuck to a schedule, arriving at rehearsal at 10:00 a.m. and leaving every day at 1:00 p.m. for lunch. I did not return in the afternoon, because Gillian Lynne would stage numbers and Ruth Mitchell, my assistant, would rehearse scenes that had already been blocked. This process continued for the duration of rehearsal, the last day of which we put the entire show together for the producers and the crew. It went beautifully, no hitches, and the storytelling and the score were in place.

As I was dismissing the company and telling them I would meet them at the theatre to begin technical rehearsals, one of the youngest ballet girls in the ensemble raised her hand and said that she had been delegated by the company to ask me a question. I nodded to go ahead. "What do you do in the afternoon?" And I replied, "Watch *Coronation Street*!" which was admittedly smart-ass.

Some afternoons, I would take Ruth away from rehearsal to the theatre to test some of the stage machinery. We had discovered that Her Majesty's is the only theatre in London that still has working Victorian machinery—traps, lifts, everything turned by hand. Maria loved that and designed the set to conform with it. The show was teched with candelabra cranked by hand from the basement. Ruth and I checked the travelator ourselves to prove that it was safe.

Late in the show, there is a moment when Raoul dives into the lake in the opera house from the travelator—it's one of the most effective moves in the show and very simply rendered. All he has to do is climb over a rail and drop through the stage floor to a pile of mattresses. Smoke is used to complete the illusion. Ruth took that drop. This is as good a time as any to mention that the chandelier was dubbed "Ruthie" in London, and to this day, it still bears her name all over the world.

We broke early after the Saturday run. On Monday, we convened in Her Majesty's Theatre, the crown jewel of London's West End. Slowly, carefully, we introduced the company to their new home. We showed them the arrival and departure points of scenery, paths, stairs, and traps, all in full light to avoid accidents. Given the nature of the material and its staging, I had ordered many more surprises than we needed. I had no idea which ones would work or, more relevantly, which would enhance the tension, the sense of unease we wished for our cast, but also for our audiences. So I ordered:

- A prop horse on which Christine could be led by the Phantom to his lair below. (The horse was so cumbersome, so heavy, that it moved tentatively and at a snail's pace. Good-bye, costly horse.)
- Six live white doves to bedeck the roof of the opera house and on cue to escape into the flies. (I had been assured by their wrangler that they would do as rehearsed. However, when they flew, it wasn't up, but rather across the auditorium and to the ceiling of the theatre, where they perched for two days until he could coax them down. Six unemployed doves.)
- A ratcatcher is discovered on the travelator. Purpose? To direct the audience's attention to a scene which followed with the ballet mistress and Raoul. The ratcatcher was directed to chase a swarm of rats with blood-red eyes. (The rats looked like a string of foot-long sausages pulled offstage, followed by a man with a net! The man with the net remains in the show, but I defy anyone to tell me what that fellow is doing—guess it doesn't matter.)

- Finally, I ordered costumes for two statues featured in the cemetery sequence, when Christine goes to visit the grave of her famous violinist father. They were to come alive along with lightning and thunder. Yes, and five jets of fire from the stage to scare the hell out of the audience The statues failed to shock. Goodbye statues, welcome jets of fire!

We teched for four weeks, and there were more orchestra calls than I have ever experienced. Andrew is a stickler for sound, probably more than any composer I've ever worked with. And it is worth it. Then there was a dress rehearsal when the chandelier refused to budge from the stage. Later, in previews, when it refused to plummet from the ceiling to the stage, no one seemed to care. Difficult to believe, but *Phantom* at its first preview was the same show that is celebrating its thirty-first year in London, and will rack up thirty years on Broadway on January 26, 2018.

Opening night in London was everything we hoped for, so the next move would be to Broadway. Cameron preferred the Martin Beck Theatre in New York (now the Hirschfeld) because it mirrored the capacity in London. The Shuberts offered the Majestic—I had played a number of shows there, and despite its much larger capacity, I knew it to have excellent sight lines and a large welcoming lobby, which is helpful when you have late arrivals. The Majestic is one of Broadway's jewels. Andrew and I called Cameron, and he agreed to book it. I am certain the Majestic is a key to our longevity. As each year passes, we become more of a New York landmark, plus of course our audience now includes our grandchildren. I know I've taken mine to see it.

Now it was time to contract our original triumvirate of stars—Crawford, Brightman, and Barton—for the Broadway opening. There was no problem with Barton, who is American, or with Crawford, who is a known star. However, Actors' Equity tossed us a grenade: not so fast! It seemed its board was refusing to accept Brightman as a star, insisting we cast an American. There followed from that spring and through the entire summer hearings before the board. Mackintosh, Lloyd Webber, the Shuberts, and I appeared separately to testify that Andrew had written the musical specially for his wife and surely that was his prerogative. In addition, I pointed out that it was a starring role and the producers were backing up the decision with a hefty investment, so if it failed they would be facing substantial losses. The whole damned dispute seemed ridiculous, but still they said, "No!" So Andrew decided to scrap the New York production. I'm not certain who made them change their minds, possibly the Shuberts. One thing was certain: if they continued, they were going to deny their membership the many thousands of jobs *Phantom* has provided over the years. They caved, and we set rehearsals for November, with a late January opening.

There were to be nine previews, the same number as in London, many of them purchased by charitable organizations. One preview night, Judy Prince and I were backstage with the cast when I suggested we skip that performance and dine in the neighborhood. We had to move through the lobby before they opened the front doors to let the audience in. We made a dash for it, but they opened those damn doors before we could get out. Judy blasted her way through the crowd and disappeared, but I was stuck behind, facing an elegantly dressed benefit crowd. Then I saw Donald Trump and his then-wife Ivana ahead. I had never met Mr. Trump before and have never been in the same room with him since. The crowd recognized him, and there was a buzz. As I reached the doors, a voice behind me shouted, "Hal!" I turned. "It's Donald!" I turned again. "Ivana, it's Hal." Ivana didn't know who the hell Hal was. The crowd in the lobby stopped to watch. So I asked, "Is this the first time you've seen the show?" He replied: "Is this the first time?! Is this the first time?! We saw it last night! And in London—twice!" I thanked them and turned to leave, whereupon he shouted, "Hal! Ivana and I are so proud of you!"

Moving on.

When we opened, the *Times* review was okay, not thrilled, but our audiences were. The advance sales indicated how successful we could be, dependent on the word of mouth, the Tony Awards (which we later won), and more importantly, whether we kept the show in mint condition. I had been a producer before, and I realized how difficult it was to get the original directors to revisit their shows. Cameron had had the same experience. So of paramount importance is keeping the quality of the performance: casting replacements up to their originals; a resident director on site every night; refurbishing and rebuilding scenery and costumes. What is it they say about not looking a gift horse in the mouth?

Phantom had three touring productions running simultaneously and one in Canada. Ruth Mitchell took charge of those until she died after a lingering illness. Arthur Masella, also in my office, took over the casting, direction, and maintenance of international companies. I oversaw as much as I could of them, but often there were conflicts. The US productions are maintained by our resident director (presently Seth Sklar-Heyn); David Caddick, our original musical director; Kristen Blodgette, his right hand; and David Lai, the Broadway music director.

In 2002, Maria Björnson suddenly and shockingly died at a young age. Soon after, there was an offer from Las Vegas for a version to play at the Venetian Hotel. It was designed by her original assistant, Paul Kelly. I believe it represented pretty much what she would have wished, but additions were needed to satisfy the Vegas audience's appetite for spectacle. Arthur Masella assisted me on every aspect of this version, cutting the show to an hour and forty-five minutes. Kelly and the designer David Rockwell transformed the theatre into a replica of the original Paris Opera—complete with boxes and filled with Victorian ladies and gentlemen, exquisitely costumed mannequins. Our chandelier this time descended right over the audience, stopping just in time to scare the hell out of them. The pièce de résistance was the exterior, in gold, of the front of the Paris Opera, delivered through the stage floor.

The production was awarded best show in Las Vegas by the local newspaper and ran for six years. On its fifth anniversary, the audience was invited to attend in costume. This was not so strange, as audiences had attended anniversary performances in London and on Broadway dressed as the Phantom and Christine. Our audience in Las Vegas arrived as a variety of characters. Two audience members in the front row even dressed as me, complete with glasses, beard, and a bald head. I met them after the show—they were a married couple. That night an audience member told me he had seen our show 175 times.

Phantom as of now has played to over 150 million people in thirty countries in fourteen languages. Aside from London and New York, there are productions playing in Japan and Sweden. But what gives me the most satisfaction, as we approach our thirtieth year on Broadway, is the number of Equity members who have found employment, and add to that musicians, stagehands, wardrobe mistresses, dressers, front-of-house, box office managers, ushers, and concessionaires. Also the small businesses that count on theatre productions for customers and, oh yes, parking lot owners!

Over thirty years ago, John Wharton, an esteemed senior partner of Paul, Weiss, suggested that pricing of tickets to Broadway shows should be on a supply-and-demand basis. It was logical. After all, it prevailed in department stores and almost everywhere anything was sold. However, our industry was appalled at the idea and rejected it. But he was right, and *Hamilton* has installed that policy. It keeps scalping to a minimum, and for those who can't afford Broadway prices, there are a substantial number of lottery tickets available at a fraction of the cost. Meanwhile, the creators of the show and its backers share in enhanced box office grosses. I wish we had listened to John Wharton thirty years ago . . .

 The Shubert Organization, Inc.   234 West 44th Street New York, N.Y. 10036   212 944-3700

TELEFAX

January 24, 1990

TO: HAL PRINCE

FROM: GERALD SCHOENFELD AND BERNARD B. JACOBS

Dear Hal:

      We both want to offer our heartiest congratulations to you upon the second anniversary of THE PHANTOM OF THE OPERA on Broadway.

      Obviously, PHANTOM has proved to be the most successful show in the history of theatre in this country and, undoubtedly it will prove itself to be the most successful show ever - worldwide. You certainly are to be congratulated.

          Sincerely,

GERALD SCHOENFELD   BERNARD B. JACOBS

GS:BBJ:pg

CHAPTER
34

G ilbert Bécaud, the French singing star and composer, found me when I was in Paris and asked me to direct a musical based on the film *Madame Rosa*. It was the story of a Jewish lady in the Arab section of Paris during the Nazi occupation who took care of young Arab children and witnessed the removal of some of Paris's Jewish population, first to a velodrome in the city, where they were incarcerated, and subsequently taken on trains to concentration camps. It was an excellent film with Simone Signoret in the leading role. I envisioned it as an intimate musical (on the scale of the original Paris production of *Irma la Douce*) and perhaps starring Line Renaud. I was interested and offered a good friend, Julian More, as the librettist. Before the advent of Lloyd Webber and Rice, Julian had great success with three musicals running simultaneously in the West End. His biggest hit was an inflated adaptation of the same *Irma la Douce*.

I agreed to direct it, providing it opened in Paris. I knew a successful Paris opening might ensure a successful move to Broadway. But Bécaud double-crossed me, preferring a direct move to Broadway, and against my instincts I'm afraid I caved. And because of that, whenever there were difficulties with the material during the writing process and in rehearsals, I guess I never forgave him—I behaved very badly. He died some years ago, but I still harbor personal guilt.

We headed for Broadway. For Roza (I have no idea why we changed the spelling of her name), we cast the great actress and singer Georgia Brown, who had been the leading lady in the original production of the musical *Oliver!*, and Bob Gunton for the male lead. I asked the Russian set designer Alex Okun to take on the assignment. It was an impossible one, as it required an entire rooming house onstage, in which Madame Roza's apartment was on the fifth floor. In other words, she would enter on the stage-left floor landing and would make her way up and around the set, which was really an

Escher box, until she arrived stage right back to the stage level again, only this time it represented the fifth floor. So: see photo!

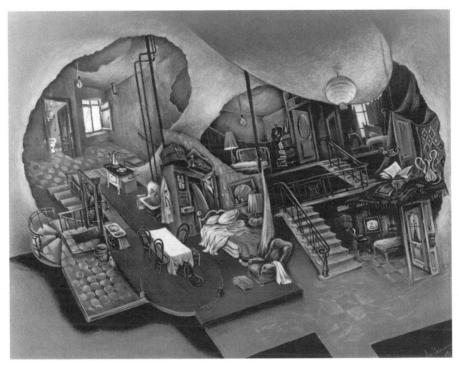

Alexander Okun's extraordinary set design for *Roza*

We finished rehearsal and opened at the Mark Taper Forum in Los Angeles. It was a huge success, selling out every night, and the reviews were fine. Then we moved to Baltimore Center Stage, where the reviews were again excellent and tickets almost immediately unavailable—it became a scalper's heyday. After a number of sold-out weeks in Baltimore, we moved to Broadway, where the reviews were hostile and we closed after twelve performances. I remain bewildered and especially regret that Georgia and Bob weren't recognized for their extraordinary performances. Georgia died suddenly and far too young, a few years later.

CHAPTER
35

In the late eighties or early nineties, I observed a seismic shift in labor union negotiations which would deleteriously affect the cost of mounting Broadway productions and change the profile of their investors. As costs continued to rise, I worried that it would affect the nature of material, and the courage of investors to take chances with uncharted territory. About that time, I received a phone call from Fred Ebb, who told me he and John Kander were considering a musical based on Manuel Puig's *Kiss of the Spider Woman*: What did I think? I thought it was a wonderful idea, particularly if we adapted Puig's novel rather than the film, which though fine was nowhere near as dense as Puig's novel.

We discovered the rights were available, and invited Puig, who lived in Rio de Janeiro, to fly up and see whether he could write the adaptation. He accepted. A slight figure, he was warm, enthusiastic, and extremely intelligent. There was an aura of fragility surrounding him; I sensed it was more physical than emotional. He was excited and agreed to take a shot at writing the libretto. Consumed by *movies*—he had written another novel with Rita Hayworth's name in its title—he would hold forth about *Gilda*, even going so far as to imitate Hayworth's first appearance. We were influenced by him to feature the glamorous elements of the forties and soft-pedal the politics. He returned to Brazil, where he began a first draft, occasionally sending us scenes. Puig did not relish the notion of a long period collaborating in New York, and it became obvious that working this way would make it impossible to come up with a libretto.

So he stepped aside, and we asked Terrence McNally to sign on, which he did, enthusiastically. Then I chose my design team: Thomas Lynch (scenery), Florence Klotz (costumes), and Peter A. Kaczorowski (lighting). Susan Stroman agreed to stage the splashy musical numbers. Terrence delivered the book, and Kander and Ebb the score, rather quickly. It appeared we were all inspired.

About the same time, I heard from a consortium headed by the producer/ general manager Martin Bell, who was working on a scheme to collect about $20 million to establish an organization called New Musicals. They would finance productions of new material, at the State University of New York in Purchase, on an experimental level to see whether they had commercial futures. SUNY Purchase had two theatres: a black box and a handsome seven-hundred-seat proscenium theatre, which could provide all the possibilities of a Broadway house. The scenery and costumes would be built on campus and production costs significantly reduced. And because it was an experimental theatre, there would be no reviews from the mainstream media or national magazines. Bell met with all of them and assured us that they would honor the embargo. New Musicals signed two more shows for its initial season and a list of candidates for three more seasons. To follow *Kiss* was a musical version of *The Secret Garden* with a score by Lucy Simon and a book and lyrics by Marsha Norman.

When we had a first draft of *Spider Woman*, I followed my usual procedure and read the book to the authors and the composers played the score—Kander and Ebb always performed their material with uncommon expertise. We began casting. John Rubinstein signed on as Molina, the Argentine window dresser who finds himself in a jail cell with a macho revolutionary. For that role we cast Kevin Gray. Our Spider Woman, Lauren Mitchell, was Puig's Rita Hayworth. We rehearsed in Manhattan. I always make room for an intern during this process, and in this case, it was a young man recommended by the Drama League named Mark Brokaw.

We opened in Purchase after five weeks of rehearsal to a welcoming neighborhood audience. The next morning, one of the New York tabloids reviewed our show, and of course the floodgates opened, and then all of the newspapers and national magazines followed suit. *Kiss* was savaged. And rightfully so. However, we weren't pretending to be ready for Broadway. (This is as good a place as any to interrupt the narrative to point out that as of 2017, the *New York Post* and the *Daily News* do not regularly review Broadway shows, nor do the national news magazines.) Anyway, we finished out the run in Purchase and closed, our future dubious. Puig had flown up for one of the final performances and he was encouraging—though I knew he knew. New Musicals folded, and the prospect of that lineup of worthy attractions sank. As for Mark Brokaw, he'd learned how *not* to do a musical.

Nevertheless, he went on to become the brilliant director of Paula Vogel's Pulitzer Prize-winning *How I Learned to Drive*. *The Secret Garden* actually made it to Broadway, but I don't know what became of the other nascent projects.

Flat emotionally, we decided to take a hiatus, but not before Fred Ebb exploded, "Whatever happened to Hal Prince? I thought I'd be working with the Hal Prince I knew." That stung. After a year, Terrence, Kander, Ebb, and I reconvened. This time I proposed we try a "Hal Prince solution" and confine our musical to prison cells—the entire show! We would make excursions into Molina's film fantasies, but always with the jail present. Our chorus, all men, would be dressed in ragtag prison gear: with torn T-shirts, filthy shorts or trousers, and an unshaven appearance—a mess.

Only the Spider Woman would be glamorous. We chose a solid-gold candidate in Chita Rivera. Then we cast Richard Thomas, the TV star of *The Waltons*, as Molina. And our revolutionary was Tony Crivello, who had followed Mandy Patinkin as Che in *Evita*. Not that we faulted any of our original artists; it was simply an effort to start anew. Still, I regret we didn't invite Susan Stroman back to the project. Subsequently, I've worked so successfully (and happily!) with her; to this day she has never referred to *Spider Woman*—some classy girl!

I asked Jerome Sirlin, an expert of projections, to design the scenery. The unit set was to be a series of jail cells, on which were projected other venues: a nightclub, a movie theatre, a warden's office. The juxtaposition of these settings on the bars of jail cells was complex emotionally and always enhanced the density of Puig's story. But who would produce our show? Given its reception, no one on Broadway was interested.

Enter Garth Drabinsky. I had worked with him when he obtained from Andrew Lloyd Webber the Canadian rights to *Phantom*, which I had directed in Toronto. Garth, who had built a handsome new theatre for *Phantom* where the show ran for ten years, wanted to know our plans. When I told him, he offered to produce the show in Toronto at the St. Lawrence Centre for the Arts. And then I was shocked to learn that Manuel Puig had died suddenly. He would never know the end of the story.

We flew to Canada for ensemble auditions when I heard that for personal reasons we had lost Richard Thomas. During those auditions, I had seen Brent Carver—well known in Canada, unknown on Broadway. He was an uncommonly intelligent and charismatic actor. We cast him.

Rehearsals went well. Vincent Paterson was our choreographer; I had seen his work in *Truth or Dare*, the Madonna documentary. We opened to fine notices for a run that entire summer. I took off for Spain, planning to return for the final week of the run. Garth intended to move directly to Broadway. I talked him out of it, because of our terrible reviews in Purchase. I suggested that we open in London's West End instead, where I predicted we'd win the prestigious Evening Standard Award. He actually believed me.

One small artistic problem remained to bother me—Chita had an important number that didn't land. While I was in Spain, John and Fred sent me tapes of a "new" one, and it was a minor rewrite of the original and wouldn't work. Another tape arrived. Again I rejected it. Fred was furious. So I asked, "Whatever happened to Fred Ebb? I thought I'd be working with the Fred Ebb I knew." It was only when I returned to Toronto that they delivered "Where You Are," a number in which Chita, à la Marlene Dietrich in a white tie and tails, sang with her boys, who in this case were filthy prisoners. Rob Marshall joined us, staging that material to perfection. It remains my favorite number in the show.

We took the company to London to the Shaftesbury Theatre. And we won the Evening Standard Award, just as I predicted.

There remained Broadway. We opened at the Broadhurst in May 1993. A curtain rose on Molina alone in his cell, and at the end of the evening, the curtain came back down as Molina kissed the Spider Woman, who represented death. Our opening-night reception was tumultuous. The show was a smash. Tony Awards that season went to our three leading players, and we were named best musical of 1993. And Florence Klotz won the Tony Award for best costumes—well, really for only *one* costume: the Spider Woman's in Act 2.

Perhaps it's worth mentioning that not a single review mentioned the Purchase experiment. We ran for 904 performances. *Kiss of the Spider Woman* was a major work and a substantial success. I don't know why it hasn't entered the pantheon of great musicals.

A few years later, Judy, Charley, and I went to Buenos Aires with *Spider Woman*, this time starring Valeria Lynch, a multitalented South American star. During this visit I located Carlos, Manuel Puig's brother, who arranged a meeting with their mother, a charming, vivacious, and extremely pretty lady. We spent over an hour reminiscing. Then I mentioned how much I regretted Manuel's absence and how I hoped somewhere, somehow, he knew we had finally done him proud. She begged off seeing the show. Carlos came to see it, and he loved it.

Around this time, a friend arranged a lunch at the Casa Rosada with the president of Argentina, Carlos Menem.

As we were ushered into his palatial office, which was humungous, I was reminded of the long walk people have described when recounting their meetings with dictators. Menem was cordial, and we sat at a round table with our friend, a translator. Everyone ordered Cokes. After twenty minutes of pleasantry, my wife said, "I'm sure you have more important things to do than to waste your time with three visitors." Whereupon he gestured to two doors off the office, and as they were opened we saw that a dining room table had been set for lunch. We stayed another hour, during which I remember specifically his asking me about the jail sequences in *Kiss of the Spider Woman*, knowing of course that Puig's book had been written about his country. What had I based these scenes on? I quickly replied, "Cuba!" Satisfied, he smiled.

After lunch, he took me out on Eva Perón's balcony; I assumed Evita's pose and Charley took pictures. While standing there, I heard a good deal of shouting from women on the street below. Menem quickly guided us back into the adjoining room and closed the doors to the balcony. We thanked him and made our way to our car.

As we left the Casa Rosada, we drove at most perhaps fifty yards to the source of the loud noise that we had heard, It was coming from older women, one standing on an egg crate and shouting into a microphone. The rest of the women were walking in a circle, each of them wearing a bandana on which was embroidered, "Grandmothers of the disappeared." These were the grandmothers of thousands of young people who during the seventies had been murdered by the generals, most of them taken by helicopter and thrown out alive into the ocean. There were few records kept of these murders, and since they had been the work of Peronista generals (Menem was a Peronista), the incidents were known by everyone but kept out of the press. The irony in all of this, of course, was that the old woman with the microphone was calling for the president to come out on the street to at least talk to them. He didn't—ever—but the protesters continued their demonstrations every Thursday at 1:00 p.m.

CHAPTER
36

In the gap year between the debacle of the first *Spider Woman* and the triumphant second version, I found myself for some months in Miami with time on my hands and a computer on my desk. Judy Prince had urged me to read the four books that comprise the autobiography of Sean O'Casey. Little compares with how engrossing they are. His story had made it to film in 1965 in *Young Cassidy*, and though I found that absorbing, there was so much more to O'Casey's story—in his own words—that was missing onscreen.

After reading the first two books, I commented on what a marvelous play they would make, and Judy persuaded me to dramatize them. I had long abandoned my goal of becoming a playwright, but as this assignment invited my using O'Casey's words, I decided to take a shot at it.

It seemed a natural for the kind of environmental staging that I'd employed in *Candide*. I called Charlotte Moore and Ciarán O'Reilly, who ran the Irish Repertory Theatre, to ask if such a project would interest them—it seemed an obvious choice to premiere the work at the Irish Rep, a company that was collecting excellent reviews and developing a devoted audience. They were more than encouraging. (All these years later, the Irish Rep is one of New York's treasures.) I went to work, and by the end of that winter I had a play, *Grandchild of Kings*, that called for three Seans: preteen, midtwenties, and the old man.

It was time to call Eugene Lee. We decided the audience would surround a playing area which included a passerelle around the entire theatre. At one end there'd be a proper stage. There would be two elevated platforms facing each other mid-theatre, and the center space could accommodate a sequence for Sean and his mother in a wagon; a schoolroom for Sean and the younger members of the cast; and a bedroom for his first sexual encounter. The stage was to be used intermittently for longer scenes. At one point there was to be a massive political demonstration featuring Maud Gonne in which ladders appeared, adding playing areas to a surrounding balcony where we would accommodate audiences. That sequence would end in a riot.

Simultaneously, we cast the show—a much easier task than you'd expect, because the Irish Rep provided employment for the best Irish actors in the United States, with visiting stars from Dublin. My first version called for four musicians and for nineteen actors to cover eighty characters. (Subsequently, schools have enjoyed taking it on because it can provide roles for eighty student actors, but other productions have used as few as thirteen performers.) I pointed out that we'd obviously need a larger venue than the Irish Rep's theatre on Twenty-First Street. Not the daunting assignment it seemed, because we located the perfect space in the Theater for the New City on Tenth Street and First Avenue. What followed was a massive and ingenious construction job.

Meanwhile, we cast the great Irish actress Pauline Flanagan as Sean's mother. Young Sean (Johnny) was played by Padraic Moyles, who went on to be the star of *Lord of the Dance*. The middle Sean (Sean) was Patrick Fitzgerald, whose charm was more than equal to his talent. The elder O'Casey (Old Sean), Chris O'Neill, was Sean. Reincarnated. In the company playing multiple roles was Brian F. O'Byrne, who went on to win a Tony Award for *Frozen* and multiple awards for the leading role in *Doubt* on Broadway.

We went into rehearsal in the space on First Avenue. The show opened in a barroom, with the entire cast ranged around a piano singing a medley of Irish songs: folk tunes, bawdy ditties, familiar ballads, rousers—the works. And everyone was tipsy. It ended on a bridge over the River Liffey, on which Sean encounters a lovely young Gypsy dancer and musicians. The music segues from "Red Roses for Me" to "Danny Boy" as Old Sean and Johnny emerge from the shadows and join Sean. Together, they share O'Casey's words, completing the second book of his biography. The rest of the company gathers as the Gypsy dances. They join hands, and Sean takes his place in the center of the circle as his family continues to move around him ceremonially. The Gypsy dances in the distance as the lights come down.

Frank Rich of the *New York Times* wrote an exuberant if critical review (I liked it), and Edith Oliver in the *New Yorker* started her notice saying that when she heard we were doing it, she thought it was an impossible task. Unabashedly, she loved it. Jerry Robbins and Steve Sondheim showed up early in the run, and surprisingly Jerry came again the next night. Subsequently, Paul Newman and Joanne Woodward made their way to Tenth and First Avenue, as did Harry Belafonte with Sidney Poitier. And Cyd Charisse came to see the show alone, and troubled to write me.

Grandchild of Kings was and still is published by Samuel French, and occasionally I hear from young actors who performed it in a school production. I wish I could say I have written a play, but more accurately I organized one. Still, I'm proud I took it on—well, more accurately, that Judy urged me to.

And the big bonus was getting to be friends with Sean's daughter, Shivaun, and his widow, Eileen, a real beauty who had been a famous Cochran girl (much like the Ziegfeld girls).

CHAPTER
37

S *how Boat*, one of America's classics, opened in 1927 with music by Jerome Kern and book and lyrics by Oscar Hammerstein II. It was in every respect a watershed production. One of the first musicals to deal with a serious subject—miscegenation—it is also (in my opinion!) a love letter to families: to the family of Cap'n Andy, Parthy, and their daughter Magnolia, and to the family of show people.

A little about show people: they are colorblind. In 1927, when this show was written, color was a shameful and paramount issue in the life of our country, but not on a showboat. Definitely not. The Hammerstein/Kern musical celebrates that. This ninety-year-old musical has an old-fashioned leavening aspect: it sugarcoats serious issues by means of block comedy sequences and considerable humor. The characters are warm, loving, and often funny.

A number was written for the original called "Mis'ry's Comin' Aroun'," and its music and lyrics are exquisite, but it was deemed too serious or perhaps too depressing for an audience in 1927, and it was cut. Also, mind you, the musical was presented by Florenz Ziegfeld, who until then had concentrated on lavish revues featuring beautiful showgirls. Because of this, he was nervous about *Show Boat*'s reception. He needn't have been, because it was a huge success on opening night and ran 572 performances—a long run in those days. The score itself contains such nuggets as "Ol' Man River" and "Can't Help Lovin' Dat Man."

It was the first time that Hammerstein dealt with an interracial relationship. During the course of the show, a mixed-race acting couple is driven off the showboat by a local Southern sheriff, and subsequently we learn that their marriage dissolved and she came on hard times in Chicago. Hammerstein returned to this subject twenty-two years later when, he wrote *South Pacific* ("You've Got to Be Carefully Taught"), and once again in *The King and I*. What's especially noteworthy about the original *Show Boat* is that it did not influence intervening musicals and that Hammerstein didn't revisit the subject for years, but that he ultimately did represents just one of his mighty attributes.

Show Boat had been revived a number of times on Broadway and across the United States, but I wasn't tempted to touch it because I didn't do revivals. Garth Drabinsky's nagging persistence is what caused me to think about it. Politically, it was right up my alley, and I love the characters. But the second act gave me some concern. Until very recently, second acts of musicals have been troublesome for a number of reasons. Often it was because they were given short shrift by their authors, depending on reprises of musical numbers from the first act and the introduction of subsidiary characters simply to keep the story ball in the air. This was not true of *Show Boat*—its problem was telling a fascinating and tragic tale in the second act that covered many years that were unaccounted for historically. A world war and a depression went unmentioned.

I resisted, until it occurred to me to write two descriptive montages to fill the periods of time missing in the original. The more important of the two describes Magnolia, our leading lady, and Ravenal, her ne'er-do-well husband, moving to Chicago and coming on hard times which break up their marriage, leaving her in a rooming house raising Kim, their little girl. Eventually, Magnolia achieves stardom in the musical theatre, Kim follows in her mother's footsteps, and the family is jubilantly reunited in Natchez, where the story originated.

Both montages would have to be staged in mime and dance (there was no dialogue). I asked Susan Stroman to take on the assignment, and she knocked it out of the park. We used source material from the score, and at the end of the major montage, she choreographed three black street dancers "inventing" the Charleston. Later in the show, when our principals returned to Natchez, the entire white company celebrated with the Charleston, which they had appropriated for their own. It was a marvelous solution.

"Ol' Man River" was clearly the theme of the show, but it was pretty much lost in the second act. Surely Hammerstein and Kern intended it as a metaphor, but in the jump across years in their storytelling, it disappeared. My solution was to thread the song through the second act. Our lighting designer, Richard Pilbrow, subtly projected the Mississippi on street scenes in urban Chicago, emphasizing the metaphor.

Garth proposed that we rehearse in Toronto, where he built a magnificent theatre in North York which would house the production. We cast Robert Morse as Cap'n Andy and my old standby Elaine Stritch as Parthy. And for Magnolia we cast my favorite ingenue, Rebecca Luker, who, aside from being beautiful and having a glorious voice, navigated a difficult assignment: she is introduced as a naive teenager and ages through the show until she achieves stardom and retires from show business. My leading man was Mark Jacoby, who had recently been our Phantom. He cut a handsome figure.

Prior to rehearsal, Garth asked me to meet with the representatives of thirty-four black arts organizations in Toronto, as they had objections to the material. I agreed, little expecting a fierce encounter. I might have guessed, however, as I had been through this before: with *Cabaret* my Jewish audience objected to "If You Could See Her Through My Eyes" ("she wouldn't look Jewish at all"), and the cast of *Grind* refused to perform the best number in the score, "We All George," which was to be enacted by a group of scantily clad black beauties dressed as Pullman porters. Obviously the number had been written to protest white passengers calling all Pullman porters "George." In that instance I caved, and the number was never seen by an audience. Retrospectively, I know it would have made a huge difference to the reception of that show.

Well, here I was in Toronto facing the same damned thing again. The arts groups protested that *Show Boat* ridiculed our black cast. They referred to Uncle Tom and Aunt Jemima and totally disregarded two facts: (1) Oscar Hammerstein was a most vocal opponent of racial prejudice, and the disapproval of segregation was central to our show. (2) The show celebrated the colorblindness of show people. For over two hours in a smallish room, the arts organizers and Garth Drabinsky and I talked past each other, and the meeting went nowhere. And then we went into rehearsal.

Oscar Hammerstein had been quoted saying, "*Show Boat* is big and must be big," and he was right. Garth was giving me everything I needed. In this case, big meant more scenery than you had ever seen in any musical, delivered with remarkable fluidity by Eugene Lee; hundreds of Florence Klotz costumes; and a perfect cast of seventy-one, half black, half white.

During those five weeks rehearsing at North York, there were picket lines every day that my cast had to cross. I gathered the company together and reminded them about Hammerstein's peerless reputation and, while acknowledging the gravity of racial tensions, pointed out that they did not exist on our showboat. The cast accepted that, and rehearsals went well. However, after two weeks I began to see that having to cross the picket line every morning made them jittery, and there was worried talk backstage. I'd bring them together again and remind them of what I had said earlier. This happened three times during the rehearsal period.

Garth, meanwhile, had contacted the famous Harvard professor Henry Louis "Skip" Gates, telling him our problem and sharing the material with him. At one point he arranged a phone conversation for the two of us, and I found Professor Gates more than sympathetic; he offered any help he could to intercede with the contentious arts organizations. Then Garth contacted James Earl Jones, familiarizing him with our problems and inviting him to see the show.

We were fortunate that on the night of the first preview, there was a torrential storm. Police on horseback were waiting for a demonstration at the entrance of the theatre, but it was dampened down by the weather. Though there were a number of people who tried to crash the theatre, no one got through to the auditorium, and we opened successfully. Mr. Jones was in the house and signed on to be the voice of our *Show Boat* in the ad campaigns. Our production was a great success from that night on. I believe it's worth mentioning that not one of the protesters bothered to attend the show during its Toronto run.

It was time to move to New York. Bobby Morse had told me originally that he did not want to move with us to Broadway: he'd had major success with his Truman Capote one-man show, and I don't think he wanted to tempt fate again. John McMartin was in the audience on the Toronto opening night, and I asked him to take over on Broadway. It's probably worth noting that Cap'n Andy is the motor of this production. As head of the family, he makes everything happen. When he isn't onstage, he's busy changing costumes and aging. There's no rest time during that three hours—and the show does run for three hours. (Parenthetically, there is a union rule that requires additional pay for everyone backstage after three hours. It was my job to get that curtain down by eleven o'clock. I made it—just about.)

The show opened on Broadway at the Gershwin Theatre in 1994. My wife suggested that on opening night during the curtain call I bring onstage everyone who was working on the show every night. Not only the orchestra, the cast, and the stagehands, but also the dressers, the makeup and wig crew. The audience loved seeing 207 people on that stage! We won five Tony Awards that year: best revival of a musical, best direction, best choreography, best costume design, and best featured actress in a musical. *Show Boat* ran on Broadway for 947 performances.

Garth then proposed sending out a national company and opening it in Vancouver, British Columbia, where, predictably, he built another magnificent theatre. And once again, *Show Boat* was a success. But Garth had not calculated how, after *Show Boat*, you could fill that theatre with enough attractions to make it pay off. Subsequently, he divested himself of it, offering it to the city for one dollar. The offer was turned down.

The New York production paid back its investment and showed a profit, as did the first national tour. Garth at that point decided to mount a second national tour. I knew that was ill advised, but nothing could stop him, and the profits of the first two companies were devoured by the third one.

Then Garth decided to open *Show Boat* at the Prince Edward Theatre in London with the entire American company. I shared with him, based on my experience with *West Side Story* many years before, that the only way to make such a company viable is, almost from the opening night, to begin replacing the American company so that within six months you have a 100 percent British company and critically lower operating costs. I went to London to get the show in front of its audience. It opened well. I offered to stay on to recast with British performers so the replacement process could begin immediately, but Drabinsky told me to leave and promised to get in touch with me soon.

About two weeks later in France, Judy Prince, while reading a British newspaper, noted that directly under the *Show Boat* advertisement was another for Garth's production of *Ragtime*, which would open in six months at the same theatre. So he'd never intended to keep *Show Boat* open, and that's why he told me to leave. I wrote Garth an angry letter accusing him of his deception, to which he replied that he'd never received anything like it before from a friend. I owed him no apology.

I knew he was in the midst of producing *Fosse*, a compilation of Bob Fosse's dances, with Mike Ovitz and Roy Furman, and we dropped the matter for the moment. A couple of weeks later, I received a call at noon from Garth—that would have been 6:00 a.m. in Toronto. It was then I learned that *Fosse* had opened the night before really well—it was a hit. And the next morning, that very morning when he was calling me at 6:00 a.m., Garth had been awakened by Ovitz and told not to bother going to his office because the locks had been changed, his computers impounded, and Ovitz and Furman were taking over. That was all I knew.

During this period, I had interested Garth in Alfred Uhry and Jason Robert Brown's *Parade*—a musical based on the Leo Frank story. However, by the time Garth was locked out of his offices, the Vivian Beaumont Theatre at Lincoln Center had taken over our show.

Show Boat closed after six months in the West End, and obviously *Ragtime* never replaced it at the Prince Edward. Garth entered a long and dreary period of litigation with the Canadian government. He was accused of defrauding investors. There were a substantial number of creditors, including seamstresses and scenic builders as well as royalty holders. He declared bankruptcy and ultimately settled for a tiny fraction of his debts. And in time he went to prison, serving seventeen months of a five-year sentence.

As I write this, Garth, with characteristic tenacity, optimism, and a healthy measure of creativity, is back in business. He is producing a musical version of the film *Madame Souzatzka*. It is written by excellent theatre veterans: Craig Lucas provided the book, and Maltby and Shire the score. It stars Victoria Clark, Judy Kaye, and Montego Glover, and he plans to open it on Broadway.

CHAPTER
38

1994 was a busy year: *Show Boat* had opened successfully on Broadway, I was informed that I would be a Kennedy Center honoree, my old friend Don Hewitt phoned to tell me that it was high time I was the subject of a *60 Minutes* interview—and I directed *The Petrified Prince* at the Public Theater.

John Flaxman, with whom I've worked on a number of projects, brought me a screenplay of Ingmar Bergman's entitled *The Petrified Prince*. In hindsight, it was for excellent reasons that Bergman abandoned it, but I thought it was a fascinating project, and I invited Ed Gallardo to write the libretto. I had seen Ed's first-rate play *Simpson Street* at the Puerto Rican Traveling Theatre. Michael John LaChiusa, a much-respected composer/lyricist, accepted an offer to write the score, and George C. Wolfe, who ran the Public Theater, was interested in presenting it.

I thought it was about how all human beings experience paralysis in one way or another during the course of their lives: there is something they want to do, but never attempt. I still believe that, but I don't think Bergman was making the same point. Once again, I was imposing something on material that simply wasn't organic. What we emerged with was a whole lot of excellent material in an inchoate project.

We opened with a puppet show in which an actress in one of the leading roles suddenly popped up on the stage, totally disproportionate to the puppets. That seemed ingenious to me. I invited Jim Henson's *Sesame Street* group to design a sequence for a lovely piece of musical material that my daughter introduced on a boat with a group of *Sesame* characters. (Yes indeed, I've cast my daughter only in failures!) In addition, I cast Alexander Chaplin opposite her. Their marriage of twenty years has been the success; the musical failed.

I wish I had unlocked the secret of that material—it had huge potential. Did I kill it simply by throwing an inappropriate metaphor at it? Or once again, as with *Merrily*, was it too damn complicated?

Moving on to *Whistle Down the Wind*: it seems to me at this point relevant to repeat that every time you have a period when your career seems to be soaring—when you have *Kiss of the Spider Woman*, *Phantom*, and *Show Boat* running simultaneously on Broadway—you're headed for a fall.

Andrew Lloyd Webber offered me *Whistle*, which he had workshopped at the Sydmonton Festival in a simple and effective presentation. The story was based on a book by Mary Hayley Bell and had been made into a hugely successful film starring her daughter, Hayley Mills. Andrew's opening number, the title song, is one of the most beautiful of any show I've ever directed. The cast consisted largely of children and a young leading man, Davis Gaines, who at that point had just finished playing the Phantom more than any other actor in its history. The lyrics were supplied by Jim Steinman, whose career was closely attached to Meatloaf. He is an intelligent man with whom I did not get along. I guess the trouble was too much theorizing and not enough action.

We opened in Washington, D.C., with an excellent cast, but the show didn't work. It had all the right elements, some in the wrong place, and there were episodes in the plot that were bizarre and difficult to accept. However, I always believed I could fix it. I still believe it could and should have been a hit. But the collaborative chemistry sank us. Over the years I have found that long memorandums from authors or producers are more debilitating than creative.

Andrew and I flew back to Washington for the final performance, at which time we were to decide whether to go on with the show or post the notice. Considering the number of kids in the cast, it was a painful quandary. However, I realized that given the nature of the collaboration, I wouldn't be able to pull it off. So we closed.

Subsequently, Andrew revisited it on the London stage with another director, and, honestly, I don't believe her version was as good as mine.

This is probably a good time to examine a question that for obvious reasons is asked of me regularly: What's the difference between working with Stephen Sondheim and Andrew Lloyd Webber? Well, for one, what's the difference between their contributions? Steve is the preeminent composer/ lyricist of this age. Andrew is a brilliant composer in partnership with a variety of lyricists, and often it works marveously.

But a better answer would address their similarities, and that's easy: both are theatre men. Both have instincts for what interests audiences. Both have a healthy respect for the empty black box and *imagination*. Both are thorough professionals. They are both artists.

A favorite photo. *From right to left*: George Abbott, Bobby Griffith, and me in tech at the St. James for *The Pajama Game*. *(Robert Phillips)*

West Side Story: the original creative team. Sondheim, Laurents, Prince, Bernstein, Robbins, and Griffith *(seated)*. *(Photofest)*

"Dance at the Gym" from the original production of *West Side Story*. *(Photofest)*

The "Politics and Poker" boys from *Fiorello!* *(Photofest)*

The first Broadway entertainment ever to play the White House. In the front row left to right are Pat Stanley, Thelma Ritter, Carol Lawrence, and Eddie Hodges. On the steps from top to bottom are yours truly, Bobby Griffith, Peter Gennaro, Frank Derbas, Sally Ann Howes, Cameron Prud'homme, Larry Kert, John Lesko, Hiram Sherman, and Hal Hastings. *(Author's collection)*

The original cast of *She Loves Me* performing "Twelve Days to Christmas."
(Author's collection)

Life magazine photo shared with the cast of *Cabaret* on the first day of rehearsal. Where was this photo taken? Nazi Germany? Nope! Little Rock, Arkansas. *(Norris McNamara/ Nancy Palmer Agency)*

Joel Grey and the original *Cabaret* company featuring Boris's mirror. *(Friedman–Abeles)*

Onstage at the Alvin Theatre, opening night of *Company*, 1970. I had just told Steve Sondheim that the *New York Times* review wasn't good. *(Author's collection)*

Top: Original cast of *Company* at the Alvin Theatre. *(Robert Galbraith)*

Right: *Company* segment in *Prince of Broadway* featuring Emily Skinner singing "The Ladies Who Lunch"—the only performer who delivered it as well as Elaine Stritch. *(Ryoji Fukuoka)*

Gloria Swanson in the debris of the once glorious Roxy Theatre. This inspired the
Aronson *Follies* set. *(Eliot Elisofon / The LIFE Picture Collection / Getty Images)*

Top: Boris Aronson's *Follies* set as it appeared at the Winter Garden. *(Robert Galbraith)*

Right: One of Florence Klotz's costumes for *Follies*. This, an homage to Erté. She executed over five hundred costumes for that show, the first of which was revealed as the curtain went up on an exquisite showgirl, who in heels and headdress measured seven feet four inches! *(Author's collection)*

Hermione Gingold (Madame Armfeldt) and her guests in *A Little Night Music. (Photo by Martha Swope © Billy Rose Theatre Division, The New York Public Library for the Performing Arts)*

Yuki Shimoda, Isao Sato, and Sab Shimono in *Pacific Overtures. (Photo by Martha Swope © Billy Rose Theatre Division, The New York Public Library for the Performing Arts)*

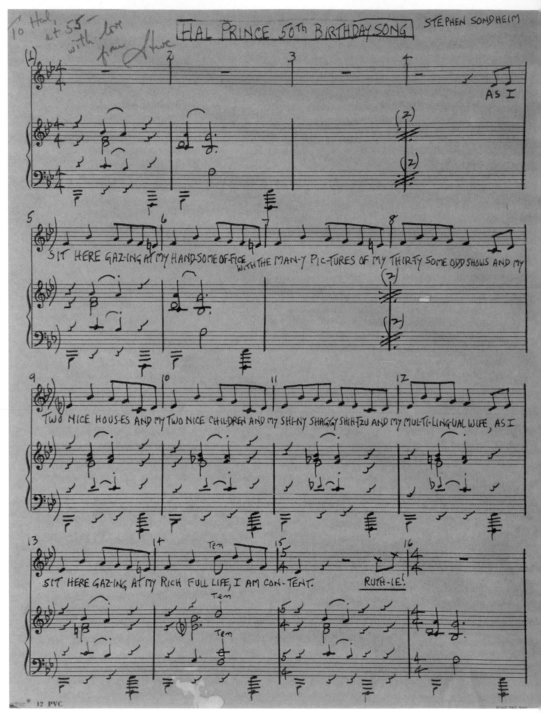

Steve wrote me a fiftieth birthday song—which was almost forty years ago.
(Author's collection)

Elaine Paige in *Evita* on the balcony of the Casa Rosada. Behind her is Joss Ackland as Perón. *(Reg Wilson/REX/Shutterstock)*

Mrs. Lovett (Angela Lansbury) and Sweeney Todd (Len Cariou) hatching their plot. *(Photofest)*

The cast of *Sweeney Todd* (sans Lansbury and Cariou) in character. *(Author's collection)*

Daisy Prince taking notes from her pop during *Merrily We Roll Along*. *(Author's collection)*

January 26, 1988, Majestic Theatre. Opening night bow, *Phantom of the Opera.* (Hope it runs!) *(Author's collection)*

Chita Rivera and the prisoners sing and dance "Where You Are"— my favorite number in *Kiss of the Spider Woman. (Photo by Martha Swope © Billy Rose Theatre Division, The New York Public Library for the Performing Arts)*

The opening night of *Show Boat* at the Gershwin Theatre. Judy Prince urged me to introduce the entire cast and backstage crew—207 people! *(Author's collection)*

The trial scene from *Parade*. Leo Frank singing the number dramatizing the false testimony given by the factory girls. *(Author's collection)*

Alfred Uhry and Jason Robert Brown at Leo Frank's grave in Atlanta. *(Joan Marcus)*

The latest reincarnation of *Candide* at the new New York City Opera. Meghan Picerno, Jay Armstrong Johnson, Linda Lavin, and Gregg Edelman. *(Photo © Sarah Shatz)*

Richard Rodgers, Ethel Merman, and I posed for this for the cover of *TV Guide* in connection with the upcoming Tony Awards. Not enough star power I guess—we were bumped for some television show long since forgotten. *(Author's collection)*

CHAPTER
39

Alfred Uhry, a first-rate playwright who has the distinction of winning an Academy Award and the Pulitzer Prize for *Driving Miss Daisy*, came to me with an idea germinated by his youth in Atlanta, Georgia, and his family's connection to an unlikely "hero," Leo Frank. Frank, the Northern relative of a prominent Southern Jewish family that owned a pencil factory in Atlanta, was invited South to be its manager. He settled there, married a Southern belle, and successfully ran the family business—until one day he was accused of raping and murdering Mary Phagan, a thirteen-year-old girl on the factory's assembly line.

The case made headlines everywhere, and though Frank was innocent, he was railroaded by the Atlanta district attorney. I recall reading that someone had said, "There are enough black men hanging from trees." That quotation appeared on front pages in the South, as well as in the North, where the case was taken up by the Jewish community and the Anti-Defamation League. For a time it seemed Frank would be exonerated, but testimony by hysterical young factory girls who had worked with Phagan resulted in a guilty verdict. He was placed in the local jail in Marietta, Georgia, where an anti-Semitic mob pulled him from his cell and hanged him. Many years later, a long-retired janitor from the factory confessed to the crime.

Alfred's interest in the story was piqued by his grandmother's Tuesday afternoon ladies' bridge club, one of whom was Lucille Frank, Leo's widow. No hesitation here: I jumped on board, and we called our show *Parade*. I asked Steve Sondheim to write the score, and at first he accepted, but then turned us down because it would have followed his musical *Passion*, a tragic love story. In other words, he wanted to diversify his next choice.

We needed to find someone else. I greatly admired Jason Robert Brown, a young composer whom Daisy Prince had discovered working late nights in a Greenwich Village café. Together they had produced, with Daisy directing,

Songs for a New World, a compilation of unrelated material, all of it stunning, with a scrumptious cast including Andrea Burns, Brooks Ashmanskas, Jessica Molaskey, and Billy Porter—every one of them a star in the making. Daisy later directed *The Last Five Years*, Brown's second musical and in my opinion a masterwork.

I wanted to work with that brilliant young composer and arranged a meeting with Alfred and Jason. They hit it off big time, and we went right to work. Garth Drabinsky, who was on the cusp of his trials, interested Andre Bishop and Bernard Gersten of the Vivian Beaumont at Lincoln Center in producing. When Jason played us "The Old Red Hills of Home," our opening, we were on our way. It was to be sung by a Civil War veteran and emphasized how divided our country was, South from North. The elements distinguishing that division have improved but, sadly, still exist.

While Alfred and Jason worked, I indulged my fascination with history: everything preceding and following the Civil War is of intense interest to me, and our project fueled that. I knew next to nothing about this story, and I had never visited Atlanta, so I scheduled a trip. I was expecting antebellum houses and to encounter Rhett and Scarlett. How wrong I was. The only connection to *Gone with the Wind* in this modern city is the Margaret Mitchell House, which stands just a few blocks from the corner where the author was struck by a car and killed. For "Rhett and Scarlett" you have to go to Savannah or Charleston or New Orleans.

I visited the Abyssinian Baptist Church and retraced Martin Luther King's steps from his childhood home to the King Center for Nonviolent Social Change.

When I returned to New York, Jason was in gear, and Alfred had written the script with great speed. We decided to heat up Leo and Lucille's relationship, which had been an arranged marriage between families. Not uncommon to the time, but for the purposes of a musical, romanticizing was a good idea. Point of fact, we developed that through our storytelling. When Leo is accused of a crime he did not commit and moves on to a brutal trial, Lucille falls in love with him, and in turn he with her. All of this culminated in a love song, "All the Wasted Time."

Jason wrote a musical through line for Leo, which I interrupted by insisting we take the audience to a happy place before plunging them into Leo's fate.

Borrowing from a short scene where Leo's jailor informs him that he has been reprieved, Jason wrote an exultant "This Is Not Over Yet."

Interruption! Many years earlier—in fact, the morning after *South Pacific* opened—when George Abbott called me into his office to ask what I had learned that night from that triumphant show, I asked him, "Why did Emile de Becque [Ezio Pinza] make such a fool of himself in front of Nellie Forbush [Mary Martin] singing and dancing 'I'm Gonna Wash That Man Right Outta My Hair'?" Abbott explained that it is valuable to place a happily giddy moment before you pull the rug out from under your principals. In this instance, the dark event was Nellie discovering that Emile has Polynesian children and she could not accept it. Flash forward: "This Is Not Over Yet" is soon followed by Leo's hanging.

Pat Birch signed on as a choreographer. She has a particular gift for dramatizing character in movement. She doesn't pay too much attention to counts, preferring to layer character onto movement. In her work, no performers dance simply to dance; they are acting through dance, which is immeasurably important. It also makes it possible for you to animate nondancers to favor their angularity and their energy, instead of having them dance pretty-pretty, which often robs a character of—what else—character. (Incidentally, Patty was a mainstay of Martha Graham's company. I was delighted when she brought Graham as her date to the opening of *Pacific Overtures* in 1976.)

Early on I thought of Brent Carver for Leo, because so much of Leo Frank's character is buttoned-down, stiff, a bit cold and unyielding. I knew Brent could mesmerize our audiences capitalizing on those untheatrical qualities. And then I got to cast a lady I'd been crazy about for years, ever since I saw her in *John and Jen*: Carolee Carmello. She was hardly my discovery; the critic who reviewed that show had been in love with her for years—I was just catching up. She has a beauty and vulnerability impossible to manufacture and also a glorious voice.

We rehearsed in New York and it went very smoothly. Jason had an office off the rehearsal room, and Alfred was always near at hand. I haven't mentioned it yet, but I don't like authors to watch rehearsals, because there's a tendency for actors to look directly at the authors and bypass the director. However, I like the authors near enough so they can come in and see if I'm on the right track.

The entire process was a labor of love and commitment by the company as well as the creators. The opening number, "The Old Red Hills of Home," is quite simply a killer. And it was delivered by an older character actor—Don Chastain—who had been my romantic lead in *It's a Bird . . . It's a Plane . . . It's Superman* thirty years earlier. He was perfect as a Civil War veteran establishing the pride of the Confederacy. Though the Civil War's effect morphs into various and unpredictable political shapes, at the heart of that war is so much that still gives us trouble.

All went well with one caveat: Brent is such a sensitive artist that he locks his dressing room door for the length of the show. It's impossible to reach him at intermission with any notes. He's not remotely difficult; it's his process. A large part of a director's responsibility is dealing with how different actors develop character. Some actors work from the outside and move in over a rehearsal period to explore motivations, while other actors start from the inside and end up putting on the false nose, the wig, and the eye shadow. Brent works unlike any actor I've ever known—no putty, no false noses. And what he achieved internally is something of a miracle.

We got through tech rehearsals smoothly, and I confess, in all my naiveté and hubris I thought what we had come up with was an Arthur Miller musical. On opening night, there was a party in the lobby of the Beaumont, where Carroll O'Connor found me and said, "You're a brave man. This is a lot for you to ask an audience to take in." I should have known then that this was a warning sign.

Our reviews were okay, some quite good and some mixed. But of course it was treated respectfully.

Judy Prince invariably gets to the point. In this case: "You walk into a theatre and there's a huge tree, and you're going to see a musical about a man who was unjustly hanged. So for the balance of the evening, you look at that tree knowing he'll be hanging from it!"

We ran for only two months. Jason and Alfred both took home Tony Awards, and subsequently our show has had a rich afterlife. Colleges love to take it on. I've seen only the NYU production, and it was first-rate.

Speaking of Jason Robert Brown, he's collected three Tony Awards. He's still a young man, but up till now he's never had anything that's run a long time. Because of my association with a number of other serious artists who have experienced the same disappointment, I've come to think of it as a badge of courage, not only of quality. I know what people want to see, but I don't pick projects with that in mind. And if I did, I'm certain I wouldn't make them hits.

Jason is currently working with the playwright Jonathan Sherman and Daisy Prince on an audacious new musical. Recent history represents a real change in Broadway's taste—new audiences are welcoming a break with tradion, encouraging young artists and fresh ideas. Maybe this time . . .

CHAPTER
40

Michael Parva, who has run the Directors Company for many years, asked me whether I would be interested in a program to develop new musical material. I was. Early on, I admired *Ness*, a musical written by Robert Nassif and Peter Ullian. It had a marvelous score, and Ullian wrote a uniquely quirky, funny, and valuable book. Ness was Eliot Ness, the crusading cop famous for stalking criminals during the Prohibition era. It wasn't quite like anything I'd seen, breaking the rules in all the right ways. When I saw it in a workshop at the Directors Company, I thought it had the makings of a swell musical. I'm not certain how this happened, but it was premiered at the Denver Center Theatre on a thrust stage, which was dead wrong. It needed a proscenium and a small space so you could isolate segments, utilizing the close-up technique that I think can be so valuable in the theatre. It failed in Denver, and it never really recovered. I should have committed myself to it, but there's more to the story.

I did commit myself to *The Flight of the Lawnchair Man*, a one-act musical by the same authors. Back up a little: there was a theatre in Philadelphia on the Avenue of the Arts which flatteringly was named for me. It was the idea of Marjorie Samoff. She had taken two small movie theatres on Chestnut Street that I was familiar with when I went to Penn and combined them to make a proper auditorium. In fact, it was quite an accomplishment. She decorated the lobby with Al Hirschfeld's portraits of all the young creative talent working on Broadway.

Because it was named after me, I figured I had better work there. The best I could do was come up with a notion of overseeing three one-act musicals called, what else, *3hree*. I would direct one, Brad Rouse in my office another, and Scott Schwartz the third. I chose a story based on an eccentric man who tied a hundred balloons to a lawn chair and lifted off to the sky. My authors created a plot, dramatizing the protagonist's obsession with flight and his rejection from flight school. They added a girlfriend and a next-door neighbor, a womanizing pilot. It was extremely funny.

Scott Schwartz chose a one-act based on an F. Scott Fitzgerald–like short story written by John Bucchino, a hugely talented composer.

Rouse's choice, *The Mice*, was the most difficult and for my money the most successful. It told the story of two people who were in love, but their affair was burdened by the fact that the man was married. They chose suicide as their solution. Ingeniously, the suicide was staged as an Astaire-Rogers dance, in which with decorous lifts the couple triggered gas tanks, which ultimately took them to another world. Difficult, eh? Well, once again the most difficult assignment was the most potently successful artistically.

However, *The Flight of the Lawnchair Man* was the winner from the critics' point of view. Michael Arnold choreographed it hilariously. The central number introduced Charles Lindbergh, Amelia Earhart, and various other aviation heroes, as well as Alex Trebek from *Jeopardy*. Our cast featured Christopher Fitzgerald, Jessica Molaskey, Rachel Ulanet, John Scherer, and other favorites of mine. Its *New York Times* reception resulted in an offer from Gordon Davidson to take *3hree* to the Ahmanson in Los Angeles. Chistopher Fitzgerald, who was stunning in the show, refused to travel with it; Eddie Korbich, our replacement, did a fine job. Gracious as Gordon was, the Ahmanson was too big a house for us; we should have played the Mark Taper Forum. The intimacy the show required was lost on that vast stage.

When we got back to New York, I suggested to the authors that we had the makings of a full musical. In other words, keep what we had as a second act and devote a first act to establish why our hero had become obsessed with flying: how he had been rejected from flight school, contemplated suicide, but ultimately came up with the balloons and the lawn chair. I thought the first act would provide heft and the second act would wrap up a successful evening. Nassif and I disagreed about the solution, and unhappily I could not persuade him to see things my way. So I left the show, the authors mounted a version at the Goodspeed Opera House, and that was the end. I still regret it, but even more I regret that Ullian and Nassif haven't had the careers they deserve.

CHAPTER
41

Carol Burnett came to me for advice. Whom would I recommend to direct a play that she and Carrie Hamilton, her daughter, had written about Carol's life? She'd had a difficult childhood with her mother, who was an alcoholic. She lived in the same apartment complex with her grandmother, whom she adored, and their escape was going to the movies. At one point Carol was an usher in the Warner Bros. Theatre on Hollywood Boulevard. I loved their play, and I asked why they hadn't thought of me to direct it. In retrospect, I think I pinned them into a corner, though Carol would deny that.

As we began the casting process, it was discovered that Carrie had developed a brain tumor, which ultimately was fatal. It was devastating for Carol and also for all of us who loved Carrie. Suddenly, the play was even more important than just Carol's autobiography. We contacted the Goodman Theatre in Chicago, managed by Roche Schulfer, a longtime friend whom I had met some years earlier through the director Greg Mosher; I admired their creativity and management skills. I sent Roche the script, and he agreed to produce it. We had titled it *Hollywood Arms* after the shabby apartment Carol shared with her grandmother.

We got to casting in New York. Linda Lavin accepted the role of Carol's grandmother. As you know from reading this, Linda has been a mainstay in my career, starting with *A Family Affair*. And as I write this, I am directing her as the Old Lady in a new production of *Candide*. We cast Michele Pawk as Carol's mother (she received a Tony Award for her performance), and Donna Lynne Champlin played Carol as an adult in the second act, launching her career on the *Garry Moore Show*. Frank Wood, a magnificent actor, played Carol's father.

We opened in Chicago to one excellent and one carping review. We worked well in Chicago. We moved to the Cort Theatre on Broadway and played only 109 performances. I know it was a terrific play and that we did right by it, but hindsight has made certain mistakes obvious.

Everyone expected the show to be hilarious, considering it was a play by their beloved Carol Burnett. I'll bet some of them even came expecting to see Carol in it. And then there was an invitation from Oprah WInfrey for Carol to be a guest on her talk show. Carol stipulated that there must be no mention of Carrie's death, and Oprah passed. I should have realized that as sensitive as this was to Carol, Oprah would have been equally as sensitive in discussing it. The Winfrey exposure might have made a difference to the outcome. Still, I respect Carol's decision. Really, it gets down to this: we never knew how to market this show—to prepare audiences for what it was really about, not *The Carol Burnett Show*. It's a fine play, and it might have had the run and the acclaim that it deserved.

Hollywood Arms was a beautiful and painful experience, and Carol and I ended up close enough friends that she refers to me as the brother she never had. And Lord knows she's the sister I never had.

CHAPTER
42

Early in my friendship with Steve Sondheim, he believed there was a musical based on Alva Johnston's biography of the Mizner brothers, Wilson and Addison, a story of two colorful and creative charlatans and their adventures in the gold rush and journalism. The only woman in their story was their mother. I believe Wilson was something of a womanizer, but I always suspected their brotherly relationship was weirdly incestuous, and therefore I was not interested.

Steve, still interested over the years, invited his frequent collaborator John Weidman to sign on. They first presented the piece, titled *Wise Guys*, at the New York Theatre Workshop in 1999, directed by Sam Mendes. I went to see it, and I didn't like it. They asked to see me in the office, and I blurted out in uncharacteristic Flo Ziegfeld fashion, "Where are the girls??? Bring on the girls!" And we did.

I suppose I talked myself into directing the show for one reason: I missed Steve. I wanted to be in a room with him again, working together. It had been such a long time, and the minute we picked up, it was as if the years between evaporated. I called Roche Schulfer again at the Goodman Theatre and offered him our project. Without hesitation, he said yes. Obviously, another Sondheim-Prince collaboration was enticing. Steve and John retitled the show *Bounce*.

John created a role for Michele Pawk, who had just won the Tony Award for *Hollywood Arms*. She would play a dance hall girl and would be the love interest for Wilson. Steve wrote a delightful love song for them called "The Best Thing That Has Ever Happened."

Most of the first act took place in the far West, and as the brothers moved across the country, the show became a kind of pioneer history of the United States. We used a covered wagon as the show's metaphorical symbol. In the second act, they settled in Palm Beach, Florida, where Addison Mizner became the most successful architect of that period. The Mizner brothers were instrumental in establishing that city as a watering hole for some of the wealthiest, most fashionable, and most powerful families in our country. So many of the great mansions in Florida were designed by Addison Mizner. His brother Wilson remained a writer.

I asked Eugene Lee to design the show, and he accepted. What I didn't know was that his production of *Wicked* was playing in San Francisco and taking up most of his time. He delivered a desultory design. There was only one moment in the second act which was up to his high standards: before the audience's eyes, a stretch of uninhabited Florida coastline transformed into huge, opulent mansions for the wealthy. Think Mar-a-Lago! But that's really all he delivered, and in fact he never revisited the show while we played in Chicago. Happily, his designs for *Wicked* have made him financially secure.

We cast Howard McGillin as Wilson Mizner. He had played the Phantom on Broadway and was an early replacement for Molina in *Kiss of the Spider Woman*. Richard Kind, a famous face and name in television, played Addison Mizner. As the mother, we cast Jane Powell, the movie star. And Gavin Creel, a newcomer, played Addison's lover. Predictably, his career has taken off—he's special. All of them were fine. And the show was fine—but just fine, not exciting, more intelligent than entertaining.

On opening night in Chicago, I recall John and Steve telling me in the bar next door how they thought we had saved the show, but we hadn't. We moved from Chicago to the Kennedy Center, but it stayed pretty much the same. We left *Bounce* in Washington, which regrettably I suppose was fine with me. Years later, Steve and John came back to it, erased "the girl," and recast the mother as a tough broad, and John Doyle directed an entirely new version. It opened at the Public Theater under a new title: *Road Show*. Steve and John liked it. I didn't any more than our version. Wilson and Addison ended up in a sleeping bag together, which I guess is why I turned the show down initially all those years ago.

CHAPTER
43

Probably the most inspired casting I've ever done was asking Lotte Lenya to be a principal in the original production of *Cabaret*. After all, she not only was the consummate artist, she was Bertolt Brecht and Kurt Weill's leading lady, and she represented Weimar Germany. Her personal story remains extraordinary. Born in an upper-middle-class family, she always sang, but her father told her she was too ugly to work as an entertainer and should probably take up streetwalking. Which she did. Briefly. However, undaunted, she auditioned for a Weill revue, he cast her, and they fell in love and married.

Then on January 30, 1933, Hitler became chancellor of Germany. Weill, being Jewish, immediately left for the United States as Lenya was touring as Juliet on the road. They divorced. Within a year, Weill sent for her, and they remarried and settled for a time in California, ultimately moving to New York.

I knew much of this even before I met Lenya, and the rest I learned over the course of working on *Cabaret*. She was a brilliant lady, and no one could sing Weill as she did. In *Cabaret*, Kander and Ebb wrote two numbers in the Brecht/Weill style for her, and she triumphed. Curiously enough, it was the first time that she had landed as a Broadway star. Earlier, Off-Broadway, she had resurrected *The Threepenny Opera* for a successful long run at what is now the Lucille Lortel Theatre on Christopher Street.

I'd always been a huge fan of German musicals, abstract and gritty as so many of them were. And I love Weill. Not so much Brecht, though since *Cabaret* many connect me to the Brecht tradition. (I would much prefer a more accurate connection to Meyerhold.) Little wonder that I thought the Lotte Lenya/Kurt Weill marriage would make a fascinating subject for a musical.

Alfred Uhry agreed, and we went to work in 2005, using Weill's songs to structure a proper musical. I asked Pat Birch to choreograph. To design the show, I chose Beowulf Boritt, a young designer I had discovered at Ming Cho Lee's clambake at the Library for the Performing Arts some years earlier. (It was the first presentation of graduating seniors from theatre design programs all over the United States. It took place on Memorial Day weekend, and over the years I've worked with half a dozen designers from those conventions.) When I first was introduced to Beowulf, I didn't have anything for him, but my daughter Daisy was directing Jason Robert Brown's *The Last Five Years* and asked whether I could recommend any young designers. I sent her Beowulf's résumé. They met and Daisy cast him for the assignment, so I guess I followed in her footsteps.

LoveMusik was the story of an open marriage. Clearly Weill and Lenya were crazy about each other, but Lenya had many affairs, and in the mid-1940s Weill even wrote *The Firebrand of Florence* for Lenya to star in, opposite one of her lovers. What Lenya did not know until rather late in their marriage (Weill died at the age of fifty) was that he had a mistress in California. At his funeral (which was attended by their next-door neighbor and collaborator Maxwell Anderson; Moss Hart, another collaborator; and a number of their friends), Lenya said good-bye to him, and then introduced a mysterious woman in black—the other person in Weill's life, and the one who Lenya felt should be the last to say good-bye to him. Now, how's that for musical material?! That was the story we told. As Kurt Weill, we cast the protean Michael Cerveris; as Lotte Lenya we chose the equally gifted Donna Murphy.

We approached the nonprofit Manhattan Theatre Club, and they accepted. It seemed the ideal place to premiere our musical. Our good friend Marty Bell found the enhancement for the show, putting together a group including Chase Mishkin, Tracy Aron, Aldo Scrofani, Roger Berlind, and Debra Black. There were other generous producers, all of whom seemed more interested in art than commerce.

We ran our fifteen weeks at MTC, but there was no possibility for a move. What mostly disappointed me was that the stars were nominated for Tony Awards, but the show wasn't. I know it should have been. A portion of Ben Brantley's review in the *New York Times* is worth quoting because it's curious:

This bio-musical about the marital and professional relationship of the German-born composer Kurt Weill and the actress Lotte Lenya, directed by Harold Prince, is sluggish, tedious and (hold your breath) unmissable—at least for anyone who cherishes stars who mold songs into thrilling windows of revelation.

On the other hand, the most notable of the other reviews was from John Simon (no pushover he!) of Bloomberg News:

If you're looking for a musical that leaves its recent and current competition miles, if not light years, behind, "LoveMusik" is it.

Judy Prince believes *LoveMusik* contains one of the most potent staging moments of my directing career. After Weill and Lenya agree to separate, he packs a bag of clothes to leave, in the course of which, alone onstage, he sings "It Never Was You," dropping the piece of luggage as he drifts out of the spotlight into the darkness. Death. The bag springs open, scattering his clothes on the stage. Lenya appears, steps into the spotlight, kneels, and places his clothes back into the suitcase. Blackout.

CHAPTER
44

In the 1930s, my father had a seat on the New York Stock Exchange, and my family lived very well indeed. We had a house in the country, a Pierce-Arrow, and a beautiful apartment opposite the American Museum of Natural History. After the Depression hit us, we moved into a small apartment where we shared the floor with an old couple. One day my mother said to me, "Be kind to our neighbors. Mr. Zweig's brother died yesterday."

His brother was Stefan Zweig, the celebrated Austrian writer. When the Nazis occupied Vienna, Zweig had relocated to Petrópolis in the hills outside Rio de Janeiro. There, unable to live away from his beloved culture, he committed suicide. I began to read, and adore, Zweig. And because of Zweig, I began to read Joseph Roth, his good friend and an important writer.

Roth had started writing what the French call *feuilletons*—random observations of life, often political—for a daily newspaper in Vienna. Then he wrote books, among them *Hotel Savoy, Job, The Antichrist*, and the amazing novel *Radetzky March*, which he followed with *The Emperor's Tomb*. I wanted to fashion a musical based on one of his novels, *The Tale of the 1002nd Night*, using songs from classic Viennese operettas. I sent the book to Richard Nelson, the esteemed playwright, who responded positively.

We went to work. Nelson fashioned a libretto that would include material from both Strausses, Johann Sr. and Johann Jr.: *Die Fledermaus, Eine Nacht in Venedig* (*A Night in Venice*), *Wiener Blut*, and *Der Zigeunerbaron*. We invited Ellen Fitzhugh to write the lyrics and titled our show *Paradise Found*.

Briefly, *The Tale of the 1002nd Night* concerns a shah with a huge harem who is unable to make love. In an effort to stimulate him, his chief eunuch takes him to the various capitals of Europe, where he fails to become inspired. When they arrive in Vienna, the shah is feted at Emperor Franz Joseph's palace, where his eyes light on an exquisite woman who awakens his dormant desire. The only problem is she is Elisabeth, the empress of the

Austro-Hungarian Empire. What follows is complicated and extremely well dramatized by Nelson.

Because the score was limited to familiar and celebrated Viennese waltzes, there was little interest in the commercial theatre for our project. We consulted Nelson's agent, Patricia Macnaughton, who unfortunately came up with the Menier Chocolate Factory, a tiny venue in the Southwark section of London. Formerly a chocolate factory, it is now a theatre with a capacity of 150. We rehearsed in New York. Susan Stroman choreographed, and our cast featured Mandy Patinkin, Judy Kaye, Shuler Hensley, Kate Baldwin, John McMartin, and Nancy Opel—all of them heavy hitters.

After four weeks of rehearsal, we had a week of invited previews in the rehearsal hall. They were warmly received, everyone loving the show. We accepted the invitation to the Menier, even though it was a polar-opposite venue for our lavish, modern Viennese operetta. That may be the worst decision I've ever made in my career, and I will not lay blame (though I'd love to).

We arrived in London to find that our scenery was lost "somewhere in France." My original arrangements were to rehearse on the set the minute I arrived with the company. But that didn't happen, and most of our tech time was taken up lighting an empty space. The sets arrived just in time for the opening, and to put it mildly, we were rejected. And they were right.

I harbor ill feelings about this experience, because I know how marvelous that material is and how much damage the decision to play the Chocolate Factory caused the project. At the time we played the Menier, there was a prevailing trend of taking large musicals and compressing them. Casts, orchestras, sets—all were reduced, and the Menier's scaled-down versions of *La Cage aux Folles*, and *A Little Night Music*, among others, had been critically acclaimed. However, our material could not be minimalized. We were as wrongheaded as the theatre that did not really welcome us.

Parenthetically, Rob Marx, who had been executive director for the Library for the Performing Arts and now is director of the Fan Fox and Leslie R. Samuels Foundation, attended the opening night with Barbara Fleischman, a close friend and a generous supporter of the arts. Many months later, he said to me what I should have done when I saw the space and in particular when the scenery did not arrive: we should have performed the rehearsal-space version, and I should have announced it as such to the audience on opening night. No scenery. No costumes. That's the only way it would have worked there. I wish to hell he'd said it to me before we opened.

I still love the *Paradise Found* material, and I hope to interest an opera company in mounting a production of it, as it should be seen. The music is irresistible, and the book and lyrics as good as they come. Enough years have passed now to revisit it, and I am determined to do so.

CHAPTER
45

S o what's in the future?

By the time this book reaches the public in mid-September of 2017, I will have opened *Prince of Broadway* (Steve Sondheim's title) at the Samuel J. Friedman Theatre for the Manhattan Theatre Club on Broadway. They're billing it as a celebration. I think of it as a biography of a sixty-two-year career.

Susan Stroman is co-directing and choreographing; and David Thompson, her frequent collaborator, has written the narrative. Jason Robert Brown is the musical supervisor and has written a number to open and close the show. Beowulf Boritt is designing the sets in homage to the originals; every set is as close to the original as possible and bears the name of its designer. The same goes for the costumes, which are the work of William Ivey Long. And my lighting designer is Howell Binkley—as talented as he is patient. (Over most of these many years I've depended on Howell and the redoubtable and equally patient Ken Billington to deliver the lighting.) John Weston is providing the sound, Paul Huntley, touched with genius, the wigs, and Angelina Avallone is doing the makeup for nine actors covering seventeen musicals. The show is cast with favorites of mine: Chuck Cooper, Janet Dacal, Bryonha Marie Parham, Emily Skinner, Brandon Uranowitz, Kaley Ann Voorhees, Tony Yazbeck, and Karen Ziemba.

None of this would have happened without the creative support of Kumiko Yoshii and John Gore of Broadway Across America, and Jeffrey Seller, who really needs this after producing *Hamilton*.

We've been working on the show for five years now. It was entirely the idea of a Canadian producer, and I backed into it. After less than a year, he dropped out, I believe because he thought it would be too costly. But by then I was hooked and my collaborators and I have stayed with it all this time. My main goal: stage it the way you would today, don't attempt to replicate the original. It takes the juice out of the process.

Our show received a bracing blood transfusion when a group of Japanese investors at the Umeda Arts Theater invited us to bring the entire production to Tokyo. Which we did in the fall of 2015, where it was received enthusiastically. We returned to New York having learned from that nine-week sold-out run what changes to make for America. In essence, the text is more specific and informative for an American audience, many of whom know these shows.

I know I have a reputation for doing "dark" musicals, and certainly I have done shows to create controversy, to make political or social statements that seemed important to me at the time. Once I found my footing, I rarely did shows "just to entertain"—it never occurred to me, though I began my career working alongside George Abbott, whose goal was solely to entertain. *Prince of Broadway* is more about entertaining the audience, and I imagine Abbott would approve.

I also realize that putting on a retrospective of your own work today may seem a farewell, but this is not my intention. I have plans, projects which excite me. And possibly, just possibly, I can schedule a meeting with authors the day after we open.

There's a revival of *Evita* in the works exactly as originally produced and directed. Larry Fuller is on board choreographing, and Tim O'Brien and Tazeena Firth's scenery and costumes are being replicated—identically. Dan Kutner, who has been in my office for over a decade and is a director in his own right, is preparing it for an opening in Johannesburg in October 2017. Fuller and I will catch up with it during rehearsals. From Johannesburg, it's set to open in Cape Town and tour Southeast Asia, Japan, Taiwan, and possibly China. Then it will be recast in Australia for an extended run at the Sydney Opera House.

I am determined to persuade Andrew Lloyd Webber and David Ian, its producer, to come back to Broadway. It will have been some time since the most recent revival, which didn't serve the material well. I'm certain that our audience is ready. *Evita* has always been one of the most satisfying experiences of my career.

Over the years, my work has taken me to Germany, to Austria, to Japan, to Russia, to Canada, to South Africa, to Mexico, and to Argentina. Unabashedly,

I'm hooked on German expressionism, on traditional Kabuki, on the work of Meyerhold, of Piscator, and of Brecht. Also, Orson Welles, Bergman, and Fellini. The list could be far longer, but the point—what is the point? They've enriched me and influenced my work in the theatre.

Mindful that for so much of my life I've worried about the balance between work and family, I've come to accept that I have two families. Just as *Show Boat* celebrates a family and the family of show people, so has my life. I've always thought I had few friends, but no, I have many friends: the actors, the authors, the composers, the choreographers, the designers—*the artists*. For those of us who work in the theatre, there are no borders. We are family.

And I suppose, because of both families, I can finally admit I did get here from there.

IN CLOSING

What follows is a keynote speech that I gave at a conference hosted by Broadway Across America that was attended by producers, directors, theatre owners, and performers. The conference took place in 2005 at The Fontainebleau Hotel in Miami.

Little known fact: I was president of the League of New York Theatres in 1964.

I had been impressed into the job by Leland Hayward and Irene Selznick, two of Broadway's most prestigious producers. I had previously shown little interest in that organization. I imagined it to be an old fogeys' establishment. And, to be honest with you, I imagined they considered me a lucky twerp.

But Leland and Irene picked me precisely because I was an outlier. To be truthful, I stayed on only a few years because I had yet to realize how important collective bargaining was. And I had an insatiable hunger to be an artist.

I had not yet realized that producers could be creative. Or, more accurately, that they should be.

Surely, they may not be writers or designers, actors or directors, but producers should have an artistic sensibility.

But today, the producing population has been infiltrated by investors who assume the job title of "producer."

In the days when I was producing, I had 175 investors. They were press agents, company managers, actors, stagehands, and, of course, a few of my parents' friends. But the names of producers above the title were never more than three.

If you are a creative producer with an impressive track record, investors should have no serious role reading a script, contributing to the casting of a show, approving its decisions, and—guess what—attending the meeting the day after a show has opened and giving advertising advice.

Look, I certainly know it was easier then. The disproportionate cost of producing today has changed the relationship between producers and potential investors. But I firmly believe that investors should bet on creative teams and let them make the decisions.

Another point: over the years, surely you know that we have accepted escalating costs and haven't sufficiently curtailed them. When I started, the cost of mounting a musical averaged $250,000 and a straight play was $100,000.

My career began with the adaptation of a book called *7½ Cents*, about a strike in a pajama factory in Dubuque, Iowa. We had no experience raising capital. George Abbott agreed to direct it and asked if he could do the first backers' audition at Howard Cullman's apartment at 480 Park Avenue. We agreed, and the Cullmans gathered about one hundred of the major Broadway investors. When the Cullmans invested, everyone followed. And if they abstained, everyone followed them as well.

Abbott began with these words: "This show is about a strike in a pajama factory." And you could feel the collective deflation in the room. The composers played selections from the score, including "Hey There," "Hernando's Hideaway," and "Steam Heat." And at the end of the presentation, we raised zero. Zip. Zilch. Nada.

So, the next day, I thanked Mr. Abbott and took over the chore of raising capital. It was not so much of a chore then; it was actually a hell of a lot of fun. That was then.

What followed were eleven auditions in friendly living rooms, passing a bottle of Scotch, some paper cups, and a couple of packages of peanuts and pretzels.

My speech began with me saying, "Our show is *Romeo and Juliet* in the Middle West. The Middle West is a very popular location these days, thanks to the Broadway hit *Picnic*, blah, blah, blah."

And in those eleven auditions, my presentation successfully raised our capital.

It took fourteen weeks to pay off our first hit musical. Of course, if you had a moderate hit, it would take longer. I know because *Company*, which I consider something of a watershed project, showed a profit after twenty-one months and, more often than not, played to 60 percent capacity.

And because you could return the investment on less than full capacity, we were able to produce a new musical every single year. And some of them were blockbusters. A long run in the 1950s and 1960s was one thousand performances. I needn't tell you how that has changed today.

We held on to our original 175 investors through the late seventies without another presentation. It's true that *Pajama Game* is not exactly *Hamilton*. Nor was *Damn Yankees*.

Of the $250,000 raised for *The Pajama Game*, we used only $169,000 to open. *Damn Yankees*, similarly capitalized, spent only $162,000, which accounts for the short payback time. We arrived at this through product placement and having negotiated contracts that were sweetened after the production paid back. We were careful that all of this activity did not compromise quality. And that takes a creative mind. It takes a creative mind to know when to say "yes" and when to say "no." Often, "no" can be as irresponsible as "yes" can be wasteful.

First-rate producing requires *taste*, as well as the ability to raise capital. But taste is indispensable.

Our next hit was *West Side Story*, and, perhaps, that was our *Hamilton*.

True, it didn't start out as a blockbuster, but, as of now, it has returned 1,521 percent on its original investment.

A little more about *West Side Story*:

I picked it up when Steve Sondheim told me that he, Arthur Laurents, and Lenny Bernstein had lost their producer and there was no—absolutely no—interest from anyone on Broadway in doing a show about gang warfare in Hell's Kitchen.

Though my partner and I were struggling in Boston with a new musical of our own, I jumped at the chance to hear the score and met with *West Side Story*'s creative team. We flew in from Boston on a free Sunday, came away with the project that no one wanted, and returned to Boston.

New Girl in Town, our Boston musical, opened on Broadway three weeks later. It wasn't good enough, but it returned its investment.

I believe even today there is no dearth of writers—playwrights, composers, and lyricists—or brilliant designers and directors. But stubbornly courageous, creative producers . . . ?

Please go back in time and regard the impact of *West Side Story*, *Fiddler on the Roof*, *Cabaret*, *Company*, *Follies*, and *A Little Night Music*. They, too, were subsidized by my 175 investors.

I am certain that none of those musicals would have seen the light of day had I not produced them. And, incidentally, every one of these shows came into being without twenty-nine-hour readings, workshops, labs, or developmental productions. Can you imagine offering a *West Side Story* twenty-nine-hour reading for investors without its choreography and its orchestra and its brilliant production values?

In 1964, I produced *Fiddler on the Roof.* Again, there was absolutely no interest from the "Broadway money" in producing that show, despite the presence of Jerome Robbins as its director and choreographer, and authors with elegant track records.

But how the hell could I turn that down?

We rehearsed for eight weeks. The production cost escalated to $375,000. And its weekly gross at capacity was $75,383. Things were different, eh? And, over the years, *Fiddler* has returned 3,904 percent on its investment.

And now I'll share with you something I deeply resent: my investors and I took the original gamble of putting unlikely shows on Broadway that ultimately made history. But when those shows have first-class revivals on Broadway, we do not participate in their success.

The subsequent revivals of *West Side Story*, the recent *Fiddler*, the countless revivals of *Cabaret*, prompt my original investors—and sometimes their heirs—always to ask me what can they expect from these productions. And I have to say, "Zero. Zip. Zilch. Nada."

In the fifties and sixties and into the early seventies, the League was equally divided between producers—the Theatre Guild, the Playwrights' Company, Rodgers and Hammerstein, Feuer and Martin, Kermit Bloomgarden, David Merrick, and me, to name just a few—and the theatre owners.

And though, from the first, it was potentially a weird marriage, over the years the balance has shifted, bringing changes which are arguably less about artistic growth and more and more about *product.*

Well, I would be a fool not to acknowledge that we are a business. And businesses provide product. But today, because of theatrical bookings, we are deluged with limited-engagement productions, usually revivals, many from the West End, featuring huge stars.

The thinking is that they guarantee paying back their investments, but with limited profit potential. And revivals, though important historically, and a stimulus to new work, are not new work. And they do not represent the now or the future of the theatre.

In the 1970s, I was a member of NEA National Council of the Arts, and I predicted that there would emerge a successful partnership between the not-for-profit theatres and Broadway. And I was roundly rejected.

But about the same time, *Candide*, which I directed for the Chelsea Theatre Center at BAM, was an early beneficiary of this process. Soon to be followed by *A Chorus Line*. And the list is long, including *Sunday in the Park with George*, *Rent*, *Avenue Q*, and *Hamilton*.

Now, let me say something—something in praise of our host, Broadway across America.

When I started in the theatre, the road was an ancillary asset. It was regarded as an opportunity to increase our profits by sending out shabby, compromised versions of Broadway productions—dubious casting with unsuitable performers with star names, plus scenery and costumes that were pale copies of the originals. It wasn't until Claudia Cassidy, the spiky critic of the *Chicago Tribune*, assuming the Carrie Nation mantle of the crusader, blasted the hell out of all of us for what we were sending out, that we realized the power of her words as our box office receipts diminished.

Thanks to Broadway across America, we now observe that the road can sizably increase our profits, that the road is a significant builder of audiences, and that the road is the virus that encourages young wannabe Broadway creators.

In addition, I have observed design teams, having learned from the original Broadway production, actually enhance what they send out on the road.

And surely it's true that theatres across the United States have adjusted their facilities to accommodate every detail of lavish touring productions. I know firsthand that the touring *Phantom of the Opera* is replicated in all its elegant detail.

So, in closing: for those of you who agree that what the theatre lacks is creative producers, I see a rosy future. To achieve it, we must define what makes our product uniquely different from television and film and build on the living relationship of live audiences and live performances. Inevitably, no two performances are exactly alike, nor is the audience's response.

Theatre is far more engaging than sitting in a seat at a movie house or on your couch at home and "receiving" entertainment.

I would urge you to forget LED walls and holograms and settle on what stage scenery does best: invite imagination.

Choose material and subject matter that surprises and often takes place in surprising locations.

Don't clone last year's hit.

Certainly, there will always be products content to entertain, to amuse an audience for two hours of sheer pleasure. But, alternatively, you must honor that audience by engaging them in ideas, in controversy, by inviting them to think.

If there is one point I passionately want to make, not only for you producers, but for your investors—the often fifty people whose names appear above the title of a two-character play—it is this: there are greater profits to be realized in courageous, groundbreaking projects, and a lasting investment, not only in quality, but in financial rewards, when you think in terms of *art*.

Sergei Diaghilev, one of the greatest producers who ever lived, urged his artists to "astonish me."

Well, today more than ever, you must astonish *them*. And if you do, you'll save the theatre—both as a product and as an art form.

ACKNOWLEDGMENTS

Aside from Foster Hirsch, who's prodded me—but in a kindly fashion—to complete this book and offered editorial advice, I want to thank the gang in my office, a small gang indeed.

While I was writing this, Ben Holtzman, who has been with me a little more than a year, asked the right questions, provoking more information and substantially urging me to enrich the text. Ben aims to be a Broadway producer and doubtless will be a creative one.

Dan Kutner has been my right hand for thirteen years. He is currently directing an original musical in Moscow, and as I mentioned earlier, he's been invaluable to the revival of *Evita*. So, we have a director and a producer.

Arthur Masella, aside from his many independent ventures, has reproduced *Phantom of the Opera* internationally for decades. He started as an intern on *Pacific Overtures* over forty years ago and became a stage manager on the original *Sweeney Todd*. He has been my associate director on the New York City Opera productions of *Candide*.

And last but far from least is Nancy Rosenband, my business manager. Having joined us as an accountant, she's been with me for thirty years and provides much needed common sense and cautionary advice.

APPENDIX

All productions listed here were on Broadway, unless noted otherwise.

THE PAJAMA GAME
OPENING: May 13, 1954, St. James Theatre
CLOSING: November 21, 1956
NUMBER OF PERFORMANCES: 1,063
Music and Lyrics by Richard Adler and Jerry Ross
Book by George Abbott and Richard Bissell
Scenery and Costumes by Lemuel Ayers
Choreography by Bob Fosse
Production Directed by George Abbott and Jerome Robbins
Produced by Frederick Brisson, Robert E. Griffith, and Harold S. Prince

DAMN YANKEES
OPENING: May 5, 1955, 46th Street Theatre
CLOSING: October 12, 1957
NUMBER OF PERFORMANCES: 1,019
Music and Lyrics by Richard Adler and Jerry Ross
Book by George Abbott and Douglass Wallop
Scenery and Costumes by William and Jean Eckart
Dances and Musical Numbers Staged by Bob Fosse
Production Directed by George Abbott and Jerome Robbins
Produced by Frederick Brisson, Robert E. Griffith, and Harold S. Prince
   (in association with Albert B. Taylor)

NEW GIRL IN TOWN
OPENING: May 14, 1957, 46th Street Theatre
CLOSING: May 24, 1958

NUMBER OF PERFORMANCES: 432
Music and Lyrics by Bob Merrill
Book by George Abbott
Production Designed by Rouben Ter-Arutunian
Dances and Musical Numbers Staged by Bob Fosse
Production Directed by George Abbott and Jerome Robbins
Produced by Frederick Brisson, Robert E. Griffith, and Harold S. Prince

WEST SIDE STORY
OPENING: September 26, 1957, Winter Garden Theatre
CLOSING: June 27, 1959
NUMBER OF PERFORMANCES: 732
REOPENING: April 27, 1960, Winter Garden Theatre
RECLOSING: December 10, 1960
NUMBER OF PERFORMANCES: 249
Music by Leonard Bernstein
Lyrics by Stephen Sondheim
Book by Arthur Laurents
Scenic Production by Oliver Smith
Costumes Designed by Irene Sharaff
Lighting by Jean Rosenthal
Entire Production Directed and Choreographed by Jerome Robbins
Co-Choreographed by Peter Gennaro
Produced by Robert E. Griffith and Harold S. Prince (by arrangement
    with Roger L. Stevens)

A SWIM IN THE SEA
OPENING: September 15, 1958 (Philadelphia)
CLOSING: September 27, 1958 (Philadelphia)
NUMBER OF PERFORMANCES: 16
Written by Jess Gregg
Scenery and Lighting by James Riley
Costumes by Hazel Roy
Directed by Elliott Silverstein
Produced by Robert E. Griffith and Harold S. Prince

FIORELLO!
OPENING: November 23, 1959, Broadhurst Theatre
CLOSING: October 28, 1961
NUMBER OF PERFORMANCES: 795
Music by Jerry Bock
Lyrics by Sheldon Harnick
Book by Jerome Weidman and George Abbott
Scenery, Costumes, and Lighting by William and Jean Eckart
Choreography by Peter Gennaro
Production Directed by George Abbott
Produced by Robert E. Griffith and Harold S. Prince

TENDERLOIN
OPENING: October 17, 1960, 46th Street Theatre
CLOSING: April 22, 1961
NUMBER OF PERFORMANCES: 216
Music by Jerry Bock
Lyrics by Sheldon Harnick
Book by George Abbott and Jerome Weidman
Sets and Costumes by Cecil Beaton
Dances and Musical Numbers Staged by Joe Layton
Production Directed by George Abbott
Produced by Robert E. Griffith and Harold S. Prince

A CALL ON KUPRIN
OPENING: May 25, 1961, Broadhurst Theatre
CLOSING: June 3, 1961
NUMBER OF PERFORMANCES: 12
Written by Jerome Lawrence and Robert E. Lee
Settings by Donald Oenslager
Costumes by Florence Klotz
Directed by George Abbott
Produced by Robert E. Griffith and Harold S. Prince

TAKE HER, SHE'S MINE
OPENING: December 21, 1961, Biltmore Theatre
CLOSING: December 8, 1962
NUMBER OF PERFORMANCES: 404
Written by Phoebe and Henry Ephron
Scenery and Lighting by William and Jean Eckart
Costumes by Florence Klotz
Directed by George Abbott
Produced by Harold S. Prince

A FAMILY AFFAIR
OPENING: January 27, 1962, Billy Rose Theatre
CLOSING: March 25, 1962
NUMBER OF PERFORMANCES: 65
Music, Lyrics, and Book by James Goldman, John Kander, and William
    Goldman
Settings and Lighting by David Hays
Costumes Designed by Robert Fletcher
Musical Numbers Staged by Bob Herget
Choreography by John Butler
Directed by Harold Prince
Produced by Andrew Siff

A FUNNY THING HAPPENED ON THE WAY TO THE FORUM
OPENING: May 8, 1962, Alvin Theatre
CLOSING: August 29, 1964
NUMBER OF PERFORMANCES: 964
Music and Lyrics by Stephen Sondheim
Book by Burt Shevelove and Larry Gelbart
Settings and Costumes by Tony Walton
Lighting by Jean Rosenthal
Choreography and Musical Staging by Jack Cole
Production Directed by George Abbott
Produced by Harold Prince

SHE LOVES ME

OPENING: April 23, 1963, Eugene O'Neill Theatre
CLOSING: January 11, 1964
NUMBER OF PERFORMANCES: 301
Music by Jerry Bock
Lyrics by Sheldon Harnick
Book by Joe Masteroff
Settings and Lighting by William and Jean Eckart
Costumes by Patricia Zipprodt
Musical Numbers Staged by Carol Haney
Production Directed by Harold Prince
Produced by Harold Prince (in association with Lawrence N. Kasha and
    Phillip C. McKenna)

FIDDLER ON THE ROOF

OPENING: September 22, 1964, Imperial Theatre
CLOSING: July 2, 1972
NUMBER OF PERFORMANCES: 3242
Music by Jerry Bock
Lyrics by Sheldon Harnick
Book by Joseph Stein
Settings by Boris Aronson
Costumes by Patricia Zipprodt
Lighting by Jean Rosenthal
Entire Production Directed and Choreographed by Jerome Robbins
Produced by Harold Prince

BAKER STREET

OPENING: February 16, 1965, Broadway Theatre
CLOSING: November 14, 1965
NUMBER OF PERFORMANCES: 311
Music and Lyrics by Marian Grudeff and Raymond Jessel
Book by Jerome Coopersmith
Production Designed by Oliver Smith

Lighting by Jean Rosenthal
Choreography by Lee Becker Theodore
Production Directed by Harold Prince
Produced by Alexander H. Cohen

POOR BITOS
OPENING: November 14, 1964, Cort Theatre
CLOSING: November 28, 1964
NUMBER OF PERFORMANCES: 11
A Play by Jean Anouilh
Translated by Lucienne Hill
Foreign Production Designed by Timothy O'Brien
American Production Designed by Jean Rosenthal
Costumes by Donald Brooks
Lighting by Jean Rosenthal
Directed by Shirley Butler
Produced by Harold Prince (in association with Michael Codron and
    Pledon Ltd.)

FLORA, THE RED MENACE
OPENING: May 11, 1965, Alvin Theatre
CLOSING: July 24, 1965
NUMBER OF PERFORMANCES: 87
Music by John Kander
Lyrics by Fred Ebb
Book by George Abbott and Robert Russell
Settings by William and Jean Eckart
Costumes by Donald Brooks
Lighting by Tharon Musser
Dance and Musical Numbers Staged by Lee Theodore
Production Directed by George Abbott
Produced by Harold Prince

"IT'S A BIRD . . . IT'S A PLANE . . . IT'S SUPERMAN"

OPENING: March 29, 1966, Alvin Theatre
CLOSING: July 17, 1966
NUMBER OF PERFORMANCES: 129
Music by Charles Strouse
Lyrics by Lee Adams
Book by David Newman and Robert Benton
Scenery and Lighting by Robert Randolph
Costumes by Florence Klotz
Dances and Musical Numbers Staged by Ernest Flatt
Production Directed by Harold Prince
Produced by Harold Prince (in association with Ruth Mitchell)

CABARET

OPENING: November 20, 1966, Broadhurst Theatre
CLOSING: September 6, 1969
NUMBER OF PERFORMANCES: 1,165
Music by John Kander
Lyrics by Fred Ebb
Book by Joe Masteroff
Scenery by Boris Aronson
Costumes by Patricia Zipprodt
Lighting by Jean Rosenthal
Dances and Cabaret Numbers by Ronald Field
Production Directed by Harold Prince
Produced by Harold Prince (in association with Ruth Mitchell)

ZORBA

OPENING: November 17, 1968, Imperial Theatre
CLOSING: August 9, 1969
NUMBER OF PERFORMANCES: 305
Music by John Kander

Lyrics by Fred Ebb
Book by Joseph Stein
Scenic Production Designed by Boris Aronson
Costumes by Patricia Zipprodt
Lighting by Richard Pilbrow
Choreography by Ronald Field
Production Directed by Harold Prince
Produced by Harold Prince (in association with Ruth Mitchell)

COMPANY
OPENING: April 26, 1970, Alvin Theatre
CLOSING: January 1, 1972
NUMBER OF PERFORMANCES: 705
Music and Lyrics by Stephen Sondheim
Book by George Furth
Sets and Projections Designed by Boris Aronson
Costumes by D.D. Ryan
Lighting by Robert Ornbo
Musical Numbers Staged by Michael Bennett
Production Directed by Harold Prince
Produced by Harold Prince (in association with Ruth Mitchell)

FOLLIES
OPENING: April 4, 1971, Winter Garden Theatre
CLOSING: July 1, 1972
NUMBER OF PERFORMANCES: 522
Music and Lyrics by Stephen Sondheim
Book by James Goldman
Scenic Production Designed by Boris Aronson
Costumes by Florence Klotz
Lighting by Tharon Musser
Choreography by Michael Bennett
Production Directed by Harold Prince and Michael Bennett
Produced by Harold Prince (in association with Ruth Mitchell)

A LITTLE NIGHT MUSIC
OPENING: February 25, 1973, Shubert Theatre
CLOSING: August 3, 1974
NUMBER OF PERFORMANCES: 601
Music and Lyrics by Stephen Sondheim
Book by Hugh Wheeler
Scenic Production Designed by Boris Aronson
Costumes by Florence Klotz
Lighting by Tharon Musser
Choreography by Patricia Birch
Production Directed by Harold Prince
Produced by Harold Prince (in association with Ruth Mitchell)

CANDIDE (Broadway)
OPENING: March 10, 1974, Broadway Theatre
CLOSING: January 4, 1976
NUMBER OF PERFORMANCES: 740
Music Composed by Leonard Bernstein
Book Adapted from Voltaire by Hugh Wheeler
Lyrics by Richard Wilbur
Additional Lyrics by Stephen Sondheim and John Latouche
Sets and Costumes Designed by Eugene and Franne Lee
Lighting Designed by Tharon Musser
Choreographed by Patricia Birch
Directed by Harold Prince
Produced by The Chelsea Theatre Center of Brooklyn (in conjunction with
    Harold Prince and Ruth Mitchell)

PACIFIC OVERTURES
OPENING: January 11, 1976, Winter Garden Theatre
CLOSING: June 27, 1976
NUMBER OF PERFORMANCES: 193
Music and Lyrics by Stephen Sondheim
Book by John Weidman
Additional Material by Hugh Wheeler

Scenic Design by Boris Aronson
Costume Design by Florence Klotz
Lighting Design by Tharon Musser
Sound Design by Jack Mann
Choreographed by Patricia Birch
Directed by Harold Prince
Produced by Harold Prince (in association with Ruth Mitchell)

ON THE TWENTIETH CENTURY
OPENING: February 19, 1978, St. James Theatre
CLOSING: March 18, 1979
NUMBER OF PERFORMANCES: 449
Music by Cy Coleman
Book and Lyrics by Betty Comden and Adolph Green
Scenic Design by Robin Wagner
Costume Design by Florence Klotz
Lighting Design by Ken Billington
Sound Design by Robin Wagner
Musical Staging by Larry Fuller
Directed by Harold Prince
Produced by Robert Fryer, Mary Lea Johnson, James Cresson, and Martin
    Richards (in association with Joseph Harris and Ira Bernstein)

EVITA
WEST END OPENING: June 21, 1978, Prince Edward Theatre
WEST END CLOSING: February 18, 1986
NUMBER OF PERFORMANCES: 3,176
BROADWAY OPENING: September 25, 1979, Broadway Theatre
BROADWAY CLOSING: June 26, 1983
NUMBER OF PERFORMANCES: 1,567
Music by Andrew Lloyd Webber
Lyrics by Tim Rice
Scenic Design by Timothy O'Brien and Tazeena Firth
Costume Design by Timothy O'Brien and Tazeena Firth
Projection Design by Timothy O'Brien and Tazeena Firth

Lighting Design by David Hersey
Sound Design by Abe Jacob
Choreographed by Larry Fuller
Directed by Harold Prince
Produced by Robert Stigwood (in association with David Land)

SWEENEY TODD
OPENING: March 1, 1979, Uris Theatre
CLOSING: June 29, 1980
NUMBER OF PERFORMANCES: 557
Music and Lyrics by Stephen Sondheim
Book by Hugh Wheeler
Scenic Design by Eugene Lee
Costume Design by Franne Lee
Lighting Design by Ken Billington
Sound Design by Jack Mann
Dance and Movement by Larry Fuller
Directed by Harold Prince
Produced by Richard Barr, Charles Woodward, Robert Fryer, Mary Lea
    Johnson, and Martin Richards

MERRILY WE ROLL ALONG
OPENING: November 16, 1981, Alvin Theatre
CLOSING: November 28, 1981
NUMBER OF PERFORMANCES: 16
Music and Lyrics by Stephen Sondheim
Book by George Furth
Scenic Design by Eugene Lee
Costume Design by Judith Dolan
Lighting Design by David Hersey
Sound Design by Jack Mann
Choreographed by Larry Fuller
Directed by Harold Prince
Produced by Lord Grade, Martin Starger, Robert Fryer, and Harold Prince
    (Associate Producers: Ruth Mitchell and Howard Haines)

WILLIE STARK
PREMIERE: April 24, 1981, Houston Grand Opera
An Opera in Three Acts by Carlisle Floyd
Based on the Robert Penn Warren novel *All The King's Men*
Scenic Design by Eugene Lee
Lighting Design by Ken Billington
Costumes Designed by Judith Dolan
Directed by Harold Prince
Produced by Houston Grand Opera and The Kennedy Center for the
   Performing Arts

A DOLL'S LIFE
OPENING: September 23, 1982, Mark Hellinger Theatre
CLOSING: September 26, 1982
NUMBER OF PERFORMANCES: 5
Music by Larry Grossman
Book and Lyrics by Betty Comden and Adolph Green
Scenic Design by Timothy O'Brien and Tazeena Firth
Costume Design by Florence Klotz
Lighting Design by Ken Billington
Sound Design by Jack Mann
Choreographed by Larry Fuller
Directed by Harold Prince
Produced by James M. Nederlander, Sidney L. Shlenker, Warner Theatre
   Productions, Joseph Harris, Mary Lea Johnson, Martin Richards, and
   Robert Fryer (in association with Harold Prince)

PLAY MEMORY
OPENING: April 26, 1984, Longacre Theatre
CLOSING: April 29, 1984
NUMBER OF PERFORMANCES: 5
Written by Joanna M. Glass
Incidental Music by Larry Grossman
Scenic Design by Clarke Dunham
Costume Design by William Ivy Long

Lighting Design by Ken Billington
Directed by Harold Prince
Produced by Alexander H. Cohen and Hildy Parks (in association with
   Samuel Klutznick)

DIAMONDS
OPENING: December 16, 1984, Circle in the Square (Downtown)
CLOSING: March 31, 1985
NUMBER OF PERFORMANCES: 122
Music by Gerard Alessandrini, Craig Carnelia, Cy Coleman, Larry
   Grossman, John Kander, Doug Katsaros, Alan Menken, Jonathan
   Sheffer, Lynn Udall, Albert Von Tilzer, and Jim Wann
Lyrics by Gerard Alessandrini, Howard Ashman, Craig Carnelia, Betty
   Comden, Fred Ebb, Ellen Fitzhugh, Adolph Green, Karl Kennett, Jack
   Norworth, Jim Wann, and David Zippel
Book by Bud Abbott, Ralph G. Allen, Roy Blount Jr., Richard Camp, Jerry
   L. Crawford, Lou Costello, Lee Eisenberg, Sean Kelly, Jim Wann, John
   Lahr, Arthur Masella, Harry Stein, John Weidman, and Alan Zweibel
Scenic Design by Tony Straiges
Costume Design by Judith Dolan
Lighting Design by Ken Billington
Sound Design by Tom Morse
Choreographed by Theodore Pappas
Directed by Harold Prince
Produced by Stephen G. Martin, Harold DeFelice, Louis W. Scheeder, and
   Kenneth John Productions (in association with Frank Basile)

GRIND
OPENING: April 16, 1985, Mark Hellinger Theatre
CLOSING: June 22, 1985
NUMBER OF PERFORMANCES: 71
Music by Larry Grossman
Lyrics by Ellen Fitzhugh
Book by Fay Kanin
Scenic Design by Clark Dunham

Costume Design by Florence Klotz
Lighting Design by Ken Billington
Sound Design by Otts Munderloh
Choreographed by Lester Wilson
Directed by Harold Prince
Produced by Kenneth D. Greenblatt, John J. Pomerantz, Mary Lea
    Johnson, Martin Richards, James M. Nederlander, Harold Prince, and
    Michael Fratzer

PHANTOM OF THE OPERA
WEST END OPENING: October 9, 1986, Her Majesty's Theatre
WEST END CLOSING: —
NUMBER OF PERFORMANCES: —
BROADWAY OPENING: January 26, 1988, Majestic Theatre
BROADWAY CLOSING: —
NUMBER OF PERFORMANCES: —
Music by Andrew Lloyd Webber
Lyrics by Charles Hart
Additional Lyrics by Richard Stilgoe
Book by Richard Stilgoe and Andrew Lloyd Webber
Production Design by Maria Björnson
Lighting Design by Andrew Bridge
Sound Design by Martin Lean
Musical Staging and Choreography by Gillian Lynne
Directed by Harold Prince
Produced by Cameron Mackintosh and The Really Useful Group

ROZA
OPENING: October 1, 1987, Royale Theatre
CLOSING: October 11, 1987
NUMBER OF PERFORMANCES: 12
Music by Gilbert Bécaud
Book and Lyrics by Julian More
Scenic Design by Alexander Okun
Costume Design by Florence Klotz

Lighting Design by Ken Billington
Sound Design by Otts Munderloh
Musical Staging by Patricia Birch
Directed by Harold Prince
Produced by The Producers Circle Company and The Shubert
    Organization

GRANDCHILD OF KINGS
OPENING: February 13, 1992, Theatre for the New City
CLOSING: May 10, 1992
NUMBER OF PERFORMANCES: 112
Adapted by Harold Prince from the Autobiographies of Sean O'Casey
Set Design by Eugene Lee
Lighting Design by Peter Kaczorowski
Costume Design by Judith Dolan
Sound Design by James M. Bay
Choreographed by Barry McNabb
Directed by Harold Prince
Produced by The Irish Repertory Theatre Company and One World Arts
    Foundation

KISS OF THE SPIDER WOMAN
WEST END OPENING: October 20, 1992, Shaftesbury Theatre
WEST END CLOSING: July 17, 1993
NUMBER OF PERFORMANCES: 390
BROADWAY OPENING: May 3, 1993, Broadhurst Theatre
BROADWAY CLOSING: July 1, 1995
NUMBER OF PERFORMANCES: 904
Music by John Kander
Lyrics by Fred Ebb
Book by Terrence McNally
Scenic Design by Jerome Sirlin
Costume Design by Florence Klotz
Projection Design by Jerome Sirlin
Lighting Design by Howell Binkley

Sound Design by Martin Levan
Choreographed by Vincent Patterson
Additional Choreography by Rob Marshall
Directed by Harold Prince
Produced by Livent, Inc.

SHOW BOAT
OPENING: October 2, 1994, Gershwin Theatre
CLOSING: January 5, 1997
NUMBER OF PERFORMANCES: 947
Music by Jerome Kern
Book and Lyrics by Oscar Hammerstein II
Scenic Design by Eugene Lee
Costume Design by Florence Klotz
Lighting Design by Richard Pilbrow
Sound Design by Martin Levan
Choreographed by Susan Stroman
Directed by Harold Prince
Produced by Livent, Inc.

THE PETRIFIED PRINCE
OPENING: December 18, 1994, The Public Theatre
CLOSING: January 15, 1995
NUMBER OF PERFORMANCES: 20
Music and Lyrics by Michael John LaChiusa
Book by Edward Gallardo
Scenery by James Youmans
Costumes by Judith Dolan
Lighting by Howell Binkley
Sound by Jim Bay
Musical Staging by Rob Marshall
Directed by Harold Prince
Produced by The Public Theatre (by arrangement with John Flaxman and
    Live Entertainment of Canada, Inc.)

WHISTLE DOWN THE WIND
OPENING: December 12, 1996, National Theatre, Washington, D.C
CLOSING: —FEBRUARY 9, 1997
NUMBER OF PERFORMANCES: 70
Music by Andrew Lloyd Webber
Lyrics by Jim Steinman
Book by Patricia Knop
Scenic Design by Andrew Jackness
Costume Design by Florence Klotz
Lighting Design by Howell Binkley
Sound Design by Martin Levan
Choreography by Joey McKneely
Directed by Harold Prince
Produced by The Really Useful Company

PARADE
OPENING: December 17, 1998, Vivian Beaumont Theatre
CLOSING: February 28, 1999
NUMBER OF PERFORMANCES: 85
Music and Lyrics by Jason Robert Brown
Book by Alfred Uhry
Scenic Design by Riccardo Hernandez
Costume Design by Judith Dolan
Lighting Design by Howell Binkley
Sound Design by Jonathan Deans
Choreographed by Patricia Birch
Co-conceived and Directed by Harold Prince
Produced by Lincoln Center Theater (in association with Livent U.S. Inc.)

FLIGHT OF THE LAWNCHAIR MAN (3HREE)
Premiered at The Prince Music Theater, Philadelphia
Music and Lyrics by Robert Lindsay Nassif
Book by Peter Ullian
Scenic Design by Walt Spangler

Costume Design by Miguel Angel Huidor
Lighting Design by Howell Binkley
Sound Design by Duncan Robert Edwards
Choreography by Michael Arnold
Directed by Harold Prince
Produced by Prince Music Theater

HOLLYWOOD ARMS
OPENING: October 31, 2002, Cort Theatre
CLOSING: January 5, 2003
NUMBER OF PERFORMANCES: 76
Written by Carrie Hamilton and Carol Burnett
Incidental Music by Robert Lindsay Nassif
Scenic Design by Walt Spangler
Costume Design by Judith Dolan
Lighting Design by Howell Binkley
Sound Design by Rob Milburn and Michael Bodeen
Directed by Harold Prince
Produced by Harold Prince and Arielle Tepper

BOUNCE
OPENING: June 20, 2003, Goodman Theatre, Chicago
CLOSING: November 16, 2006, Kennedy Center, Washington, D.C.
Music and Lyrics by Stephen Sondheim
Book by John Weidman
Set Design by Eugene Lee
Costume Design by Miguel Angel Huidor
Lighting Design by Howell Binkley
Sound Design by Duncan Robert Edwards
Choreographed by Michael Arnold
Directed by Harold Prince
Produced by The Goodman Theatre and The Kennedy Center for the
    Performing Arts

LOVEMUSIK
OPENING: May 3, 2007, Biltmore Theatre
CLOSING: June 24, 2007
NUMBER OF PERFORMANCES: 60
Music and Lyrics by Kurt Weil
Featuring Songs with Lyrics by Maxwell Anderson, Bertolt Brecht, Howard
    Dietz, Roger Fernay, Ira Gershwin, Oscar Hammerstein II, Langston
    Hughes, Alan Jay Lerner, Maurice Magre, Ogden Nash, and Elmer Rice
Book by Alfred Uhry
Scenic Design by Beowulf Borritt
Costume Design by Judith Dolan
Lighting Design by Howell Binkley
Sound Design by Duncan Edwards
Musical Staging by Patricia Birch
Directed by Harold Prince
Produced by Manhattan Theatre Club (in special arrangement with Marty
    Bell, Aldo Scrofani, Boyett Ostar Productions, Tracy Aron, Roger
    Berlind/Debra Black, Chase Mishkin, and Ted Snowdon)

PARADISE FOUND
OPENING: May 26, 2010, Menier Chocolate Factory, London
CLOSING: June 26, 2010
Music by Johann Strauss II
Lyrics by Ellen Fitzhugh
Book by Richard Nelson
Scenic Design by Beowulf Borritt
Costume Design by Judith Dolan
Lighting Design by Howell Binkley
Sound Design by Gareth Owen
Choreographed by Susan Stroman
Co-Directed by Harold Prince and Susan Stroman
Produced by Menier Chocolate Factory (in association with Jeffrey Berger,
    Tony Ponturo, and Tim Kashani)

INDEX

B

as project no one wanted, 299
reviews, 38–39
Sondheim and, 33, 34
ticket pricing and, 40
Wharton, John, 249
"What a Lovely Day for an Auto da Fé," 197
Wheeler, Hugh
 Candide and, 189, 190, 196
 A Little Night Music and, 175
 Sweeney Todd and, 223, 224
"Where Do I Go from Here?," 62
"Where You Are," 256
Whistle Down the Wind, 270
White House, 43
Wicked, 284
Willie Stark, 233–34
Wilson, Sandy, 136
Winfrey, Oprah, 282
Winter Garden Theatre, 198
Winterset, 183
Wise Guys, 283

Wolfe, George C., 269
Wood, Frank, 281
Wood, Peggy, 45–46

Z

Ziegfeld, Florenz, 263
Ziegfeld Follies, 161
Ziemba, Karen, 293
Zien, Chip, 236
Zipprodt, Pat, 105
Zorba
 Aronson and, 141–44
 casting of, 141, 142
 as disappointment, 143
 in Europe, 143
 Kander and Ebb, 141, 144
 mine disaster in, 142
 Quinn and, 144
 sets for, 141–42
Zweig, Stefan, 289